THE *ILIAD*, THE *RĀMĀYAṆA*, AND THE WORK OF RELIGION

HERMENEUTICS: STUDIES IN THE HISTORY OF RELIGIONS

Kees W. Bolle, Editor

Richard Marks, *The Image of Bar Kokhba in Traditional Jewish Literature: False Messiah and National Hero* (1993)

Joanne Punzo Waghorne, *The Raja's Magic Clothes: Re-Visioning Kingship and Divinity in England's India* (1994)

Devin DeWeese, *Islamization and Native Religion in the Golden Horde: Baba Tükles and Conversion to Islam in Historical and Epic Tradition* (1994)

Gregory D. Alles, *The* Iliad, *the* Rāmāyaṇa, *and the Work of Religion: Failed Persuasion and Religious Mystification*

Gregory D. Alles

THE *ILIAD*, THE *RĀMĀYAṆA*, AND THE WORK OF RELIGION

Failed Persuasion and Religious Mystification

The Pennsylvania State University Press
University Park, Pennsylvania

Library of Congress Cataloging-in-Publication Data

Alles, Gregory D.
The Iliad, the Ramayana, and the work of religion: failed persuasion and religious mystification / Gregory D. Alles.

p. cm.
Includes bibliographical references (p.) and index.
ISBN 0-271-01319-2 (cloth : alk. paper). — ISBN 0-271-01320-6 (paper)
1. Homer. Iliad. 2. Epic poetry, Greek—History and criticism. 3. Vālmīki. Rāmāyaṇa. 4. Epic poetry, Sanskrit—History and criticism. 5. Literature, Comparative—Greek and Sanskrit. 6. Literature, Comparative—Sanskrit and Greek. 7. Hinduism—In literature. 8. Religion—In literature. 9. Greece—Religion.
I. Title.
PA4037.A612 1994
883′.01—dc20 93-37998
CIP

Printed in the United States of America

Published by The Pennsylvania State University Press,
University Park, PA 16802-1003

Contents

For Sarah,
who has taught me more than she knows.

Acknowledgments

At times it seemed as if I would spend my whole life writing this book, despite its relative brevity. I have certainly acquired enough intellectual and professional debts to last a lifetime. So first let me acknowledge the obvious: I cannot enumerate every debt here. As a result, I mention only those that the formality of the occasion seems to require. I hope all those whom I do not mention learned of my gratitude long ago.

This book owes a great deal to my teachers. For my general "cultivation" in the academic study of religions, I must thank Mircea Eliade, Joseph Kitagawa, Frank Reynolds, Kurt Rudolph, and, as an undergraduate, Ted Ludwig and Ed Senne. I am sorry that the first two cannot see this book in print. More special thanks are due to Wendy Doniger, Arthur Adkins, and Anthony Yu, who guided earlier reflections on speech making in the *Iliad* and the *Rāmāyaṇa,* the subject of my doctoral dissertation.

A Fulbright grant for research in India changed the shape of this book—indeed, the shape of my life. For hospitality, practical advice, and intellectual stimulation, I must especially thank Sharada Nayak and Dileep Patwardhan (U. S. Educational Foundation in India), R. T. Vyas and B. N. Bhatt

(M. S. University of Baroda), G. U. Thite (University of Pune), S. N. Dubé (University of Rajasthan, Jaipur), and U. N. Roy (University of Allahabad). I would be terribly remiss if I did not also mention people like Sheikh, Malek, and Mahebub, three of the many good people who staffed the guest houses where I stayed. When I left for home, I told them they had been like a second family. I meant every word.

Of friends, four deserve special thanks for making valuable contributions along the way, despite their being neither Ramayanists nor Homerists: Norman Girardot, Richard Maxwell, Leif Vaage, and Eric Ziolkowski. To what extent they agree with what I have written is not for me to say.

My gratitude naturally includes publishers present. The people at Penn State Press have without exception maintained that difficult balance between being professional and kind. It also extends to publishers past. Odd portions of this book appeared previously in "Wrath and Persuasion: The *Iliad* and Its Contexts," *Journal of Religion* 70, no. 2 (April 1990): 167–88 (© 1990 by The University of Chicago. All rights reserved). Thanks are also due to The University of Chicago Press and Princeton University Press for permission to reprint portions of Richmond Lattimore's translation of the *Iliad* (Copyright 1951 by The University of Chicago. All rights reserved) and from the Goldman et al. translation of the *Rāmāyaṇa* (*The Rāmāyaṇa of Vālmīki: An Epic of Ancient India,* trans. Robert P. Goldman et al., 4 vols. to date. Copyright © 1984, 1986, 1991 by Princeton University Press. Reprinted by permission of Princeton University Press).

I want to begin one last word of thanks with an observation: in at least one respect, giving birth to a book is the opposite of giving birth to a baby. In childbirth the mother suffers the labor pains, but the close relatives get to enjoy the new arrival. "Bookbirth" is just the opposite. The author gets most of the pleasure, but the close relatives suffer most of the pain. Thanks to Mary, Timothy, Cassandra, Zachary, and especially Sarah for suffering the labor.

Introduction

I

To an Indian audience—at least, to most Indians I know—it seems self-evident that the *Iliad* and the *Rāmāyaṇa* can and should be compared. To an American audience, it is less so.

The *Rāmāyaṇa*—to be more precise, Vālmīki's *Rāmāyaṇa* (there are many, many others)—is the *ādi-kāvya,* the first work of "high letters" in Sanskrit literature.[1] It weighs in at a little under twice the size of the *Iliad* and the *Odyssey* together, containing about 24,000 two-line *śloka*s divided into seven books known as *kāṇḍa*s. Vālmīki's Sanskrit version, although revered, is not popularly read today, but the Rāma story continues to exert a major influence on Indian life through just about every communicative and artistic medium and genre imaginable.[2] How pervasive that influence is can be judged from a quick anecdote. In August 1989 I asked a class of more than seventy English students at Anand Arts College in Anand, Gujarat, which of them had watched the "Ramayan" serial regularly on Doordarshan, Indian TV. (The serial aired in forty-five-minute episodes every Sunday morning from January 1987 to July 1988.) Too many hands went up to count, so I asked who had *not* watched the serial every week. Not a single hand was raised. The same incident also illustrates the nature of the story's influence. When I asked about favorite characters or episodes, one young woman immediately and typically replied that her favorite character was Sītā, because "Sītā is the ideal woman."

The Rāma story is profoundly and pervasively intertwined with the Indian self-consciousness. In today's world, the experience of colonialism, followed by almost half a century of independence, has given one kind of comparative commentary on that tale self-evident value: the comparison of the classic version, Vālmīki's Sanskrit "original," with the analogous, classic "first poems" that were profoundly and pervasively intertwined with the self-consciousness of the former British rulers. That is, in colonial and postcolonial India it has made obvious sense to compare Sanskrit classics with their Greek counterparts. One could thereby assert, for example, that India was culturally and socially equal, if not superior, to Britain. The value of that accomplishment should not be underestimated. It vigorously countered a political domination that implicitly or explicitly, but always improperly, called Indian self-worth into question. One supposes, then, that as "the Indian mind" becomes progressively decolonized, the need to compare Sanskrit classics with Greek ones, as opposed to other literary works, will lose its self-evidence.[3]

For Americans and Western Europeans, the situation is rather different. There may have been a time when a desire to justify cultural colonial programs—religious proselytization, medical missions, educational missions—would have provoked "Westerners" to compare Greek with Sanskrit epic. The political ambitions of the British and their immediate colonial competitors also provided compelling reasons to pursue a Greek-Sanskrit comparison. Thus, in the colonial context, it was self-evidently important when someone like the German Indologist, Albrecht Weber, theorized that the *Rāmāyaṇa* was derived from Homeric epic. It was also important, as well as predictable, that someone like Kashinath Trimbak Telang write a rebuttal.[4]

But if there was once a time in America and Western Europe when the value of comparing Greek and Indian classics seemed self-evident, that time is no more. The postcolonial British attitude toward India seems, from a transoceanic distance, to oscillate between two poles. On the one hand, there has been an intense, imaginative fascination with the India of the past one hundred years, evident in nostalgic enthusiasm for the Raj (*A Passage to India, The Jewel in the Crown*) and in aesthetic enthusiasm for Anglo-Indian writers like Raja Rao and Salman Rushdie. On the other hand, there is terror, realistic or not, at the prospect of Indians and other previously colonized people actually overrunning Britain itself.

The attitude toward India in the United States does not oscillate between nostalgia and terror but disinterest and fantasy. In politics and economics, India has steadfastly refused to play the American game; America has responded with at best flagging political and economic interest in India. At the same time, and perhaps as a result, the American mind tends to fantasize India as either heaven or hell: either a realm of supremely intense, universal spirituality (Gandhi, but also Rajneesh), or one of complete material degradation (poverty, hunger, overpopulation, disease).[5]

In this book I undertake to compare the *Iliad* and Vālmīki's *Rāmāyaṇa,* primarily for an American audience and principally from the perspective of the study of religions.* There is nothing in either the American or Western European self-consciousness to make that comparison immediately compelling today. To be sure, I have academic reasons for my venture; the remainder of this introduction will present them. Nevertheless, as the preceding observations suggest, a comparison, any comparison, of two culturally foundational works like the *Iliad* and the *Rāmāyaṇa* cannot avoid broader social and political implications altogether. Before turning to academics, I want to touch briefly on those implications, because one set of them—a specific dynamic of decolonization, if you will—attracts my attention to these two poems. It also determines the attitude I bring to them.

The world today is being increasingly divided into two hemispheres, North and South, rich and poor. (The future of the formerly communist countries remains uncertain.) Clearly, the most important factors driving North-South relations are economic. I say that without at all endorsing the simplistic view that economic-material reality is the only genuine historical force. At the same time, the *Iliad* and the *Rāmāyaṇa* have provided and continue to provide cultural paradigms for very large numbers of Northerners and Southerners, respectively. My hope is that by treating these two

*Because I intend this volume for a more general audience than philologists with a mastery of both Greek and Sanskrit (surely not a large crowd), I have kept citations from the original languages to a minimum, and I have tried to make the discussions accessible to readers with no knowledge of either Greek or Sanskrit. When the terms I use are likely to be unfamiliar to these readers, I gloss them in footnotes.

paradigmatic poems as equals, I can help assert a common dignity that economic disparity has tended to erode. Besides, in a world of intense suffering and conflict such as our own, my specific theme—an examination of how Homer and Vālmīki adjudicated the peril of failed persuasion (the collapse of diplomacy, the resort to violence and war)—can claim some topicality.

II

Cross-cultural comparison has been out of fashion in academia for quite some time. That is understandable, because the comparative approach so common in humanistic studies about a hundred years ago encouraged misinterpretation and self-promotion. Recent scholars have preferred instead to cultivate what Clifford Geertz has called "local knowledge," often under the pretext of reproducing the world "from the native's point of view."[6] But although it may be understandable that comparison is out of fashion, it is also unfortunate. A multicultural world is here to stay, in intellectual life as in every other kind. If multicultural studies are to mean anything besides atomized, specialized accounts of different peoples, places, and times juxtaposed at random, cultural scholars will need once more to compare, and compare seriously and vigorously.

One of the most sophisticated recent accounts of the comparative enterprise, certainly the most sophisticated recent engagement with comparison in the study of religions, is that of Jonathan Z. Smith.[7] The second chapter of his book, *Drudgery Divine: On the Comparison of Early Christianities and the Religions of Late Antiquity,* systematically develops a career's worth of reflections on comparison.[8] I seriously doubt that Smith has written the last word on comparison, but at least in broad terms, the present book, which was conceived and initially drafted before *Drudgery Divine* appeared, recalls Smith's recommendations.

For present purposes we can distill Smith's richly textured reflections into three basic assertions. First, comparison does not aim either to demonstrate that one cultural artifact possesses unique, superlative status, or to postulate that several cultural artifacts are the same. Instead, Smith says, comparison must develop a "discourse of 'difference.' "[9] To quote him (quoting himself): "It is axiomatic that comparison is never a matter of identity. Comparison requires the acceptance of difference as the grounds of its being interesting, and a methodological manipulation of that difference to achieve some stated cognitive end."[10] Second, comparison should be analogical, not genealogical. Scholars may attempt to compare to establish genealogies, that is, to determine which artifact came first and who borrowed from whom. Nevertheless, "all comparisons are properly analogical."[11] They reflect a principled manipulation of similarities and differences in the scholar's mind. As a result, genealogical comparison is really an obscurantist endeavor; it replaces the scholar's concepts and purposes, the real determinants of the comparative enterprise, with a simplistic and deceptive chronological frame. Third, comparison does not faithfully preserve either "phenomenological whole entities" or "local meanings." Instead, it selects and utilizes specific elements from different contexts to elucidate a scholar's theoretical concerns. "It is the scholar's intellectual purpose—whether explanatory or interpretative, whether generic or specific—which highlights that principled postulation of similarity which is the ground of the methodical comparison of difference being interesting."[12]

Smith's immediate aim in making these assertions is to critique the forms of comparison prevalent in the study of religions in the recent past. He directly criticizes scholars of early Christianity for their concerns with the uniqueness of Christianity, concerns that are both taxonomic (the "Christ-event" was unique in human history) and genealogical (any similarities between pagan figures and Jesus are due to borrowings from Christianity). Just over the critical horizon stand projects like James George Frazer's evolutionary anthropology and the universalizing morphology of Mircea Eliade. Viewed against the excesses of these enterprises, Smith's strictures and axioms make a good deal of sense. In a pluralistic world, it is no longer possible to identify one tradition, text, experience, or event as a unique, absolute repository of meaning and value—aside from making an arbitrary leap that scholarship can never admit, because it would require us to abandon the possibility of questioning anything and everything.[13] Furthermore, it is widely recognized how wrong evolutionists like Frazer were in trying to construct chronological sequences from essentially taxonomic schemes. And Smith himself is in large part responsible for exposing the interpretive missteps in Mircea Eliade's work, the most recent general synthesis in the history of religions. Given the excesses in the inherited models of comparison, Smith has identified, I am convinced, the kind of comparison appropriate in religious studies today. It is by and large the kind of comparison in which I try to engage.

But in a more general sense, Smith's account does not succeed. His universal claims are universal in appearance only, as emerges first of all from his rhetoric. If any axiom is left today at all, it is that there can be no hard and fast axioms. To write "it is axiomatic," as Smith does, immediately disturbs the *manes* of Nikolay Lobachevsky, János Bolyai, and Bernhard Riemann, who in the nineteenth century abandoned Euclid's axioms and developed entirely new and significant fields of geometry. Smith's rhetoric of axiom invites us to consider, then, the extent to which his directives can be sustained. The answer is, not as far as one might like.

Smith's first stipulation, that comparison is interesting only to the extent that it manipulates differences, is convincing only when it conflates several kinds of difference. One kind is the difference that is a prerequisite for comparison: the difference that allows us to speak of two or three items to be compared, for example, two or three different poems. Another kind is the difference that helps define relations between specific aspects of the items being compared: two or three different poems are different *or similar* with regard to aspects *x, y,* or *z.* Finally, there is the difference that makes the comparison—or any assertion—interesting. That difference is not to be found in the objects being compared but in the relation between the comparison and its scholarly context. That is to say, what is interesting in academia is (to borrow from Marshall Sahlins's analysis of fashion) an account that differs from customary academic practice in a respect major enough to seem significant, but not so major that it seems dilettante or "off the wall."[14] Smith's insistence that comparison develop a discourse of difference provides a good example. It is interesting not so much because it is true, but because it provides an alternative to the kind of comparison practiced by the most influential recent comparativists, such as Mircea Eliade, comparison as the discourse of similarity. It is a pretty safe bet that a future generation of scholars, inheriting a tradition of comparison fashioned in the image of difference, will find intensely interesting precisely the concern for similarity that Smith rejects.

Like his remarks on comparison as a discourse of difference, Smith's strictures against genealogical comparison are attractive as directions for present practice but questionable as universal prescriptions. In an academic context dominated by the question of whether early Christians or late antique pagans first developed certain religious features, it is indeed interesting to argue, as Smith does, that the most significant features appeared in both traditions more or less concurrently, then developed in parallel. In other words, early Christianities and late antique religions relate by analogy, not genealogy. But the fit between this empirical argument and Smith's theoretical stipulations is too constricting. When Smith rejects genealogy in favor of taxonomy, he creates a conceptual space that cannot comfortably contain any empirical conclusions other than those at which he wants to arrive. In other words, he falsely transforms empirical conclusions into procedural principles. It is far from clear why a historian should refrain entirely from speaking about influence or borrowing between two or more religions (for example, the "influence" of Taoism on Buddhism in China during the first millennium C.E.).[15] In fact, there are no reasons, aside from reasons of fashion, why concerns with taxonomy should be any more legitimate than concerns with history. And how could history proceed at all without comparison of some sort?[16] The problem is not, as Smith seems to think, with genealogical comparisons per se. It is, on the one hand, with an inherited tradition that treated taxonomies as genealogies, and on the other, with the inability of Smith's synchronocentric analysis to deal satisfactorily with the complexities of time, at least on the level of theory.[17]

On one point, however, I agree with Smith without hesitation: a scholarly comparison is instructive only to the extent that it addresses scholarly, theoretical purposes. Inasmuch as the present comparison does not aim to develop a comparative mode alternative to the one Smith advocates, we may place my reservations about Smith's universal strictures gently to one side and turn to the comparison at hand.

In Smith's terms, this book is not a genealogical enterprise but an analogical one. Contrary to the expectations that a reader of a book on Greek and Indian epic may have, it is not a book in Indo-European studies. A case can probably be made that the *Iliad* and the *Rāmāyaṇa* are remote products of a common tradition of Indo-European poetry,[18] but it is not made in this book, which focuses instead on the poems themselves. The choice of focus does not reflect any conviction that genealogical comparisons are in principle illicit so much as a reaction to the current state of scholarly writing on Greek and Indian epic and Indo-European themes more generally. There is today considerable room for skepticism about the presuppositions underlying much of Indo-European comparative mythology, heavily indebted as it is to the probably flawed work of Georges Dumézil.[19] As a result, I do not at present see much room for developing convincing, substantive, and significant comparisons of the two epics along genealogical lines. Instead, I shall treat them analogically. The commonalities that serve as the basis for the comparison have much more to do with the character of the poems than with their putative common roots: the two epics are recognized as "first poems" by two major cultures; they are formulaic poems, sharing, among other things, the difficulty of precisely inscribing the boundaries of the formula; they are constituted to a great degree not by descriptive narration but by direct address, that is, by speeches; in developing the oratorical dimension, they provide two paradigmatic instances in which the central narratives of foundational "first poems" articulate the same tension, the failure of persuasion and the resulting threat of social disintegration; and they negotiate that failure and resulting threat by religious means advanced through fiction.

These characteristics provide the commonality on whose basis the comparison proceeds, but they are the frame of the comparative cart, not its cargo, which is a discourse not of similarity but of difference. In making this comparison I am not concerned with identifying patterns common to the two poems (archetypes, morphologies, what have you) that manifest some universal structure or other (the collective unconscious, the shared structures of human consciousness, . . .). Nor am I interested in identifying basic patterns that characterize the genre to which we ordinarily assign the poems, epic literature. I explore instead the differentials by which the two poems articulate and negotiate the threat of failed persuasion. My burden is both to explicate and account for these two moves in their limited particularity. In doing so, I will, of course, reveal something of the specifics of ancient Greek and Indian civilization, of the two epic poems, and of how the civilizations as well as the poems differ from one another. At the same time, I will address issues in the academic study of religions. It is to those issues that we now turn.

III

During the twentieth century, one of the most significant approaches to the academic study of religions, especially in the United States, has gone by the name "history of religions." The title of the series in which this book appears underscores one characteristic of that approach: it has been heavily hermeneutical. In the somewhat dated words of one leading practitioner, it has sought to interpret and to understand "the religious meaning of humankind's religious experience and its expressions through the integration and 'significant organization' of diverse forms of religious data."[20] At the same time, the history of religions has consistently emphasized that a comprehensive picture of religion is its goal, and it is this "priority of the whole" that, in part, compels me to break with tradition and to look for another model than hermeneutics with which to conceive of my task.[21]

Joachim Wach, for example, adopted the essentially romantic notion that meanings were expressions of genuine experience, expressions by means of which historians could "recognize" (*erkennen*) what had been previously "cognized" (*gekannt*). Wach modified the romantic notion of meaning in two ways. First, he thought of experience not as "psychological experience" (*Erlebnis*) but as empirical experiences or encounters (*Erfahrungen*). Second, he insisted that external expressions or objectifications had structures that merited study on their own—what he once called the "objective *Geist*."[22] Within this framework, Wach advocated an "integral study of religious expressions": a "full linguistic, historical, psychological, technological, and social enquiry, in which full justice is done to the intention of the expression and to the context in which it occurs, and in which this expression is related to the experience of which it testifies."[23]

Wach's formulation contains an inevitable tension between his universal intent and his particular conceptions. The "struggle of experience for expression"[24] does not describe religion in general; it characterizes a specific, limited type of religion. In Wach's context, this image ultimately derives, through F.D.E. Schleiermacher, from Evangelical Pietism.[25] To be sure, Wach does not simply transpose Pietism into a general academic description. Pietism privileged emotional experience, whereas Wach includes thought and will along with feeling in what he calls the "integral" religious experience.[26] But in either case, the emphasis on experience as the source of religion—the fount of *true* religion (compare the title of Johann Arndt's meditations with Wach's talk of false and incomplete religions)[27]—arose in opposition to a Protestant scholasticism that vehemently proclaimed salvation quite apart from any experiences, a scholasticism that sought to give assurance of salvation *despite* all experience. In that assurance lay any profundity the teachings of the scholastics might have had. Thus, when Wach derives all religious expression from religious experience, he does not identify what all religions share. He favors a particular type of religion, and as a result, his *Religionswissenschaft* fails to achieve the comprehensive vision to which it aspires.[28]

Perhaps the most famous historian of religions, Mircea Eliade, centers the history of religions on a loosely existentialist notion of meaning with quasi-Kantian overtones. For him, religious symbols reveal Being and thus make authentic existence possible, but they do so as structures of (the archaic) human consciousness. Thus, Eliade advocates a morphology of the sacred that exploits structural homologies in identifying the elementary constituent forms according to which the sacred manifests itself. At the same time, he envisions a history of religions that is a "total hermeneutics." On the one hand, historians of religions must not be content to study the context of their "documents" by every means available; they must understand them on their own plane of reference. On the other hand, historians of religions must not simply decipher the meaning of religious phenomena; they must locate them historically and elucidate their cultural contributions. "*Homo religiosus,*" Eliade insists, "represents the 'total man.'"[29]

Eliade's psychological depth and his profound sensitivity to the general dynamics of religious symbols make for much more powerful accounts than Wach's arid generalizations. Still, Eliade's notion of meaning requires him to insist on the irreducibility of the sacred, even when he advocates his "total hermeneutics": "A religious datum reveals its *deeper meaning* when it is considered on its plane of reference, and not when it is reduced to one of its secondary aspects or its contexts."[30] This "paradigm of the hierophany" frustrates any ambitions Eliade's *grand système* may have toward comprehensiveness. It transmutes any attempt to consider religion apart from the modalities of the hierophany into an act of disciplinary *hybris,* an improper longing for Being at the Center. Consequently, Eliade finds it impossible to deal with some religious phenomena that are entirely accessible—and of intense interest—to Wach. A prime example is religious authority.[31] Concerned to do justice to the one irreducible element in religion, Eliade develops a history of religions that is capable of doing only that and little else.

Of course, one might argue that historians of religions only need to take a sufficiently sophisticated, up-to-date notion of hermeneutics as their model, such as the philosophical hermeneutics of Hans-Georg Gadamer and Paul Ricoeur or, better yet, the hermeneutical, symbols-and-meanings anthropology of Clifford Geertz.[32] For several reasons I prefer a different approach. As recent work in other humanities has underscored, hermeneutics has no monopoly on human understanding. In the study of art, for example, scholars like Michael Baxandall have developed incisive social histories and in the process exposed some elaborate, high-iconographic interpretations as so much academic pretentiousness. More of a maverick, David Freedberg has rejected not just iconography but social history, too, in an attempt to locate the universal, essentially psychological ways in which human beings respond to images.[33]

Scholars of religions have also begun to recognize the limits of hermeneutics. Ronald Grimes has pointed out that applying Ricoeur and Geertz's metaphor of the text to rituals may very well impede analysis. Frits Staal has argued vigorously that rituals are meaningless, that in asking about the meaning of rituals we are asking the wrong question. The anthropologist Renato Rosaldo has distinguished two kinds of rituals, those which reveal cultural depth (and, we might add, are fit subjects for hermeneutical analysis) and those, filled with platitudes, which act to catalyze emotional processes, which then continue over long periods of time. Rosaldo notes that in his experience most rituals belong to the latter class, not the former. That corresponds to my experience, too.

Besides these examples, there may be reasons of principle why hermeneutics is too narrow a model on which to build a general history of religions. The proper task of hermeneutics is to retrieve and apply (*hermeneuein*) communicated meanings, traditionally in theology, literature, and law. To be sure, there are countless particular instances of communicated meanings in religion, and historians of religions need to treat them. But when the whole to be understood is not a particular communicated meaning, such as a sacred text, but religion, and not even a particular religion but religion as it appears throughout the world, can one really use the interpretation of communicated meaning as a model? Who would be communicating on such a global scale, and to whom?[34]

There is good reason to suspect, then, that a history of religions conceived as hermeneutics is too narrow. Its focus on meaning neglects some very interesting topics and at times presents a distorted image of religion. I prefer, then, to replace "meaning" with "event" as the central category for the history of religions. My mode of investigation is not hermeneutics but history—not history as the recovery of the past but as a principled and systematic exploration of events in which religion occurs, including events of meaning.[35] I correlate my approach quite deliberately with a metaphysics that assigns priority to actuality rather than to idea and an "anthropology" that views human thought as a form of activity (*praxis*).

Given the hermeneutical predilection for meaning, one set of religious phenomena presents a particularly pointed example of the kind of approach I have in mind, written works. A sacred text, like any literary work, is not simply a repository of disembodied religious meanings. It is also an act, or rather, a set of acts, among them, the composition of the text, the portrayal and retrieval of the text, the effects of the text on the religious community, and vice versa. Epic poems illustrate nicely why it is important for the history of religions to conceive of its work as a principled investigation of this broader set of events rather than as a creative translation of meanings. That is why I have chosen to examine two epics in this book.[36]

In the hermeneutical tradition, epics have counted as only indirectly religious. Either they represent mythologies that have lost their religious content and become literary works, as Eliade thinks happened with Greek mythical works like the *Iliad,* or they began as secular folklore and were then mythologized by a later religious imagination, as Robert Goldman suggests happened in the case of the *Rāmāyaṇa.*[37] But such a narrow view misses a crucial point. If one considers the actions that both of these poems performed, and in some senses continue to perform, rather than the meanings they conveyed, one can recognize both of them as genuinely religious works.

The book in hand aims to elucidate that action or work. It does so by attending to one particular manner in which Homer and Vālmīki represent meaning as being rendered and used. The central narratives of both poems share a significant thematic. When ordinary persuasion fails and no usual possibility of recourse remains, society threatens to collapse. At that point, religious elements intervene. In the *Iliad,* it is the gods who restore order; in the *Rāmāyaṇa,* it is Rāma's supreme virtue. In their different ways, then, the two narratives accomplished a serious and significant religious purpose in ancient Greece and India. They instilled and enforced a confidence that even when the social order is shaky, the religious order will hold.

Given the traditional, comparative thrust of the history of religions, it seems best to illustrate my points by examining not one but two epics. Among other things, that procedure will eventually allow some preliminary comments on the differential character of religious events. Practical considerations motivated the choice of the *Iliad* and the *Rāmāyaṇa* (I read Greek and Sanskrit but not, for example, Swahili), but so have several considerations related to content: both the *Iliad* and the *Rāmāyaṇa* are identified as "first poems" in their respective cultures; both are formally similar in ways that can be designated, not unproblematically, as formulaic; both can boast of a full range of secondary literature as well as carefully compiled critical texts; and both share a significant thematic, the failure of persuasion, realized under differing cultural conditions.

The goal of this study is by no means to expound a full theory of religion or even to reveal the religious dynamics of epic poetry in general. The range of evidence considered is simply too narrow to accomplish either task. Instead, its aim is therapeutic: to raise questions about some basic issues in the history of religions and to suggest directions in which future inquiry might proceed.

IV

The topic of failed persuasion in the *Iliad* and the *Rāmāyaṇa* allows us to address some basic issues in the history of religions, but it articulates with other practices in religious studies as well.

Over the last decade and a half, a critic of romantic literature, Jerome McGann, has made many perceptive observations about the study of classic literary texts. A scholar firmly rooted in the practice of textual criticism, McGann has exposed the notion of "text" with which hermeneutical and poststructuralist thinkers have become accustomed to operate as abstract and attenuated and championed the significance of concrete texts in their social and institutional contexts.[38] In addition, he has emphasized that poems are not simply collections of self-referential, nonpositive discourse systems but always "works": events of language, or as he says, "specific and worlded engagements in which meaning is rendered and used."[39] Most to the point here, McGann sees value not in "interpreting" poems, which simply makes them "vehicles for recapitulating and objectifying the reader's particular ideological commitments," but in taking poems as "culturally alienated products," which confronts "readers with ideological differentials that help to define the limits and special functions of . . . current ideological practices."[40] In just this manner, the topic of failed persuasion in the *Iliad* and the *Rāmāyaṇa* articulates with two powerful ideological practices in religious studies.

One such practice is interreligious dialogue, sometimes called interreligious-interideological dialogue to include Marxists and atheists in the discussions. There are many different conceptions of what dialogue is and ought to be, not all of which are commensurate. But in general, dialogue provides an alternative to more traditional enterprises in the practice and study of religions. From within a dominant perspective (such as the Christian), dialogue replaces proselytization, acceptance replaces condemnation, in defining the manner in which one interacts with those who practice other religions. From within the academic perspective, dialogue replaces analysis and critical evaluation in defining the manner in which scholars of religions relate to the (human) subjects they study.

Especially in the last two decades, dialogue has borne great expectations. Leonard Swidler's introduction to a recent discussion of dialogue by four leading Christian theologians provides a good example. It begins, "The future offers two alternatives: death or dialogue. This statement is not over-dramatization." Swidler continues:

> Today nuclear or ecological, or other, catastrophic devastation lies just a little way further down the path of monologue. It is only by struggling out of the self-centered monologic mindset into dialogue with "the others" as they really are, and not as we have projected them in our monologues, that we can avoid such cataclysmic disasters. . . . Since our religion or ideology is so comprehensive, so all-inclusive, it is the most fundamental area in which "the other" is likely to be different from us—and hence possibly seen as the most threatening. Again, this is not over-dramatization. . . . Hence, if humankind is to move from the Age of Monologue into the Age of Dialogue, the religions and ideologies must enter into the movement full force.[41]

It is instructive to observe the very problematic role of persuasion in the discussion that follows these remarks. Of the four interlocutors, John Cobb may take persuasion most seriously. "Real dialogue," he writes, "consists in the effort of both sides to persuade the other." Thus, "dialogue is the ideal context for evangelistic witness, not its opposite."[42] But Swidler could hardly disagree more. Persuasion in a strict sense, he objects, violates the very spirit of dialogue.

> My understanding of what fundamentally makes dialogue different from other kinds of intellectual encounters is that each partner comes to the encounter *first of all* to learn. If I want (especially, first of all) to persuade, I don't go to a dialogue, but to a debate, an argument, a teaching situation, or the like. . . . On the one hand, in dialogue, rather than trying to persuade my partner of something, I try to explain my understanding of it as clearly as possible precisely within that particular dialogue context so as to clarify *for myself* my understanding of the matter under discussion. . . . On the other hand, also in dialogue rather than trying to persuade my partner of something, I try to explain my understanding of it as clearly as possible as a *quid pro quo,* that is, as a

> response to my partner, who *also* comes to the dialogue primarily to learn.[43]

It seems clear enough that a significant, perhaps irreconcilable difference separates the images of dialogue that Cobb and Swidler advance, but dialogic conventions dictate that the participants come to some sort of consensus on this as seemingly on all important matters. The book concludes with a set of numbered "Consensus Statements." The tenth statement attempts at least partially to overcome (in questionable syntax, if not thought) the distance between the various participants on terms like "persuade" and "confront."

> The differences among us are partly because we each have a different "feel" for the words involved, but probably even more because we were speaking of different stages in the dialogue and at times had different dialogue participants in mind. We do agree, however, that at the beginning stage of a new dialogue we very much need to stress listening carefully and sympathetically to our partner and the seek our [*sic*] areas of agreement assiduously. At that stage we do not need to "persuade" or "confront," for we had been doing that for decades or even centuries.[44]

Does this statement actually reconcile the differences between Cobb and Swidler, or does it advance a third option inconsistent with the other two? In any event, for the best of motives (an abundance of good will, a magnanimous commitment to compromise), these dialoguers seem disappointingly eager to grab at any means necessary to explain away differences of opinion and deny genuine conceptual disagreement and intellectual debate.

Persuasion presents problems for advocates of interreligious-interideological dialogue. For that reason, a contrast of the practice of dialogue with what we find in the *Iliad* and the *Rāmāyaṇa* can be expected to highlight significant limitations of an ideological practice that attributes social thriving to mutual communication, especially religious communication. Persuasion is also similarly marginal to another recent view, but because that view attributes thriving not to dialogue and communication but to religious violence. This is the position of the French literary scholar and cultural theorist, René Girard.

As the later, rather apologetic book, *Things Hidden Since the Foundation of the World,* makes clear, Girard's views have significant roots in the

Christian tradition, especially in Christian teachings that emphasize the sacrificial nature of Jesus's death.[45] But Girard's best-known and most influential exposition, *Violence and the Sacred,* relies heavily not on a Christian theology of vicarious atonement but an exegesis of Greek tragedy.[46]

As Girard sees it, the potential course of human social interaction is something like the plot of Aeschylus's *Oresteia.* Just as Agamemnon's murder provokes Clytemnestra's murder and then renders her son and killer, Orestes, deserving of death, so every human society is threatened by a chain reaction of violence. To be more specific, vengeance represents the culmination of those forces of dissension that threaten to tear human community apart. As a result, human society is constituted only to the degree that it avoids "an interminable outbreak of vengeance," "an internal process of self-destruction." For reasons that will soon be apparent, Girard refers to this threatened chain reaction as a "sacrificial crisis."[47]

But if the potential course of human social interaction, as Girard sees it, resembles the *Oresteia,* the ending of Girard's story differs remarkably. "Violence," Girard insists, "is not to be denied, but it can be diverted to another object." Communities protect themselves from the violence of vengeance run amok through acts of violence that carry no risk of vengeance. In other words, they sacrifice. Through sacrifice, "the community's spontaneous and unanimous outburst" of violence is defused by being deflected onto the sacred, that is, onto a sacrificial victim. "The victim . . . is a substitute for all the members of the community, offered up by the members themselves. The sacrifice serves to protect the entire community from *its own* violence; it prompts the entire community to choose victims outside itself." The process of deflection works by a double substitution. First, a part substitutes for or takes on the guilt of the community as a whole, for example, a sacred king. Then, this representative of the community's self is replaced by the other, that is, by a ritual victim "drawn from categories that are neither outside nor inside the community, but marginal to it." The slaughter of the surrogate transforms the total disorder that violence threatens to release into a total order that violence produces.[48]

Like Swidler and company, Girard has great expectations. (Precisely what the practical implications of his view are is difficult to say.) His "hypothesis" or "theory," he claims, makes possible the first genuine "science" of religion by enabling the formulation of rigorous definitions. "Any phenomenon associated with the acts of remembering, commemorating, and perpetuating a unanimity that springs from the murder of a surrogate victim can be termed 'religious.'" At least to Girard, the methodological advantages of such a position are clear and irresistible. "The surrogate victim theory avoids at once the impressionism of the positivist approach and the arbitrary and 'reductivist' schemata of psychoanalysis."[49]

But Girard is even bolder. Adhering to what would seem an outmoded view of the historical and logical relations between religion and culture, he writes, "All religious rituals spring from the surrogate victim, and all the great institutions of mankind, both secular and religious, spring from ritual." What Girard aims at, then, is a science of human culture in its entirety, and one that reveals a truth necessarily hidden. "In order to retain its structuring influence the generative violence must remain hidden; misapprehension is indispensable to all religious or postreligious structuring." This requirement, Girard maintains, continues to mesmerize modern scholars, making it impossible for them to understand religion.[50] Worse still, modern cultural scholarship—ethnology in the manner of Frazer, psychoanalysis in the manner of Freud—are themselves sacrificial misunderstandings, symptomatic of a contemporary sacrificial crisis. And so Girard's book ends with as much poetic vision as scholarly analysis: "The essential violence returns to us in a spectacular manner—not only in the form of a violent history but also in the form of subversive knowledge. This crisis invites us, for the very first time, . . . to expose to the light of reason the role played by violence in human society."[51]

The present introduction is not the place to engage either interreligious dialogue (as conceived by Swidler) or sacrificial violence (as conceived by Girard). That will come at the end of the book. It is enough for now to note that the two ideologies account for social thriving in ways that render persuasion problematic and marginal: communication (as sharing) and violence. Homer and Vālmīki present a critical contrast. They recognize in persuasion a central source of social well-being, and they perceive in its failure the threat of ultimate disaster.

V

One final introductory task remains: to introduce briefly some of the conceptual apparatus that the argument will use. Three topics deserve comment here: the nature of the configurations (or patterns or structures) that the argument eventually invokes; the manner in which the book envisions the work of the epics and how that differs from currently popular talk about the literary or discursive construction of reality; and the sense I attribute to a term that might evoke misunderstanding, the term "mystification."

In his influential book, *The Order of Things,* Michel Foucault practices an archaeology of knowledge that claims to unearth configurations of a specific kind.[52] Excavating the epistemological layers on which the human sciences stand, he identifies the particular *epistêmes* that have enabled and organized knowledge since the Renaissance. Then he locates the human sciences within the modern *epistême.* His book ends with a tantalizing question: are we about to witness a death of humanity, parallel to Nietzsche's death of God, and the subsequent emergence of an *epistême* that will give the human sciences strictly conceived no place?

The present book is congruent with Foucault's archaeology in at least one significant way: it identifies configurations that operate on a broad scale. But how it diverges from Foucault's project is probably more significant than how it continues it. Foucault's approach is antihumanistic; his configurations are abstract *epistêmes* that define entire eras. My approach aspires to be humanistic; deliberately suspicious of such era-wide abstractions, it deals with configurations or patterns that appear in two specific poems. Foucault's configurations cut horizontally. They exclusively define entire (European) cultures at given periods. The configurations in this book cut longitudinally. Leaving room for cultural plurality at any given moment, they identify significant patterns that perdure over time. *The Order of Things* quarantines knowledge. In identifying the patterns that shaped knowledge, it deliberately ignores contextual features that might explain or account for those patterns. (To be sure, Foucault's later writings investigate how knowledge evidences a will to power.) This book contextualizes. It inserts the configurations into the contexts that evoked the epics and on which they acted. Perhaps most significant, Foucault's configurations pattern knowledge; they postulate relations between "words and things" (the French title). The configurations in this book are about rhetoric. They identify patterns of words in action.

One often reads today about one particular kind of verbal action, the construction of worlds of meaning.[53] There are, indeed, very important contexts in which it is appropriate and correct to speak of just such a construction, for example, the sense in which feminists talk of gender roles as socially constructed rather than given by nature. Gender, racial, and class differentials are indeed neither universal nor necessary. They are (to borrow Lévi-Strauss's well-worn distinction) cultural, not natural, the result of nurture rather than instinct. But although I do find it useful and necessary to talk about the cultural construction of social realities, I find the notion less than helpful in discussing the *Iliad* and the *Rāmāyaṇa.*

There is one sense of construction that I might want to use in talking about these poems. Some Homerists and Rāmāyaṇists, along with many if not most nonscholarly readers, have believed that the *Iliad,* the *Rāmāyaṇa,* or both describe worlds and perhaps events that the authors experienced directly. Careful scholars have shown, however, that the worlds of both the *Iliad* and the *Rāmāyaṇa* are composites, mixing historical features from different ages with nonhistorical ones.[54] Any unity these composites possess results from the fabricative capacity of the poetic imagination. In that sense, then, Homer and Vālmīki did construct poetic worlds, and we reconstruct poetic worlds every time we construe the poems. But what Marx said of history goes for the *Iliad* and the *Rāmāyaṇa,* too: the poems' authors and audiences may construct poetic worlds, but they do not and cannot construct them exactly as they please.

One implication of that statement is crucial here. The specific work of the *Iliad* and the *Rāmāyaṇa* cannot have been to construct epic worlds, because Homer and Vālmīki inherited traditions of epic poetry whose conventions by and large determined the worlds of the poems and even the specific themes and actions that might appear in them. As a result, it would actually obscure the manner in which these two poems articulated and continue to articulate with their contexts if we were to make the imaginative construction of worlds to be the specifically poetic work. Instead, the poetic imaginations worked to construct specific solutions to problematics given in the worlds the poets inherited. Audiences cared about those solutions because the problematics that they resolved were common to both the imagined worlds of literary reality and the experienced worlds of lived reality.[55]

If the argument of this book is correct, the imagined-literary and experienced-literal worlds in early Greece and India shared one problematic in particular, the practice of civic persuasion. In both settings, Greek and Indian, persuasion was conceived as necessary to harmonious, patterned social interaction; consequently, the failure of persuasion marked the limits of that interaction and threatened social chaos. But the horizons of the imagination are much more remote than those of experience, and the greater extension of imagined reality made the distinctive work of the *Iliad* and the *Rāmāyaṇa* possible. The two poems transcended in the imagination those limits of social interaction which appeared insurmountable in experience. In doing so, they performed an essential, religious work. They mystified the threat of chaos and made the configurations of social interaction fundamentally tenable. They also enabled them to perdure, as they have up to the present day.

In briefest summary, that is my argument. But before developing it in detail, I want to clarify a term just alluded to. The term is "mystification," and René Girard has given us reason to pause before we use it. He writes: "The notion that the beliefs of all mankind are a grand mystification that we alone have succeeded in penetrating is a hardy perennial—as well as being, to say the least, somewhat arrogant. The problem at hand is not the arrogance of Western science nor its blatant 'imperialism,' but rather its sheer inadequacy. It is precisely when the need to understand becomes most urgent that the explanations proposed in the domain of religion become most unsatisfactory."[56] It is truly puzzling that, having so eloquently recognized the arrogance of demystification, Girard then does his best to exemplify it. He unmasks (so he claims), for the first time in history, the true role of violence in society.

Somewhat more congenial are words that the historian Carlo Ginzburg wrote some years ago about a cult in modern Italy: "In wretched and disintegrated conditions, religion helps men and women to bear a little better a life in itself intolerable. It may not be much, but we have no right to despise it. But precisely because they protect believers from reality rather than prompting or helping them to become aware of, and change it, such popular cults are in the end a mystification."[57]

Unlike Ginzburg's subject, the *Iliad* and the *Rāmāyaṇa* do not permit us to dismiss religious practices on the basis of class. They recall the religio-ideological practices of the upper strata of Greek and Indian society, not the popular cults of peasants. Nevertheless, our distance from the poems renders the imaginative solutions that Homer and Vālmīki provide to the threats of failed persuasion unconvincing. Enthusiasts like Walter F. Otto and Károly Kerényi notwithstanding, most academics cannot believe in Homer's gods as most Greeks did, to the point of actually worshiping them. But such faith is crucial if the *Iliad*'s resolution is to be entirely successful. The situation of the *Rāmāyaṇa* is only a little different. Modern scholars, Indians and others, who have wished to embrace the *Rāmāyaṇa* as more than a pretty story have generally taken refuge in wholesale historicization: the monkeys, bears, and demons alongside and against whom Rāma fought were really tribal peoples; Rāvaṇa's fortress-city Laṅkā was not the island southeast of the Indian peninsula but an island in the middle of a lake in southeast India; the events in the poem took place not at the traditional date, the transition from the Tretā to the Dvāpara yuga some 869,000 years ago, but roughly in the sixth century B.C.E. The inevitable distance from which we approach the poems paints their work with the color of mystification. To speak less metaphorically, our distance from the poems opens a gap between the worlds of experience and imagination, a gap that historicizations try to bridge. We postulate a difference that those for whom the poems worked and continue to work do not accept. In our eyes, but not theirs, the poems imagine solutions that are unavailable in the world of experience and are therefore unconvincing. For that reason, I call those solutions mystifications.

This terminology calls for extreme delicacy. The slightest misstep will snap Girard's trap of intellectual arrogance shut. Let us recall, then, that falsification is separate from verification. It is possible to know that a proposition or solution is wrong without knowing which proposition or solution is correct. For that reason, I would suggest, identifying an ideological practice as mystification is not the same as demystifying it. Demystification entails the added step of revealing the forces or processes that are really at work, the forces and processes that mystification serves to obscure or screen. That grander, perhaps more arrogant task is not what this book intends. Its more modest aims are to explore two ancient literary works that confront us "with ideological differentials that help to define the limits and special functions of . . . current ideological practices." If the *Iliad* and the *Rāmāyaṇa* worked religiously to mystify the threat of social dissolution that appears when persuasion fails, a truly serious confrontation with that work invites us to self-reflection. What place does persuasion assume in our own social, political, and religious ideologies and practices? What faiths mystify the inadequacies of those ideologies and practices and their tenuousness? What gaps between our imagination and experience will other people discern? Above all, what, if anything, can be done to avert violence and promote social and political thriving when persuasion fails, as it has so frequently and so disastrously over the last hundred years?

It may well turn out that mystification of some sort is inevitable, that true demystification is impossible. Perhaps human beings live only by the grace of imagined solutions to experienced problems. Perhaps, as Moses learned long ago about God, human beings cannot look reality straight in the face and live.

1

When Persuasion Fails

I

Persuasion fails in the *Iliad.* In fact, it fails over and over again. But no one who has read the poem seriously can forget when persuasion fails in book 9.

At the beginning of the *Iliad,* Agamemnon, the leader of the Achaian* expeditionary force against Troy, had stolen Briseis, Achilles' favorite female captive. Stung, the mighty and indispensable Achilles retired to his ships on one end of the camp. Not to be deterred, Agamemnon marshaled his forces and set out to fight. But without the best of all the Achaians, he found himself fighting against the violent current of battle. As book 8 ends, the Achaians are in danger of being overwhelmed among their ships.

Suddenly, a small crag of hope juts out from the stormy sea. Agamemnon

*Herodotus saw the Trojan war as foreshadowing the later war between the Greeks and Persians. Following his lead, people often refer to Agamemnon's forces as Greeks. But this is an anachronism. In the poem, they are variously called Achaians, Danaans, and Argives. I will generally call them Achaians.

sends Odysseus, Phoinix, and Ajax to the ships of Achilles. "I repent. Plead with him to fight." Odysseus, renowned for his command of clever words, speaks first.

> Your health, Achilles. You have no lack of your equal
>   portion
> either within the shelter of Atreus' son, Agamemnon,
> nor here now in your own. We have good things in
>   abundance
> to feast on; here it is not the desirable feast we think of,
> but a trouble all too great, beloved of Zeus, that we look
>   on
> and are afraid. There is doubt if we save our strong-
>   benched vessels
> or if they will be destroyed, unless you put on your war
>   strength.
> The Trojans in their pride, with their far-renowned
>   companions,
> have set up an encampment close by the ships and the
>   rampart,
> and lit many fires along their army, and think no longer
> of being held, but rather to drive in upon the black ships.
> And Zeus, son of Kronos, lightens upon their right hand,
>   showing them
> portents of good, while Hektor in the huge pride of his
>   strength rages
> irresistibly, reliant on Zeus, and gives way to no one
> neither god nor man, but the strong fury has descended
>   upon him.
>
> (*Il.* 9.225–39)

Before he is through, some seventy or so lines later, Odysseus will enumerate the many gifts that Agamemnon has promised Achilles.

Achilles declines the lengthy offer, politely but firmly. Then Phoinix speaks, the aged friend of Achilles' father Peleus. His words are equally long and eloquent. Unfortunately for the Achaians, they are also equally effective. Then the baton passes to that stout defensive tower, Ajax. A man of deeds, not words, Ajax recites only a few, bitter lines, then the emissaries return. The Achaians receive their report in stunned silence.

In the *Rāmāyaṇa,* persuasion also fails. The most dramatic and disastrous failure occurs toward the beginning of the second book. Daśaratha, the king of Kośala* and father of the righteous Rāma, has decided the time has come to hand his scepter down. He will inaugurate his righteous son as heir apparent. But Rāma's stepmother, Kaikeyī, gets other ideas. Long ago Daśaratha had given her two boons: "Ask whatever you wish. . . ." Now Kaikeyī states her wishes. "Inaugurate my son Bharata," she demands. "Send Rāma to the forest for fourteen years." Daśaratha swoons. He cannot even remain conscious long enough to give Rāma the bad news. Strikingly, Rāma accepts this misfortune with perfect calm and equanimity.

But how inevitable is Rāma's misfortune? Lakṣmaṇa, one of Rāma's younger brothers, does not think it is inevitable at all. He tries to persuade his brother at length:

> Now is not the time for panic, the source of this sheer folly.
>
> Could a man like you talk this way were he not panicked, fearful of losing people's respect because of some infraction of righteousness?
>
> You are a bull among kṣatriyas [warriors], as powerful as fate is powerless. How in the world can you blame fate, a contemptible, feeble thing?
>
> How is it you harbor no suspicion of those two evil people? Don't you know, my righteous brother, that there are cunning people who wear the guise of righteousness?
>
> A thing the whole world would find despicable is under way: someone other than you is to be consecrated. I despise that "righteousness," my king, which has so altered your thinking, and about which you are deluded.
>
> Even if you think it fate that framed this plot of theirs, still you must reject it. I cannot approve of this course at all.
>
> For it is only the weak and cowardly who submit to fate; heroic men, strong of heart, do not humble themselves before fate.
>
> (*Rām.* 2.20.5c–11)

*One of the two most important of the legendary sixteen "republics" (*mahājanapadas*) in northeast India that preceded the rise of the Magadhan empire. Essentially, Kośala extended north from the confluence of the Ganges and Jumna rivers, where Allahabad is today.

Rāma's mother, Kausalyā, adds her own eloquent voice to Lakṣmaṇa's, but Rāma's response is the same. "Father must keep his word. I will go to the forest." He assents to only this much: Sītā, his wife, and Lakṣmaṇa may accompany him.

It is a contemporary truism that any piece of literature can sustain a variety of interpretations and analyses. In this book I develop only a single, limited analysis of the *Iliad* and the *Rāmāyaṇa.* I concentrate on the thematic of failed persuasion in each poem's *defining narrative.* I do so in order eventually to elucidate the religious work of the two poems.

II

Let me begin by explaining the term I just used, defining narrative.

The *Iliad* that you and I read is not Homer's *Iliad,* even if we read a critically edited Greek text. It is something like that poem's great-great-grandchild, assembled by European scholars attempting to re-create the original. The great-grandchild, now deceased, was a text established by the librarians of Alexandria. The grandchildren were the various city-texts used according to legend for purposes of competitive recitation, on which the Alexandrian text was based. The children—how many were there?—were the various versions recited orally by wandering singers called rhapsodes. And since every lineage must begin somewhere, maybe there was even a patronymous ancestor named Homer, who, to judge from modern practice, written as well as oral, would have varied the *Iliad* over his lifetime as the circumstances required.

The state of the *Iliad*'s text is bad enough. The received text of the *Rāmāyaṇa* is even worse. Unlike the *Iliad,* the *Rāmāyaṇa* is not an only child. It is more like a set of Siamese triplets abandoned on our doorstep. We know three major versions of the poem, preserved in Northeast, Northwest, and South India. But whose children are they? There are very few clues. Modern scholars are now circulating what they claim is a composite sketch of the parent text, a critical edition reconstructed according to principles developed for editing texts from ancient Greece, Rome, and Israel. But unlike works of European antiquity, the *Rāmāyaṇa* does not seem to have ever had a fixed text, so it is not entirely clear just what text the critical edition is actually trying to reproduce. Have the editors, then, successfully reconstructed a member of the previous generation, or are we really looking at a "first foto" of the next one?

For some critical purposes, a poem's questionable descent does not pose serious difficulties. The New Critics taught us long ago to interpret the poems that we have and toss the historical scraps to the pedants. But for the purposes at hand, the questionable descent of the *Iliad* and the *Rāmāyaṇa* poses very real problems indeed. The aim of this book is not to recover the religious meanings of the poems but to elucidate their religious work. To state the problem most pointedly: how can we talk about the work in antiquity of poems that only came into existence in the forms we know during the past hundred years? The difficulties are real, but there is no need to abandon our project and retire into the transcendent isolation of a New Critical "text," whichever text that happens to be. One way around the difficulties is to concentrate on what I call the defining narrative.

The potential for variation within the *Iliad* is great. The possibility of adding to or subtracting from the poem has been both nightmare and paradise for the analyst.* But all versions of the *Iliad* that would have stood out as such from the background of oral-formulaic poetry would have had to have shared one common feature: the story of Achilles and Agamemnon, Achilles and Patroklos, and Achilles and Hektor, either in whole or, for partial recitations, in fragmentary form.

In the *Rāmāyaṇa,* the analyst's dream has become reality: we know three—now four—distinct versions of the poem. But Camille Bulcke, the best *Rāmāyaṇa* scholar of an earlier generation, made a very perceptive observation. Most of the variations, he noted, heighten descriptions, lengthen speeches, draw out battles, and otherwise add to the impressive appearance of the poem, but they do not significantly alter the story.[1] All recensions, indeed all texts, of Vālmīki's *Rāmāyaṇa* are defined by a narrative, handled in a way that differentiates it from other Rāma tales and from other, later versions of the *Rāmāyaṇa,* such as Tulsi's or Kamban's or, in Sanskrit, the *Adhyātma-rāmāyaṇa.***

*For most of the nineteenth century and the first half of the twentieth, Homeric scholars were divided between two camps. The unitarians insisted that the *Iliad* and the *Odyssey* were each the products of a single hand, if not the same hand. The analysts insisted that they were composites, and tried various means to identify the different layers that made up the completed poems.

**Retellings of the *Rāmāyaṇa* are almost beyond enumeration. Tulsi Das (sixteenth century) composed in Hindi what is today the most popular *Rāmāyaṇa* in North India. Kamban's Tamil version occupies an analogous position in the far south. The *Adhyātma-rāmāyaṇa* is a medieval version with a heavy philosophical overlay.

Here, then, is what I mean by "defining narrative": the common tale or narrative thread that a poem would have to have told in order to count as a version of the *Iliad* or Vālmīki's *Rāmāyaṇa.* The burden of this chapter is to examine the thematic of failed persuasion in those narratives.[2]

III

Homer frames his narrative at the beginning of the poem: *Mēnin aeide, thea, Pēlēïadeō Achilēos*—word for word: "The wrath sing, o goddess, of the son of Peleus Achilles." Whatever else it may be, the *Iliad* is a poem about the wrath of Achilles, and it is as a direct result of that wrath that persuasion fails.

From the point of view of contemporary critical scholarship, the theme of the wrath of Achilles is something of an antique, if not entirely antiquated. Contemporary scholars have been more disposed to find in the *Iliad* a tragedy of nature versus culture or a confrontation with the aporias of life and death.[3] But for the ancient Greeks the situation seems to have been different. A textual variant, apparently intended to link the *Iliad* to the *Cypria,* the preceding poem in the epic cycle, mangles our *Iliad*'s first nine lines but at the same time preserves the theme of wrath. Although ancient audiences tolerated various openings for the *Iliad,* they apparently found the frame of Achilles' wrath compelling, and we would do well not to throw it out too quickly.

A couple of standard objections make it seem that Homer's opening prayer—"Sing, goddess, the wrath of Achilles"—goes unfulfilled.[4] The first is philological. *Mēnis,* it is said, is a noun that along with its verbal cognates, denotes a particular kind of anger felt only by Achilles and the gods. Unfortunately for the opening frame, the last time this kind of anger appears—in fact, the last time the noun *mēnis* appears—is when Achilles renounces his wrath at Agamemnon in book 19, just when tension really starts to build.

Philological arguments are impressive by their very learnedness, but I find this argument less convincing than I once did. First, *mēnis* is not a workhorse in Homer's vocabulary. After appearing as the first word of the poem, it appears only three times more, once in book 9 and twice in book 19.[5] Statistically, we should not expect it again until somewhere around book 29, well into "Iliad II." Second, Homer does not appear to be as aware of verbal nuances as his commentators. He uses other terms, such as *cholos,* to describe Achilles' emotional state without any discernible indications of subtle differences, even when Achilles is allegedly renouncing his *mēnis* in book 19 (compare 1.217 and 19.15). In fact, the later Greeks themselves did not seem to feel the sense and force that we attribute to *mēnis* today. The textual variant of the *Iliad* that I alluded to reads: "Tell me now, o Muses who dwell on Olympos, how *mēnis* and *cholos* came upon" Achilles and Apollo. Third, *mēnis* is the very first word of the poem, obviously an intentionally forceful position. It is quite possible that Homer chose *mēnis* because—given the conventions of his meter—it is the only word for wrath that can occupy this position. Another noun, such as *cholos,* would have made the opening much weaker.

The second objection is more weighty: *mēnis* or not, Achilles' wrath does not seem to be the subject of the poem we have before us. After Achilles becomes enraged in book 1, he drops out of sight. The poet treats us to what Hermann Fränkel perspicuously identified as a synopsis of the war at Troy. Starting in book 9, Achilles begins to reappear. But when he finally stands at center stage in book 19, he *renounces* the anger that the poem is supposed to be about, is reconciled with the Achaians, and fights valiantly to a very dramatic climax. Either the momentum of the story carries Homer on to a grand finale that is unannounced and out of place, or Homer sings a single, unified poem but stumbles over the first few lines, unable to articulate his grand theme.[6]

This objection is forceful, but it can be overcome. The problem is that it tries to discuss Achilles' wrath in sterile, lexical isolation. Reinsert that wrath into the system of interactions to which it clearly belongs, and Homer's claim, in effect, to "sing the wrath of Achilles" makes more sense.

The proem of the *Iliad* articulates half, but only half, of this system: wrath produces suffering, in this case, immeasurable suffering for the Achaians and death for mighty heroes. The other half of the system appears, for example, in one of Homer's memorable similes: ". . . like a strong-bearded lion whose whelps a stag-hunter has seized from out of the thick wood; and the lion, when it returns, grieves [*achnutai*] and traverses many vales, scenting out the tracks of the man, if somewhere he might find him. For especially sharp anger [*cholos*] seizes him" (18.318–22; my translation). Wrath not only produces suffering; it also results from suffering. Gregory Nagy puts the two halves together, but with French overtones that reify evil more than I find appropriate in the *Iliad:* "The word *akhos* [distress, anguish] signals *le transfer du mal:* the *akhos* of Akhilleus leads to the *mēnis* of Akhilleus leads to the *akhos* of the Akhaians."[7]

In brief, Homer's theme is the cyclical interaction of affliction and wrath centered on Achilles, "the best of the Achaians." It is that cyclical interaction which makes persuasion fail.

IV

The cyclical interaction of affliction and wrath seems to have been something of a typical theme in early Greek epic. Generalized, it appears on the famous shield of Achilles in *Iliad* 18.[8] Even more pointed, Homer recounted another instance of this theme at length in the embassy to Achilles in book 9. There Phoinix warned Achilles to relent, lest he suffer the fate of Meleagros—Meleagros, who, affronted by his mother, retired from battle in anger and sulked, resisting every attempt at persuasion except that of his wife, Cleopatra; when Cleopatra finally did persuade her husband, he returned to battle and fought valiantly, but he had lost the rewards that would otherwise have been his.

The cycle of affliction and wrath underlies the architecture of the story of Meleagros. It also underlies the architecture of the *Iliad*'s defining narrative. But how the *Iliad*'s tale differs from the Meleagros tale are instructive. For one thing, Homer shows more psychological insight than Phoinix. An enraged hero does not seek his own betterment (as the moral of Phoinix's story implies); he seeks revenge. For him, the cycle of affliction and wrath must end where it began, not with the hero but with the person who affronted him. The result is a narrative constructed of two successive cycles that take affliction and wrath to their ultimate expressions.

The first cycle begins with an escalating spiral: the wrath of Chryses and Apollo leads to the wrath of Agamemnon, which leads in turn to the wrath of Achilles. Achilles contemplates drawing his sword and running Agamemnon through, but Athena restrains him. So begins the theme of the enraged and sulking hero who is not willing to destroy society completely and thus must be content with inflicting suffering by refusing to act. Homer's treatment of the situation is masterful and bold. Phoinix dwells on the sulking Meleagros and the attempts to persuade him. Homer has Achilles return to his ships—and ignores him. Instead, he patiently and persistently shows what is at stake in the sufferings that Achilles' anger inflicts: the whole Trojan campaign. The Achaian hopes rise with Diomedes' *aristeia** in books 5 and 6, only to be crushed by a Trojan onslaught that brings the Achaians to the brink of despair.

At this point, Achilles reappears, but only because his appearance is mandated by what is of more interest to Homer than Achilles himself, the consequences of Achilles' wrath. Desperate, the Achaians attempt to close the cycle of affliction and wrath by means that placate even the gods (see *Il.* 9.499ff). They send Odysseus, Phoinix, and Ajax to offer Achilles Agamemnon's gifts. Their failure leaves both the Achaians and Achilles in impossible positions.

The Achaians are brought from the brink of despair to the brink of annihilation. Under the cover of night, Diomedes and Odysseus manage a successful raid, but Homer simply uses this passage (usually athetized) to add to the pathos of the next day's events. The Trojans breach the walls, overcome every hero but the steadfast Ajax (Achilles' antitype), and set fire to the ships. At the same time, Achilles finds that a strategy of nonaction involves him in contradictions that inevitably cause the cycle of affliction and wrath to snap another turn. Despite his intentions, Achilles cannot be both inside and outside the camp. Faced with the entreaties of Patroklos, he is caught between action and nonaction, wrath and friendship. The contradiction is embodied in the fateful, implausible instructions Achilles gives Patroklos as he tries to be both places at once: fight while you are being beaten; when you start to win, stop. Patroklos is an inevitable if unintended casualty of Achilles' great rage.

The first cycle of affliction and anger is never really resolved; it is simply replaced. Achilles does make up with Agamemnon, but only because, after he has rolled in the dust in anguish for his lost comrade, a new "anger [*cholos*] came harder upon him, and his eyes glittered terribly under his lids, like sunflare. He was glad, holding in his hands the shining gifts of Hephaistos" (*Il.* 19.15–18). Wrath at an ally gives way to wrath at an enemy. The anger of nonaction becomes the rage of action. The story of Achilles' wrath now becomes the story of Achilles' deeds. Achilles refuses to eat; only with difficulty does he allow others to do so. Beside himself with rage, Achilles lashes out even at the gods. He kills Hektor, but he would prefer to eat his flesh raw. In his rage, he entirely forgets to bury Patroklos, until reminded of his duty by Patroklos's own ghost. Finally, he

*A heroic poem, or a part of one, in which a hero demonstrates his prowess or *aretē*.

drags Hektor's corpse about Patroklos's pyre for twelve days running. Homer has described rage pushed to its absolute limit. There are no *algea,* no sufferings, that, once inflicted, will dispel Achilles' wrath. Within the limits of human society, the situation has become utterly impossible—until a force outside society, a compelling force, intervenes.

There are marked differences between this story and the tale of Meleagros.[9] First, consider the setting. Meleagros refuses to fight for a settled community over which his family has control. The communal model echoes the extended family of the *oikos,* the household writ large. Achilles sulks among a group of male warriors bound together on a foreign shore not by kinship or *oikos* but simply by the force of their common enterprise.[10] Second, in the tale of Meleagros, Cleopatra saves the city by persuading her husband to fight. In the *Iliad,* Achilles' closest companion, Patroklos (whose name inverts the two elements of Cleopatra's name), only compounds the misery. On the banks of Troy, companionship counts for something, but the familial structures that made for order at home do not. Finally, Meleagros is the champion of his city, but so are Agamemnon, Diomedes, Ajax, Odysseus, and the rest of the heroes we meet on the Ilian shore. Achilles is unique, and it is his uniqueness that makes his rage truly remarkable. He is the best of the best, "the best of all the Achaians," and he embodies the strength that the Achaian camp needs to survive. But for Homer, the very quality that gives Achilles the capacity for tremendous good also gives him the capacity for tremendous rage: the great *thumos** that Phoinix cannot persuade Achilles to tame. The paradox is nothing less than the paradox of Homeric society itself. The hero on whom survival depends is, when enraged, its greatest threat, and no human, social force can constrain him.

V

Homer uses another theme to play a continuous counterpart to the cyclical interaction of affliction and wrath, the theme of persuasion. The relation between the two is tight, for to yield to persuasion is to relent from anger. Persuasion is the force of harmony and order, anger the force of disrup-

*In Homeric "psychology," the *thumos* is the organ of action and emotion, the *psuchē* is the spirit or breath of life that departs at the moment of death.

tion and war. In the active voice, the verb *peithō,* "to persuade," *effects* order and harmony; in the middle voice, *peithomai,* it *reflects* it, as when Achilles bids Patroklos to welcome his guests, and Patroklos "is persuaded" to do so.

That Achilles' wrath excludes persuasion is clearly marked. He rejects the entreaties of Odysseus, Phoinix, and Ajax in no uncertain terms. He repeatedly insists that he cannot be persuaded.[11] The dying Hektor breathes out: "I know you well as I look upon you, I know that I could not persuade you, since in your breast is indeed a *thumos* of iron" (*Il.* 22.356–57; translation slightly altered). But there is an extra sharp edge to Achilles' implacability. Homer's world sets a limit to legitimate anger, a limit given in the paradigm of the gods and heroes of old, who, when enraged, were and are placated with gifts and persuaded with words (*Il.* 9.497–526). Achilles violates this limit, and this is a point that Homer does not want us to miss. He places the divine paradigm at the beginning of the entire poem and links Achilles' wrath with that of Apollo in (both versions of) the proem. When Apollo is enraged at the offense to Chryses his priest, Kalchas the seer suggests that the Achaians propitiate the god, for "thus we might persuade him" (*Il.* 1.100). But unlike Achilles, the god relents.

As the poem proceeds, two forms of persuasion enjoy some measure of success. One of these is the persuasion of Achilles' companion, Patroklos. The day after the visit of Agamemnon's emissaries, Achilles sends Patroklos to Nestor on the pretext of wanting to learn the identity of a wounded warrior. Nestor seizes the opportunity and asks Patroklos to intercede with Achilles. "With a god's help," he says, "you might move him. For the persuasion of a companion is a strong thing" (*Il.* 11.792–93, 15.403–4). We already know that Patroklos will achieve only limited success, for when he first answered Achilles' summons, Homer commented, "this was the beginning of his misfortune" (*Il.* 11.604). And before Patroklos has breathed a word of entreaty to Achilles, we have overheard Zeus tell Hera all that will happen (*Il.* 15.60–71). In effect, Patroklos only persuades Achilles to condemn him to death. With this death, Homer transforms what had typically been an instrument of hope—the persuasion of a *hetairos** (such as Cleopatra)—into a vehicle of disaster. Against the contradictions of Achilles' rage even the most potent human instrument of social order is useless.

With Patroklos dead, there is only one recourse left, the persuasion of

*"Companion"; when referring to a woman, the usual translation is "concubine."

those who are outside human society, the ghosts and the gods. In *Iliad* 23 the shade of Patroklos reminds Achilles of a most sacred duty, the funeral rites owed to a dead companion. Achilles obeys at once. He cremates the corpse, then sponsors the games. With these rituals, Achilles helps reconstruct what he had so furiously shattered. He reestablishes relations in which persuasion does not fail. The climax comes at the end of the book. Achilles speaks:

> "Son of Atreus [Agamemnon], we know how much you surpass all others,
> by how much you are the greatest in strength also among the spearthrowers.
> Therefore, take this prize and keep it and go back to your hollow
> ships; but let us give the spear to the hero Meriones;
> if so you wish it in your heart. This I beseech you."
> Thus he spoke, and Agamemnon, lord of men, did not fail to be persuaded.
> (*Il.* 23.890–95; translation altered)

Verbal and thematic echoes recall events earlier in the poem: the assembly when Agamemnon took Briseis, the embassy when Achilles refused to relent. But this time persuasion does not fail. Within the Achaian camp order has been restored.

But outside the camp, disorder still prevails. In that setting no common ancestors can persuade, so the task of persuasion falls to the gods.

When anger first arises in Achilles' breast, Athena descends from Olympos. "I have come to calm your fury, if you will obey," she says—that is, "if you will be persuaded [*pithēai*]" (*Il.* 1.207). Achilles is at once a model of placability: "It is necessary to observe your words, goddess, even though I am enraged [*kecholōmenon*] in my *thumos.* For thus it is better. The gods hearken especially to the person who 'obeys' [*epipeithētai*] them" (*Il.* 1.216–18; my translation). Appearances notwithstanding, Achilles is at pains to follow the specific instructions of the gods throughout the poem, and in the end, it is the gods who overcome Achilles' rage. Thetis appears to her son and informs him of Zeus's plan. Remarkably, Homer gives us not even a hint that Achilles hesitates: "So be it. [Priam] can bring the ransom and take away the body, if the Olympian himself so urgently bids it" (*Il.* 24.139–40).

But Achilles' rage has gone very far, and the quelling of this rage requires the violation of several conventions. Priam's liaison with Achilles must take place by cover of night. It defies common sense and normal cooperation: *oude me peiseis*—"you will not persuade me"—Priam tells Hekabe, and Hermes tells Priam (*Il.* 24.219, 433). Mortal enemies share the most intimate sign of communality, a meal, and then sleep under the same roof. Like all conventions, these conventions must be broken by a specialist. Priam is escorted by Hermes, the same god who escorts souls to that other most untamable being, Hades.

When at the end of book 9 Odysseus had told the assembled Achaians that Achilles was implacable, Homer noted the response: "Thus he spoke, and they all remained silent, marveling at his speech, for he spoke very powerfully" (*Il.* 9.693–94; my translation). When the aged Priam stands at Achilles' door, we are again in the presence of the profound. "[Priam] stood close beside him and caught the knees of Achilles in his arms, and kissed the hands that were dangerous and manslaughtering and had killed so many of his sons. . . . [And] Achilles wondered as he looked upon Priam, a godlike man, and the rest of them wondered also, and looked at each other" (*Il.* 24.477–80, 483–84). In the ensuing encounter, Achilles struggles to control himself. Priam's misery inevitably reminds Achilles of his own suffering, and his anger threatens to erupt (*Il.* 24.568–86). But in the end, as Achilles himself notes, the will of the gods must prevail. Achilles' wrath and the suffering that it wrought are finally extinguished with the last flickers of Hektor's pyre.

VI

It is difficult to say whether Vāimīki, like Homer, framed his defining narrative at the beginning of the *Rāmāyaṇa.* No one is quite sure where Vālmīki began. As the poem now reads, it does, of course, have a beginning. But the entire first book, the *Bāla-kāṇḍa,** is filled with traditional tales that

*The *Rāmāyaṇa* consists of seven *kāṇḍa*s or "books," each with its own name: (1) the *Bāla-kāṇḍa,* about the boy (*bāla*) Rāma; (2) the *Ayodhyā-kāṇḍa,* in which Rāma leaves his capital Ayodhyā; (3) the *Araṇya-kāṇḍa,* which recounts Rāma's years of exile in the forest (*araṇya*) and Sītā's abduction by Rāvaṇa, king of demons; (4) the *Kiṣkindhā-kāṇḍa,* in which Rāma makes an alliance with Sugrīva, the monkey king of Kiṣkindhā; (5) the *Sundara-kāṇḍa,* which describes the monkey Hanumān's visit to beautiful (*sundarī*) Laṅkā, capital of Rāvaṇa; (6) the *Yuddha-kāṇḍa,* Rāma's battle (*yuddha*) with Rāvaṇa; and (7) the *Uttara-kāṇḍa,* the last (*uttara*) book, a sampler of mythological odds and ends.

relate loosely, if at all, to the *Rāmāyaṇa*'s defining narrative. It contains stories of Rāma's boyhood, and stories for which Rāma's boyhood seems simply to have provided a convenient occasion. Most European scholars, writing history according to the canons of narrative unity, have regarded the *Bāla-kāṇḍa* as added later. Most traditional Indian scholars, writing history according to canons of spiritual unity, are inclined to let it stand.

Although the *Bāla-kāṇḍa* contributes little or nothing to the *Rāmāyaṇa*'s defining narrative, there is good reason not to ignore it entirely. Its opening, in which Vālmīki, the poem's traditional author, invents the poetic verse known as the *śloka** and learns of Rāma's deeds, provides an important clue about how most, if not all, ancient audiences heard the *Rāmāyaṇa.*[12]

> Ko tv^asmin sāṃpratam loke guṇavān kaś ca vīryavān
> dharmajñaś ca kṛtajñaś ca satyavākyo dṛḍavrataḥ?
>
> Is there anyone at all in this world today who is
>   possessed of virtues and valor,
> knowledgeable in precepts and practices, speaking truth
>   and firm in intention?
>
> (*Rām.* 1.1.2; my translation)

At the beginning of the *Rāmāyaṇa* Vālmīki himself poses this question to the great sage Nārada. Nārada responds by outlining the story of Rāma, the defining narrative of the *Rāmāyaṇa.* Among other things, Vālmīki's question sends a subtle signal about the poem we are about to hear. The *Iliad* may be a poem in which the effects of the wrath of Achilles are more important than Achilles himself, but the *Rāmāyaṇa* is a poem in which Rāma's character stands front and center. It is Rāma's virtue that makes persuasion fail.

VII

Like Daniel and Job in ancient Canaan, the virtuous Rāma appears to have been something of a standard figure in ancient Indian literature.[13] He ap-

*The workhorse of Indian meters. It consists of four *pāda*s (feet) of eight syllables each. The first four syllables in each *pāda* are free (x); the length of the last four syllables is prescribed:

xxxx ˘--˘ ¦ xxxx ˘-˘- ¦ ¦ xxxx ˘--˘ ¦ xxxx ˘-˘-.

pears in several literary works. He is even the hero of one of the *jātakas,* stories about the Buddha's previous births.[14] That story, the *Daśaratha-jātaka,* is a precious historical gem. It allows us to contrast the *Rāmāyaṇa* with a variant of the same general tale and in this way discern some of Vālmīki's distinctive concerns.

In the *jātaka* the wise Rāma (Rāma-paṇḍita), the heir apparent of Banaras (not Ayodhyā), is sent with his brother Lakkhaṇa (for Lakṣmaṇa) and his sister (not wife) Sītā to the Himalayan foothills (not the southern forests), and he is sent not for harm but for his own good: to await in safety the death of his father Daśaratha, fixed by the astrologers at twelve years in the future. But nine years later, Daśaratha dies prematurely of grief. When Rāma hears the news, he maintains not just a striking composure but a startling, perfect equanimity. He feels no emotion at all. Then he insists that his father's words be upheld and refuses to return home until the full twelve years are up. He sends his sandals home to rule instead.

The differences between the *jātaka* and the *Rāmāyaṇa* are instructive. Both authors use Rāma to illustrate the virtues of equanimity and, even more, of voluntary restraint from rule. But although the *Rāmāyaṇa* is far longer than the *jātaka,* Vālmīki writes the tighter story. The *jātaka* is an occasion and demonstration story. In it Rāma's exile is entirely unrelated to his virtue. It only provides a setting in which that virtue can eventually be seen. But in the *Rāmāyaṇa* Rāma's exile is an inseparable consequence of his virtue. The difference introduces a new dynamic into the poem. In the *jātaka* Rāma's insistence on hardship inconveniences no one but himself; in the *Rāmāyaṇa* it produces misery for as much of the world as Vālmīki wishes us to see. As a result, Vālmīki renders the defining narrative of the *Rāmāyaṇa* as a problem and resolution story, not an occasion and demonstration one. The problem afflicts the entire world, and it requires the entire narrative for its resolution.

Vālmīki defines the *Rāmāyaṇa*'s problematic in terms of two moral categories: *dharma* (righteousness or virtue) and *sukha* (pleasure). In function, these terms are analogous to anger and affliction in the *Iliad,* but in meaning, they are their contraries.[15] *Dharma,* from the verb root *√dhṛ** (to support or sustain), is the ordered activity that sustains all things. It is categorical duty, and it defines how one acts. *Sukha* (pleasure)

*In Sanskrit all verb forms, and most noun forms, are generated by altering verb roots. In transliteration, the unpronounced siglum "√" indicates that a collection of letters is a verb root rather than a generated form.

comprises especially two elements, *artha* (wealth and rule) and *kāma* (sensual enjoyment). It defines not action but experience—the good kind of experience, enjoyment, as opposed to the bad kind, *duḥkha* or suffering. Vālmīki's narrative results not from an *Iliad*-like cyclical interaction between *dharma* and *sukha,* virtue and pleasure, but from a dialectical tension between the two.

The tension between *dharma* and *sukha* is at heart a conflict between what ought to be and what one ought to do. *Dharma* and *sukha,* virtue and pleasure, ought to be congruent. The just should enjoy life, the unjust should suffer. Thus, Sītā, who is beautiful in body and soul, ought to prosper, but the demoness Śūrpaṇakhā ought not to. Hideous to behold, she offers to eat Sītā and stalk the forests at Rāma's side. The ideal appears in a reminder Sītā gives Rāma. One does not gain pleasure from pursuing pleasure, she says. "Prosperity [*artha*] comes from *dharma;* pleasure comes from *dharma,* too. Through *dharma* one acquires everything. The whole world rests on *dharma*" (*Rām.* 3.8.26; see also 27d; my translation).

The problem is, as a guide for action—what one ought to do as distinct from what ought to be—*dharma* stands opposed to *sukha,* virtue stands opposed to pleasure. To act according to *dharma* is to act without regard for, indeed, despite consequences in the world of experience. That is because in Vālmīki's world virtue is a characteristic of one's hidden, inner nature. Rāma's epithets constantly proclaim that he has conquered his senses (*jitendriya*) and realized his true self (*ātmakṛt*), his nature as *dharma* (*dharmātmā, dharmabhṛt*). Rāma's demonic archenemy, Rāvaṇa prince of thieves, abandons *dharma* for enjoyment in the form of material prosperity (*artha*) and carnal lust (*kāma*). Held captive by his senses, he deceives and is deceived by appearances (*māyā*).[16] The tension between *dharma* and *sukha,* between what ought to be and what one ought to do, provokes the events of the *Rāmāyaṇa.*

King Daśaratha recognizes Rāma's tremendous virtue and realizes that his son ought to rule. He begins preparations for Rāma's inauguration as coregent. But his favorite wife, Rāma's beautiful stepmother Kaikeyī, gets in the way. Spurred on by her hunchback servant Mantharā, Kaikeyī acts for the benefit (*artha*) of herself and her son Bharata, away on vacation.[17] She enters the house of wrath and rolls in the dirt. When her distraught husband comes, she asks for the fateful double boon: Rāma's fourteen-year exile and Bharata's inauguration. Vālmīki's *dharma* insists that King Daśaratha be true to his word.[18] Rāma insists that the king be truthful, too. Despite eloquent pleas from Lakṣmaṇa and Kausalyā and a repeated but rather inelegant plea from Rāma's fainting father ("O Rāma . . ."), the plans for the inauguration are called off. Rāma may act as he ought and insist that others do likewise, but those who pursue *sukha* to the exclusion of *dharma* seem to benefit instead.

In the rest of the *Ayodhyā-kāṇḍa* (*Rām.* 2.30–111), Vālmīki dramatizes the magnitude of the difficulty. Audiences watch and mourn as Rāma, Sītā, and Lakṣmaṇa make their slow, stately, royal procession through the streets of Ayodhyā, filled with mourning crowds that had gathered for Rāma's inauguration, past Śṛṅgaverapura and across the Ganges, through the hermitage of the Vedic sage Bharadvāja at the confluence of the Ganges and Jumna, and across the Jumna to the mountain retreat of Citrakūṭa. Left behind in Ayodhyā, Daśaratha dies of grief, and Kaikeyī's son, Bharata, is recalled. With that recall, *dharma* finally begins to assert itself, but it only begins. Instead of assuming the reins of government, Bharata denounces his mother's acts and treks off with the army in search of Rāma. In the shade of Citrakūṭa Bharata, his minister Jābāli, and his preceptor Vasiṣṭha work hard to persuade Rāma to return. Like all others before them, they fail, but they do not return home empty-handed. Bharata installs Rāma's sandals on the throne in Ayodhyā, then retires to the village of Nandi to wait out the appointed years of exile.

The first stage of Vālmīki's narrative articulates a profound moral problem.[19] What Rāma, the best of all human beings, ought to do (retire to the forest) completely frustrates what he ought to be (the prosperous ruler of Kośala). Supremely virtuous, Rāma never considers for a moment contravening duty in the interests of pleasure. But his moral virtuosity only results in disaster. The epitome of virtue seems intolerably helpless when confronted by anyone and everyone who would pursue the aims of pleasure. As for those who pursue virtue, Rāma's actions offer them nothing but *duḥkha* (suffering) and death.

Vālmīki has posed not only a moral problem but a narrative one as well. He cannot conclude his story the way the *jātaka* concludes, by having Rāma insist on spending a certain number of years in the forest. That would confirm the problematic, not resolve it, and it would make for a rather pitiful story besides. Rāma would then be nothing more than an easily manipulated pawn. At the same time, Rāma cannot simply retake by force a kingdom that he has vehemently and voluntarily renounced. If he did, he would be not virtuous but inconsistent, and rather than resolving the disjunction between *dharma* and *sukha,* the poem would simply confuse it.

Boldly and brilliantly, Vālmīki evades the two horns of this apparent dilemma. He adds a second stage to his narrative, unknown in the *jātaka,* that elegantly solves both the moral and procedural problems. Rāma experiences a new affliction that continues the threat posed by his exile. This affliction provides an opportunity for him to confront and overcome beings who epitomize action on the basis of pleasure, the *rākṣasa*s (demons).[20] It also permits a solution that is commensurate with the affliction of Rāma's exile. Rāma does what ought to be done, and as a result he brings about what ought to be. Enter Rāvaṇa, prince of demons, lord of Laṅkā.

Rāvaṇa appears by way of an escalating spiral of encounter and defeat. As Rāma, Sītā, and Lakṣmaṇa push deeper into the unknown south, they are more and more beset by demons. The demon Virādha tries to abduct Sītā; the two brothers quickly dispatch him to heaven. The demoness Śūrpaṇakhā tries to run off with Rāma; Lakṣmaṇa cuts off her ears and her nose. Her brothers Khara and Dūṣaṇa lead armies of thousands to avenge their sister's injury; Rāma and Lakṣmaṇa massacre them. With bodies thickly strewn, the stage is finally set. Śūrpaṇakhā calls on her mighty brother Rāvaṇa, invincible before the strongest creatures in the universe. She describes Sītā to him and kindles lust in his heart.

Driven by his passions, Rāvaṇa seeks help from the demon Marīca. But Marīca has tangled with Rāma once before and knows a bad idea when he hears one. He tries and tries to convince Rāvaṇa of his folly; in fact, he speaks the longest speech in the entire poem. But his attempt at persuasion fails. So he assumes the form of a golden deer, and draws first Rāma, then Lakṣmaṇa away from the hapless Sītā. While Marīca spills his lifeblood, Rāvaṇa appears to Sītā disguised as a brahmin. But he finds that he cannot win her heart, so he carries her off to Laṅkā by force. There, in a grove of aśoka trees, she mourns and patiently waits for deliverance.

The abduction of Sītā makes it possible for Vālmīki to resolve his dilemma. What ought to be converges with what one ought to do. The ideal husband, Rāma ought to kill the demons and rescue his wife. But Rāma and Lakṣmaṇa cannot redress the violation of virtue right away. A master storyteller, Vālmīki plays for dramatic interest by delaying the end. He draws the story out over three and a half books, heightening Rāma's longing and Sītā's suffering. From the bird Jaṭāyu Rāma and Lakṣmaṇa learn that Sītā has been abducted by Rāvaṇa. On Jaṭāyu's instructions they ally themselves with another exile, the once and future monkey king Sugrīva. By the dubious means of murdering Sugrīva's brother Vālin, they restore him to his forest kingdom, Kiṣkindhā. Finally, after the monsoon retreat, the monkey general Hanumān, son of the wind, locates Sītā in Rāvaṇa's capital Laṅkā. When he reports back, the armies prepare for battle.

The victory of virtue over pleasure has been a long time in coming, but when it comes, it takes on eschatological proportions. Rāvaṇa's spies try to enumerate the hosts ranged against them, but they must give up: "The rest of the strong, quick-footed monkeys cannot be counted; there are too many of them" (*Rām.* 6.18.41). The successive encounters between mighty warriors, like the crumbling walls of Laṅkā, recall universal destruction: "Laṅkā looked like the ocean at the end of the world" (*Rām.* 6.62.20cd). One by one, the demon-generals are cut down, then Rāma and ten-necked Rāvaṇa meet. Rāvaṇa's long-expected death and Sītā's long-awaited release bring to a close the period of Rāma's exile. Riding in the flying chariot Puṣpaka, Rāma and Sītā return to Ayodhyā, where Rāma is installed on the throne.

By relentlessly pursuing what he ought to do, Rāma has finally brought about what ought to be. *Dharma* and *sukha,* virtue and pleasure, converge; the tension between them is resolved. The outcome befits the beginning of a new age. The demonic enemies of virtue are all dead. Those who made the ultimate sacrifice for *dharma* are raised to a new and prosperous life. In the end, the *Rāmāyaṇa*'s defining narrative confirms Sītā's observation: the greatest pleasure derives from pursuing virtue, not pleasure.

VIII

Another thematic appears in the *Rāmāyaṇa* as a necessary complement to the conflict between what ought to be and what one ought to do: the failure of persuasion. In Vālmīki's world persuasion is the ordinary instrument by which human beings reconcile the tension between *dharma* and *sukha.* At the same time, when it is most needed, persuasion fails, consistently, disastrously, and unavoidably.

The Greek verb *peithō,* we have seen, is more versatile than the English verb "persuade." Only in the active voice does *peithō* mean "to persuade"; in certain middle or passive voices it means "to obey." Vālmīki's Sanskrit is rather different. It has no verb meaning "to persuade" at all. In the *Rāmāyaṇa* people who persuade simply "speak," "reply," "ask," or occasionally "command."[21] A single word, well-known to most English-speakers, nicely illustrates the broad range of Vālmīki's words for verbal activity, the word *mantra*. A *mantra* may be, as we usually think, a ritual formula. As such, it addresses another being as the object or recipient of action. It acts directly on that being. But *mantra* may also denote a piece of counsel or bit of advice. In that case, it addresses another being as the agent of action (compare *mantrin,* "minister or counselor"). More generally, the verb √*mantr,* which probably derives from the noun *mantra,* simply means "to speak," "to relate."[22]

Characters in the *Rāmāyaṇa* do not often use *mantras* in the first sense. They rarely act to change another being directly by means of words. Perhaps they cannot; at times they choose not to. When the captive Sītā confronts Rāvaṇa in Laṅkā, she says she could reduce her captor to ash with a single word, but she will not do it. She does not have her husband's permission (*Rām.* 5.20.20).

The characters in the *Rāmāyaṇa* prefer *mantra* in the second sense: they generally address other beings as agents rather than objects of action. That is, they generally try to persuade. Sometimes they succeed. When Sītā and Lakṣmaṇa ask Rāma's permission to accompany him to the forest, he grants their request. When the sages ask Rāma for help against the demons, he scolds them for thinking they had to ask. Killing *rākṣasa*s is, he says, the reason he has come to the forest (*Rām.* 3.5). But at the two most important junctures of the duel between what ought to be and what one ought to do, persuasion fails. These two junctures correspond to the two stages of Vālmīki's narrative.

Any number of speakers try to persuade Rāma not to go to the forest. Lakṣmaṇa's speech in *Rāmāyaṇa* 2.20 is a good example. Moved to rage by Rāma's resolve, Lakṣmaṇa urges his brother to resist the schemes of Daśaratha and Kaikeyī. Impetuously, he accuses Rāma of surrendering to fate like a coward and offers to defend Rāma's inauguration with irresistible force. But he pleads to no avail.

In the second stage, the speeches that preeminently fail address not Rāma but Rāvaṇa. Examples include Marīca's verbal marathon, the longest speech in the poem (*Rām.* 3.35–37, 39); Sītā's short, stern, eloquent refusal of Rāvaṇa's advances (*Rām.* 5.20); and the last, futile attempt by Rāvaṇa's virtuous brother, Vibhīṣaṇa, to avert the final battle (*Rām.* 6.9, but compare 6.7). The poem's historical context gives this second failure of persuasion further significance. In the *jātakas,* which are rough contemporaries of the *Rāmāyaṇa,* persuasion was a preferred method of handling demons. In those tales, the demons would hear the Buddhist *dhamma* and reform. But the events of the *Rāmāyaṇa* show how misplaced Buddhist hopes are. No speech can dissuade a prince of demons like Rāvaṇa. Demons must be confronted; indeed, they must be killed.

There are good reasons why persuasion fails in the *Rāmāyaṇa* when it is needed the most. As Vālmīki sees it, action proceeds from the inner being or character (*antarātman*) of an agent. Secluded from the world of appearances (*parokṣam,* "beyond physical sensation"), character cannot be manipulated by physical means. To address it directly one must use the privileged, nonmaterial instrument of words, *mantras* in either the first or second sense of the word.

But in Vālmīki's universe, virtuous and vicious heroes remain unaffected by words of any kind, almost by definition. *Mantras* as ritual formulas cannot harm them. The ability to withstand such supernatural weapons is a prime mark of a high heroic nature. At the same time, when it matters the most, *mantra* as advice cannot sway them, either, because a heroic character, whether virtuous or vicious, is above all one that is firm and resolved. It acts without swaying to the left or to the right and without the possibility of being swayed, either. In this world, then, the failure of persuasion becomes the necessary prelude to great action. In the narrative's first stage it demonstrates Rāma's pure but problematic virtue. In the second stage it demonstrates Rāvaṇa's pure but problematic vice. Together, the two failures set the mightiest beings in the universe on courses that must collide.

Unlike Homer, however, Vālmīki can only use persuasion to develop his problematic, not resolve it. If persuasion were eventually to succeed, Rāma and Rāvaṇa would no longer be true heroes, the *Rāmāyaṇa* would no longer be a heroic poem. Vālmīki can only fully release the tension between *dharma* and *sukha* and resolve the conflict between what ought to be and what one ought to do in one way: by presenting a being wholly devoted to virtue who confronts and overcomes another being wholly given to pleasure. That is, Vālmīki can only successfully execute his theme if, at the moments of the greatest dramatic interest, persuasion consistently and disastrously fails.

IX

In this chapter I have explicated the defining narratives of the *Iliad* and the *Rāmāyaṇa* with special reference to the development of a similar thematic, the failure of persuasion. How do the two narratives compare?

Both the *Iliad* and the *Rāmāyaṇa* articulate an ultimate threat that arises when persuasion fails. Achilles retires from battle, and the Achaians cannot hold the Trojans back. They face the imminent firing of their ships, then certain death by water or the sword. When Rāma retires to the forest, his father's subjects watch their hopes for flourishing wither and decay. The cool moonlight of Rāma's face is eclipsed, and the people plunge headlong into an underworld of dreary darkness.

There are striking similarities between these two tales. Some of them are almost more than one would expect from poets working in cultures as remote in time and space as Homer's Ionia and Vālmīki's India. For example, in both the *Iliad* and the *Rāmāyaṇa* the fortunes of society depend on a single, male hero. When persuasion fails, that hero retires from society. He leaves his community to suffer in his absence.

Even more interesting, both Homer and Vālmīki use this hero's retiring to articulate, then resolve a problem framed in terms of absolute goodness.[23] There are many ways to be good; Achilles epitomizes one of them. True, he violates norms of social order that even the gods observe; he sends his best friend to death; he fights with the gods; he forgets to bury Patroklos; and he refuses to return or bury Hektor's corpse. But Achilles has his own particular virtue, too. Arthur Adkins has insisted that, among the early Greeks, results-oriented competitive virtues (Adkins's *aretē,* "excellence") were more important than intention-oriented cooperative ones (such as *philotēs,* "friendship"). Achilles epitomizes the former class: he is good at fighting.[24] In fact, he is "the best of all the Achaians." As Homer's narrative makes clear, Achilles' virtue encapsulates the resources Achaian society needs most to survive. Unfortunately, it also makes Achilles impossible to persuade.

Rāma's goodness corresponds more closely to the categorical virtues of duty and self-renunciation. That kind of goodness evokes from Rāma and Daśaratha a most unusual response to Kaikeyī's demand. The expected response appears in the *Daśaratha-jātaka.* "The king snapped his fingers. 'Out, vile jade!' he said angrily. . . . [He] would not give her his gift." Rudely dismissing his wife, Daśaratha took measures to prevent Rāma's assassination.[25] But Vālmīki's characters are moral absolutists, committed to virtue at all costs. Vālmīki's Daśaratha only manages to faint, his Rāma only helps the king to die.

There are, then, some striking similarities between the defining narratives of the *Iliad* and the *Rāmāyaṇa:* both poets frame the problem of failed persuasion in terms of absolute goodness; absolute goodness is incarnate in the person of a single male hero; when persuasion fails, the hero retires from social activity; his absence produces communal suffering and threatens decay and death. At the same time, Homer and Vālmīki dispose this common theme in very different ways. They differ on how to pose the problem, how to solve it, and how to incarnate it in a narrative.

Homer and Vālmīki pose the problem of failed persuasion differently. First, they place it in different settings. The Achaians inhabit a temporary military encampment on foreign shores; Daśaratha's subjects inhabit settled territory. Perhaps for this reason the two heroes retire to different places. Achilles threatens to sail home, but in fact he does not leave camp. He remains by his ships on a remote flank. Rāma retires much farther. Unlike Bharata, he does not stay in a village on the edge of his father's kingdom. Unlike the Rāma of the *Daśaratha-jātaka,* he does not even go to the rather tame northern wilds of the Himalayan foothills. Instead, he pushes into the deep south, until he reaches a point, past Citrakūṭa, where Vālmīki's knowledge of geography seems to fail.

Second, Homer and Vālmīki develop the problem of failed persuasion in terms of different values. Achilles epitomizes a consequentialist ethic: he is virtuous because he gets things done. To this extent, Homer's *aretē* resembles Machiavelli's *virtu.* Rāma epitomizes a categorical ethic. It identifies right action apart from, even despite, the consequences of action. To this extent, his *dharma* resembles Kant's duty. The different ethics influence the role of persuasion. In the *Iliad* the failure of persuasion is an issue only in the case of the virtuous. If Thersites, for example, had entirely refused to be persuaded, that would have presented no real danger. But the *Rāmāyaṇa* associates the failure of persuasion with vice as well as virtue. In Vālmīki's world beings who adamantly reject virtue are almost as dangerous as those who adamantly cultivate it.

Third, Homer and Vālmīki enact the problem of persuasion against a backdrop of different emotions and social activities. When persuasion fails, Achilles is furious. He speaks vigorous, antagonistic words. Athena herself must descend from Olympos to prevent him from drawing his sword and running Agamemnon through. Rāma's emotions and behavior are just the opposite. At the beginning of the *Ayodhyā-kāṇḍa* Vālmīki describes his hero: "His *ātman* is always calm. His speech is always kind. When he is addressed harshly, he says nothing in reply" (*Rām.* 2.1.15; my translation). When Kaikeyī demands Rāma's exile, the audience sees just how painful Rāma's dedicated an-agonism can be. Kaikeyī sends Rāma to the forest; Rāma opens his mouth only to consent. Achilles' and Rāma's different emotions and behavior imply two different motivations. Achilles acts to avoid pain; Rāma acts to avoid all pleasure that would compromise his virtue.

Having posed the problem of persuasion differently, Homer and Vālmīki differ on how to solve it. In both cases the resolution reverses the moods that characterize the initial stages of the two poems. Thus, a delightful calm settles on the Achaian camp at the end of the games, then a profound, somewhat fitful calm settles on Achilles' hut when Hermes and Priam appear at the door. The *Iliad* may be celebrated as a poem of battle and death, but it restores order in the camp and creates a temporary truce on the plain of battle by successful persuasion. As the *Rāmāyaṇa* proceeds, however, quite the opposite occurs. Rāma's initial, profound an-agonism evaporates. The violent antagonism of battle comes to dominate. Although India is at times celebrated as a land of peace and nonviolence, Vālmīki solves the failure of persuasion not with successful persuasion but with war and killing.

In effect, Homer and Vālmīki use different instruments to effect their solutions. Homer uses sources that are external not just to the dispute between Achilles and Agamemnon but to the particular locality where that dispute occurs: the ghosts and the gods. Vālmīki has no use for external forces. He knows the gods, but they play little active role in his narrative. His solution arises from manifesting the inner force of Rāma's virtue and being. The different instruments produce different results. Homer restores the rather unsatisfactory status quo of an army encamped for battle. The truce is only temporary; so is the peace in the Achaian camp. Vālmīki's solution is more stable and permanent. He establishes a glorious age of flourishing, the *Rāma-rājya,* that still inspires Indians today. As a result, the end of each narrative arouses different emotions. The *Iliad* ends with a silence born of awe mixed with fatigue. The *Rāmāyaṇa* ends on a note of excited jubilation.

Besides posing and solving the problem of persuasion differently, Homer and Vālmīki choose fundamentally different structures for their narratives. Homer devotes most of his poem to developing the problem. Cycles of affliction, wrath, and affliction roll steadily toward disaster until in the last two books some sort of halt is finally achieved. One could say that Homer disposes his problem dynamically, then appeals to a structural innovation, the ghosts and the gods, to resolve it. By contrast, Vālmīki hurls his problems quickly and with devastating force. Then in a slow, stately, irresistible procession his narrative moves toward its final solution. If Homer's problem is dynamic, Vālmīki's is structural, the social complications in which the paragons of virtue find themselves entangled. And if Homer's solution is structural, Vālmīki's is dynamic. Like Homer's problem, it develops steadily throughout much of the poem.

Because of these different architectonic choices, persuasion fails at different places in the two poems. The failure of persuasion pervades the *Iliad,* from book 1 to book 24. The speech by Odysseus with which this chapter begins is a good example. One of the first and most forceful attempts to persuade Achilles, it occurs about a third of the way through the poem. In the *Rāmāyaṇa* persuasion fails most remarkably when Vālmīki is stating his problem: when he introduces Rāma's exile, then when he introduces Rāvaṇa. Lakṣmaṇa's speech to Rāma, cited at the beginning of this chapter, is another good example. A vigorous speech, it occurs almost at the very beginning of the defining narrative. When persuasion fails later in the *Rāmāyaṇa,* after the introduction of Rāvaṇa, it most often comes as a brief reminder of the direction that the initial failure established.

In the realm of imagined, literary reality, then, both the *Iliad* and the *Rāmāyaṇa* image a problematic that centers on the failure of persuasion. Persuasion is needed for the communities within the poems to thrive, but when it is needed the most, persuasion dismally fails. To move from this literary account to a contextual analysis, we must ask, how did this imagined, literary problematic intersect with the experienced, literal worlds in which Homer, Vālmīki, and their audiences lived?

2

Poetic Works and Their Worlds

I

The *Iliad* and the *Rāmāyaṇa* rehearse what happens when persuasion fails. Achilles takes to his hut, and the order of society is not fully restored until the Olympians intervene. Rāma retreats to the forest and does not return until he has slain the mightiest demon of all.

It has been quite some time since American scholars, at least, have argued seriously about whether these events actually occurred. Most of them simply assume that the stories we have are fictitious, whatever actual events might have inspired Homer, Vālmīki, or their predecessors. Discussions about the universes of the poems have been more serious. Within living memory, respected scholars like M. I. Finley and S. N. Vyas have tried to reconstruct "the world of Odysseus" and "India in the *Rāmāyaṇa* age" partly from literary, partly from archaeological sources.[1] But so far as I can see, their critics are more nearly correct. The worlds of the *Iliad* and the *Rāmāyaṇa* are artificial composites—imagined, literary realities—that never existed as experienced, literal totalities.

This chapter takes up questions of history from a different angle. It transposes those questions from the events and worlds within the poems to the poems themselves as events, to the poetic work, if you will. We know that ancient audiences cared about the *Iliad* and the *Rāmāyaṇa.* We know, too, that poems about which audiences care somehow articulate with their audiences' concerns. Otherwise, they would simply be ignored. The task at hand is to determine, so far as we are able, the manner in which the treatments of failed persuasion articulated with the concerns of their authors and early audiences. In other words, where did literary and literal realities intersect?

My suggestion is this: in imagining fictive solutions to problems of failed persuasion, Homer and Vālmīki were mystifying fundamental threats to the worlds in which they lived. That is, they addressed pressing problematics in the worlds of experienced, literal reality, but they addressed them with solutions that were, strictly speaking, available only in the worlds of imagined, literary reality. That, I will suggest, was the religious work of the poems. This suggestion will emerge more clearly, however, if before turning to actual history we assess other, plausible accounts of the work of the poems.

II

Ancient Roman rhetoricians identified three purposes for verbal activity: to please, to teach, and to move someone to act. This list is a convenient place to begin reflecting on the work of the *Iliad* and the *Rāmāyaṇa.* It helps organize the kinds of work previous scholars have ascribed to both poems.

On one view, Homer and Vālmīki sang their poems because, for motives ranging from noble to base, they were trying to please their audiences.[2] This view is easy to discount, but we should not dismiss it completely. Stories and poems do please, and at some time or other stories as long as the *Iliad* and the *Rāmāyaṇa* had better have pleased a great deal, lest Homer and Vālmīki find themselves without audiences and, perhaps, back tilling the fields. But saying that Homer and Vālmīki composed their poems to please their patrons and audiences does not tell us much that we specifically want to know. It does not identify what attracted the poets to the theme of failed persuasion, nor does it indicate why audiences would have listened with pleasure, as they obviously did, to tremendously long poems that used that theme.[3]

Other accounts conceive of the epics as teaching. Homer and Vālmīki were, so to speak, the educators of ancient Greece and India. The *Rāmāyaṇa* has indeed taught—defined and transmitted—ideal social roles. Recall the young woman's remarks about Sītā that I reported at the beginning of the introduction. Another anecdote illustrates how these roles actually operate, even among people who are not particularly devout. Reflecting on the experience of being illegally demoted and locked out of his office, a professor of archaeology once told me (I'm paraphrasing), "My sons wanted me to fight it, but I asked myself, 'What would Rāma have done?' So at first I was inclined to let it be."

Almost thirty years ago Eric Havelock developed a pedagogical view of Homer in the context of his work with orality and formulaic composition.[4] In a nonliterate world like early Greece, he argued, formulaic expressions and themes constituted the prime source of knowledge, the *Iliad* and the *Odyssey* were the first *Enkyklopedia Hellenikē.* Underlying Havelock's view is the position that in oral-formulaic poetry the medium is the message, and the stories are unimportant. But this position is difficult to maintain for works like the *Iliad* and the *Odyssey,* whose narratives possess a unity, power, and economy unique among the epics of Greece.[5] Worse yet, the establishment and transmission of social paradigms can hardly be the specific work of a narrative whose central thematic is a contravention of a social paradigm that no one should emulate and that cannot be redressed by ordinary human means. One can at least emulate Rāma, but that still does not tell us why audiences cared about the narrative.[6]

In the last several years, another view of the work of the *Iliad* and the *Rāmāyaṇa* has become fashionable. In this view, the two poems moved their audience to act or, rather, not to act. Each epic was composed to legitimate the position and interests of a ruling figure, stratum, or class in ancient Greece or India. Once again, I think, our nets come up empty. An appeal to legitimation does not elucidate why or how Homer's and Vālmīki's literary and lived worlds intersected at the failure of persuasion. But this point requires separate and extended treatment for each poem. In the course of that treatment, my own position—that the poems worked to mystify ultimate threats to social and even universal existence—will begin to emerge.

III

Those who find meaning in the *Iliad*'s structures—its world or style as opposed to its narrative—have viewed the epic as a device to legitimate the position of the highest class (using the word "class" in a nontechnical sense).[7] The world of which Homer sings is a world of heroes, of the *agathoi* or leading members of society; all others are inconsequential. It is a quick jump to assume that Homeric epic provided the model for the supremacy of the *aristoi* in Homer's day, whether that class was actually ascendant or, as Ian Morris has recently suggested for late eighth-century Athens, in (temporary) retreat.[8]

There are good reasons to connect Greek formulaic epic with the *aristoi* of Homer's day. Some eighth-century funerals seem to have emulated Homeric practice, just as funerals today are often signs of social pretension. Leading figures on the Asia Minor coast bore such Homeric names as Agamemnon and Hektor and such patronyms as Neleid (after Nestor of Pylos, whose descendants allegedly came east *via* Athens). Narrative heroic art begins to appear at this period, presumably to cater to the fancies of the well-to-do, and some have connected the nascent cults at Mycenaean tombs with familial social ambitions.[9] It does seem, then, as Ian Morris has suggested, that the *aristoi* of the eighth century liked to think of themselves as Mycenaean heroes,[10] and it is easy to imagine Homer and his fellow bards providing entertainment at rich men's feasts, as Demodokos, Phēmios, and even Odysseus himself do in the *Odyssey.* (But is Homer's depiction of bards accurate history or useful ideology? That I cannot tell.)

It is important to be clear about what these features establish. They strongly suggest that eighth-century *aristoi* were using epic materials to further their social pretensions. But as vase paintings show, the epic materials they used certainly encompassed more than the *Iliad* and the *Odyssey.* On one count only about 10 percent of painted narrative scenes derive from Homer's poems; the rest of the Homeric cycle* provides many more subjects. And the 10 percent that do come from Homer are made up of only a limited stock of favorite stories.[11] At the most we can say that traditional heroic epic provided a resource for the upper crust in its play for power and prestige. If we speak of "Homer" here, that is only a sort of synecdoche. As the practitioner of heroic epic whose name we know best, Homer is made to stand for the whole.

There are solid reasons, I think, why the *Iliad*'s defining narrative, centered on wrath, affliction, and the failure of persuasion, should not be seen as

*The series of ancient Greek epics that related the Trojan war from start to finish: *Cypria, Iliad, Aithiopis, Ilias parva* (Little *Iliad*), *Iliu persis* (Sack of Troy), *Nostoi* (Returns), *Odyssey,* and *Telegony.* Usually only the *Iliad* and the *Odyssey* are ascribed to Homer himself.

an attempt to legitimate the position of the *aristoi.* Hans Robert Jauss has developed a typology of the various ways audiences identify with heroes.[12] To my tastes, his typology is somewhat naive sociologically. Nevertheless, he makes sense when he connects the emulation and imitation of heroic models with a particular type of hero and a particular type of "receptive disposition." According to Jauss, a person emulates or imitates a "perfect" hero, one whose capacities are greater than one's own can ever be, because that person identifies with the hero through admiration. Think of how certain Christians, for example, have admired and thus identified with saints.[13]

The *Iliad* certainly contains its share of admirable and emulatable figures. As a matter of routine, both Achaian and Trojan heroes perform tasks that are impossible for mortals of today. Even among them, certain heroes stand out. My personal favorites are Ajax, Hektor, Diomedes, and perhaps Odysseus. We admire such figures. In fact, we have to. If Hektor or Ajax or Diomedes were not admirable, the *Iliad* would not work.

The reason the *Iliad* would not work is that these admirable figures provide the necessary background against which Homer sets the defining narrative. They effect a process of identification that allows us to recognize the significance of the events portrayed. The narrative itself, however, focuses on something far different from the emulatable hero. It depicts the "perfect" hero, and he turns out to be a hero whom it is impossible to emulate or really admire.

Why can we not admire Achilles? We cannot in part because Homer builds a critique of Achilles into the *Iliad,* a critique that we find compelling because we hear it from those we do admire. When Achilles' rage starts to contravene the accepted paradigms of persuasion, Phoinix says correctly, "Until now there was nothing wrong [*ou ti nemessēton*] with being angry" (*Il.* 9.523; my translation). But beginning with the failure of persuasion in book 9, there is something wrong with Achilles' anger. After Phoinix's speech, the critique continues in the tense relations between Zeus and the other gods in the middle of the poem; is taken up by Patroklos when he speaks for the Achaian cause, only to be rewarded with death (see 16.21–45); rises one notch when Odysseus demonstrates in *Iliad* 19 that Achilles' demands are unreasonable and another notch when the raging Achilles, in danger of losing his life at the hands of gods he has so boldly attacked, must be rescued by divine intervention. Once Hektor is killed, the dead Patroklos must plead with his former companion for burial. Finally, in the divine council of *Iliad* 24, even Zeus, Achilles' ultimate partisan, concedes that he has had enough.

Achilles is not an admirable and emulatable hero. He is an ambiguous hero. His rage and unpersuadability represent the internal forces of social disintegration raised to their highest power. They threaten to destroy the heroes and their world of consensus. But Achilles' rage and rejection of persuasion can pose this threat only because Achilles is the "best of all the Achaians." He is capable of great destruction, but only because he is first capable of great good. The most powerful hero is the one most needed for survival, but as the *Iliad* shows clearly, he is also the most dangerous.

How does an audience respond to such a hero and such a tale? Homer hints at how he expects his audience to respond, for he builds an audience into his poem, again an audience made up of those whom Homer's audience would admire. Confronted with the account of Achilles' rage and implacability, the great heroes of old all sat in stunned amazement at the powerful words (*Il.* 9.693–94). Achilles' rage is stunning; silent, dumbfounded amazement is the appropriate response. But Homer is not content to leave his audience in amazed awe at his hero's capacity for implacable rage and at the unraveling of the social fabric. In the end he transforms awe at the problem into awe at the solution. The stunned amazement of the Achaians is eclipsed by the profound nocturnal peace that accompanies the quelling of Achilles' great rage in *Iliad* 24, in fact, by the awe of Achilles himself as he looks on the aged Priam. Human obstinacy is great, but in the end divine persuasion is greater.

The leading class of Homer's day may have used the resources of epic to legitimate their position, but it does not make much sense to say that Homer's thematic of failed persuasion furthered their efforts. The central figure is one we cannot emulate, imitate, or admire, and the turn of events is one that everyone would try to avoid. Instead, Homer seems to be articulating powerfully an ultimate threat to human, social existence, and then providing a religious, social fiction to mystify that threat and thereby overcome it.

IV

We cannot apply the same argument against legitimation to the *Rāmāyaṇa.* Unlike Achilles Rāma is a perfect hero whom hundreds of millions of people still emulate and adore. Nevertheless, to suggest that Vālmīki composed a narrative centered on *dharma, sukha,* and resistance to persuasion in order to legitimate political privilege would, I think, again miss the point.

To be sure, the *Rāmāyaṇa* has been used to legitimate political privilege for at least the last two thousand years. The Sātavāhana king Vasiṣṭhīputra Pulumāvi (mid second century C.E.), in an inscription found in a cave at Nasik in western India, eulogized his father by comparing him with Rāma, probably Vālmīki's Rāma.[14] Almost two millennia later, in the state elections of July 1988 Arun Govil, who played Rāma in the televised "Ramayan," campaigned in costume for the ruling Congress (I) party in Uttar Pradesh. In the national elections of June 1991, the same serial's Sītā, Deepika Chikaliya, was elected, as a member of the Bharatiya Janata Party (BJP), to the Indian National Assembly (Lok Sabha) from Vadodara (Baroda) in Gujarat. Her costar, Arvind Trivedi, who played Rāvaṇa, successfully contested the seat for Sabarkantha, also in Gujarat, as a representative of the BJP. More broadly, during the late 1980s and early 1990s the BJP, or "Indian People's Party," rose from obscurity to become the nation's largest opposition party—largely by proclaiming a crusade to rescue Rāma's birthplace from Muslim squatters.[15] So there can be no question that the *Rāmāyaṇa* has been used for political legitimation. The question remains, is that why its defining narrative was composed?

Romila Thapar, arguably the leading historian of ancient India alive today, suggests that it is.[16] Bards like Vālmīki, she points out, inhabited royal courts. There they both lauded the ruler and tended the mythological treasures, the traditions of *itihāsa-purāṇa.** They often combined the two functions by prefixing traditional tales to praises as a way of legitimating the ruler's pedigree. That, says Thapar, is just what the bard or bards responsible for the *Rāmāyaṇa* did. They started with the theme of an exiled prince common in Buddhist "foundation legends." Then they formulated a tale in which the heir of the ancient kingdom of Kośala brought civilization to the wilds south of Prayāg.** In this way, they gave legitimacy to a new dynasty (and kingdom) of Southern Kośala.

Thapar's account makes a number of questionable assumptions. It as-

*Collections of tales, in simple poetic meters, that relate past events. As a genre, *itihāsa-purāṇa* usually comprises the larger of India's two epics, the *Mahābhārata,* and the various mythological collections called *Purāṇas,* but not the *Rāmāyaṇa.*

**The conjunction (*prayāga*) of the rivers Gaṅgā (Ganges) and Yamunā (Jumna), today the site of the city of Allahabad. In the *Rāmāyaṇa* Prayāg, and more particularly the hermitage (*āśrama*) of the sage Bharadvāja on its banks, forms a sort of pivot in Rāma's journey south. It is the last distinctly marked geographical location that Rāma visits. As noted earlier, Kośala is a region (*mahājanapada*) to the north of this site. But ancient Indians also referred to a region south of Prayāg as Kośala, or more accurately, Dakṣiṇa-Kośala, "Southern Kośala."

sumes that the *Rāmāyaṇa*'s defining narrative (as distinct from its constituent materials) experienced a long period of gestation; that the *Rāmāyaṇa*'s original nucleus had nothing to do with morality; that Vālmīki was a court poet; that Laṅkā was originally situated in Southern Kośala; that the point of the original story was to place Vibhīṣaṇa on the throne of Laṅkā; in fact, that certain Buddhist stories are foundation legends.[17] But even more serious than these assumptions is another obstacle to deriving the *Rāmāyaṇa*'s defining narrative from a desire to legitimate. That obstacle is the narrative itself, and I think it is insurmountable.

Notice how the *Rāmāyaṇa* legitimates in the examples already cited. It donates virtue, above all, Rāma's virtue. This donation is possible because, unlike Achilles, Rāma is a supremely admirable figure. He has to be. Otherwise his exile would pose no problems, and his victory would breed no delight. Vālmīki ensures that his audiences admire Rāma in at least two ways. He inserts into the poem audiences with whom we identify, and these audiences clearly admire Rāma. He also introduces a cast of lesser characters against whom Rāma's virtue can be judged: Kaikeyī and Daśaratha, Śūrpaṇakhā, the monkey-king Vālin, to a lesser extent Vālin's brother Sugrīva, then above all Rāvaṇa. The relation between Rāma and the other characters in the poems reverses the relation between Achilles and the kings and amplifies Rāma's stature. As a result, a favorable comparison with Rāma or any of his close associates—Sītā, Lakṣmaṇa, Hanumān, Kausalyā, or Bharata—becomes useful as an instrument of legitimation.

But the crucial point is this: the *Rāmāyaṇa* only works to legitimate to the extent that those who use it systematically neglect the problems that Vālmīki's narrative raises, then resolves. Not only does the desire to legitimate provide no motivation for a tale about the confrontation between what ought to be and what one ought to do and the failure of persuasion to resolve it; these themes, essential to the present discussion of the poem, only obstruct its legitimatory utility.

Vālmīki could have easily legitimated rule in, say, Southern Kośala without ever introducing the distinctive features of the *Rāmāyaṇa*'s story as follows: "Plagued by the attacks of demons, the inhabitants of the forests south of Prayāg ask Daśaratha, lord of Ayodhyā, for help. In response, Daśaratha sends his son Rāma, who defeats the demons, stays to rule, and fathers a dynasty." Some variants could replace "stays to rule . . . ," with "and appoints as governor Vibhīṣaṇa, father of the current dynasty." This rather trite tale would do the job of legitimation nicely, but it is distinctly not the defining narrative of the *Rāmāyaṇa*.[18]

Even more important, the features of the narrative that are our concerns—the conflict between what ought to be and what one ought to do and the failure of persuasion—fundamentally obstruct any attempt to legitimate. They emphasize a lesson that any poet serious about legitimation would work hard to avoid: the king's virtues and person and office are problematic. Vālmīki's narrative begins innocently enough. It rehearses the sort of cant virtues that praise poets have always propagated. "His *ātman* is always calm; his speech is always kind. When he is addressed harshly, he says nothing in reply" (*Rām.* 2.1.15; my translation). But it abruptly undercuts that praise. These very virtues require Rāma to renounce the kingdom and enter the forest.[19] Like all great poets, then, Vālmīki opens our eyes to the profundity of life. Among other things, he demonstrates that if we take the cant virtues of the praise poets seriously, they lead to events whose consequences everyone would want to avoid.

To be sure, it remains entirely possible that Vālmīki—whoever he might have been—was a court poet, despite tales in the *Uttara-kāṇṇa* that place him in a hermitage. In that case, it is almost certain that the royal cultivation of poetry served to legitimate the ruler's power, not just blatantly through the activity of praise poets, but more subtly through the act of sustaining the creative arts. A court that, if tradition is correct, produced the first Sanskrit *kāvya* would have some (just?) cause to brag. In that sense, the *Rāmāyaṇa* may have always helped to legitimate, even if the earliest solid evidence for the active legitimatory use of the poem dates no earlier than the second century C.E., some time after the poem was composed (see section 7 of this chapter). Nevertheless, it does not make much sense to say that the desire to legitimate provided the impetus to compose the defining narrative that we find in the *Rāmāyaṇa.* On the one hand, legitimation cannot account for the poem that was written. On the other, the *Rāmāyaṇa* legitimates only to the extent that it can invoke Rāma's virtues without invoking the problems that the narrative works so assiduously to develop.[20] Instead, Vālmīki seems to have powerfully articulated an ultimate threat to human social existence: what ought to be done threatens to upset entirely what ought to be, and the ordinary force of social control, the force of persuasion, is helpless before it. Having drawn that threat, Vālmīki then composed a masterful fiction to mystify it and thereby overcome it. The lesson of the *Rāmāyaṇa* reads: despite initial appearances, acting in accordance with *dharma* and ignoring practical advice will eventually produce what ought to be.

V

This, I suggest, was the poetic work of Homer's and Vālmīki's defining narratives: they mystified ultimate threats. First, they articulated the threats of social and universal collapse that arose when persuasion failed. Then, they imagined solutions to those threats in narrative form. The solutions are mystifications because, however compelling they may seem, they remain unavailable in our ordinary lives. Zeus and the Olympians do not send messengers to us on earth. Evil does not present itself in the form of demons that we can physically kill.

For these mystifications to have worked, the imagined, literary realities of the poems must have intersected with the experienced, literal realities of their audiences. What problems in the worlds of experience did these mystifications address? Our knowledge of ancient Greece permits a more finely grained answer than our knowledge of ancient India does. For Homer, we can distinguish the context of initial composition from the contexts of later dissemination. For Vālmīki we must discuss both concurrently.

Let us assume that the scholarly consensus is correct and that the *Iliad* came into existence in Ionia in the mid eighth century B.C.E. What was its originary context like?

There is much room for caution. Knowledge of the social and cultural institutions in which Homer would have composed is essential to any convincing analysis, but it is simply not available. We know a little about later bards, such as the rhapsodes who recited Homeric poetry and Hesiod who won first prize in a competition on Euboea. But for Homer and his Ionian associates, G. L. Huxley is depressingly sober and depressingly correct: "There is little evidence for the circumstances in which the Asiatic Greek poets were accustomed to recite their epics."[21] As for the circumstances of Homer's audience, new archaeological discoveries and ever more sophisticated analytical techniques promise increasing elucidation, but much of what we would most like to know remains dismally obscure. About Asia Minor in the eighth century, J. M. Cook writes, "[Archaeology] cannot relieve our ignorance of the constitutional history of these early settlements."[22] On the best known location in all of Greece, Snodgrass observes, "We still do not know enough of Attica in the second half of the eighth century to speak with any confidence about the likely intellectual and spiritual concerns of its artists."[23] Nevertheless, there are a few hints of the *Iliad*'s originary context, and they are tantalizing.

If Homer lived in eighth-century Ionia, it seems that he lived in the wrong place at a very exciting time. By the eighth century, Ionia was one of Greece's cultural backwaters. It was, ironically, isolated from the oriental influences that had sparked off bursts of cultural activity in other parts of the Greek world.[24]

But Ionia did have a proud past. Precisely when and why and how Greeks had come to settle on the western coast of Asia Minor is unknown, but come they did, beginning somewhere around the eleventh century B.C.E. They seem to have brought with them the roots from which a flourishing tradition of oral poetry would grow. It is difficult, of course, to know the precise place of oral poetry in Ionic life. All that we have are tasty hors d'oeuvres that do nothing to sate our hunger for the main course. Homer's references to phyla and phratries as military and kinship units seem to echo the phyla and phratries of Ionia.[25] Features of Ionian settlements seem reflected in similar characteristics in Ionian epic.[26] Homer's audiences would probably have included the leading men on the Asia Minor coast, whose suggestive names and patronyms I have already had occasion to mention (see page 52).

Ionia could also boast of another major achievement, although given the recent discoveries at Lefkandi on Euboea it must now share its bragging rights.[27] Early on, Ionia developed large, settled communities. We do not know how the settlements were patterned. Toward the end of the eighth century some communities were gathered about an elevated citadel (what Homer calls a *ptolis*) with an open area (for assembly?) flanked by a temple and what is presumably the hut of the leading man.[28] Fortification walls were not unknown—Smyrna and Emporio-on-Chios had them—but they seem to have been rare.[29] The scarcity of fortifications should not be taken, however, as indicating a scarcity of strife. Inter-Ionian struggles were not entirely quelled when later the twelve leading Ionian cities banded together to form a league, centered about a common sanctuary.[30]

These characteristics are hopelessly broad. They are nothing like the refined historical detail available to critics of modern literature, who may be able to correlate the words of a poem with events contemporary to the month or even the day of its composition.[31] But rough as they are, they may contain a clue to the significance of Homer's originary context. Many have noted that Homer's (imagined) perspective is that of an Ionian colonist. His Ionia is deliberately archaizing: for example, in the *Iliad* Miletus is not a Greek city, although by the eighth century it was.[32] The Achaian camp on the Ilian shore is reminiscent of the situation of the first Greek colonists who came to Asia Minor. Do the experiences of colonization and the development of larger settlements provide a context against which we can read the *Iliad*'s defining narrative?

The potential is certainly present, for these situations posed a problem, and the Ionians utilized a solution, that are familiar from Homer. Colonization and the subsequent coalescence of larger communities required a shift in patterns of authority. So far as we can tell, "dark age" Greeks lived in a patriarchal society. Authority resided in the *aristos,* the "best man" in charge of the *oikos* or "extended household." Colonization and urban coalescence would have disrupted this pattern by removing individuals from the context of the *oikos* and bringing them together as relative equals for joint ventures. That is, it would have created a community based on mutual persuasion and consensus.[33]

The problem is that in such a setting the traditional pattern of authority (the dominance of the single *aristos*) and the inevitable, clear interest of the *aristos* in the affairs of his family and retainers would no longer apply. What would ensure successful persuasion and consensus in the face of dissent, dissent that would be especially disastrous on a foreign shore? Social problems were never solved in ancient Greece without recourse to religion. Later colonizers received their commissions from the god. At the center of cities stood temples; under the watchful eyes of their inhabitants the citizens performed their duties and observed the laws. The general pattern seems clear: where mortal authority was ill defined, the Greeks invoked a higher authority made in their own image, the gods.[34]

The defining narrative of the *Iliad* is built around the same tensions. The story of Meleagros shows that the enraged *aristos* had been an important theme in the formulaic tradition prior to the *Iliad.* But the Meleagros tale is not set in a community of consensus. It works by playing the enraged hero's obstinacy off against the persuasion by those in whom he has an interest, his relatives and retainers. Its effect within the patriarchal community is clear from the moral Phoinix draws: an *agathos* must suffer personal affronts and maintain the position of his household as soon as it is threatened, otherwise he loses.

By contrast, Achilles' destructive wrath dramatizes the fragile nature of the community of consensus:[35] not just the precariousness of an Ionian existence susceptible to fragmentation and annihilation as a result of unpersuadable rage but also the recognition that those on whom the community of consensus depends the most pose the greatest threat. The *Iliad* does not simply objectify and dramatize this threat; it also mystifies and obscures it. For it dramatizes, operating behind the scenes, a world of divinities who although they fight among themselves, take an interest in human affairs. The authority of these gods, especially of the greatest among them, Zeus, resembles that of the old *aristos,* for it is both universally recognized and unavoidable. Even the greatest hero of them all, when enraged beyond all bounds, felt compelled to obey it. The central, social fiction of the *Iliad* reads: when the consensus of human persuasion fails, the persuasion of the gods will stand firm.

VI

It is at least conceivable that the tensions inherent in Ionian colonization and urban coalescence, along with the religious resolution of these tensions, provided the stimulus by which a poet or group of poets transformed traditional tales of rage, such as the story of Meleagros, into the masterpiece of the *Iliad*'s defining narrative. But what accounts for the widespread dissemination of this story throughout Greece in the eighth century and the intense attention that, given the *Iliad*'s careful construction and full elaboration, the narrative must have received?

By the eighth century, Greece was emerging from the dismal decline that followed the end of the Mycenaean world and experiencing what scholars since the early eighties have called a renaissance.[36] The real excitement was back by the mainland at places like Euboea, Corinth, and Athens. Some alleged developments of the time are debatable: a shift from pastoral nomadism to sedentary agriculture, the quadrupling of the population of Athens in the last half of the century, or, alternatively, the rise of a populist movement at Athens in mid-century that was suppressed as the seventh century began.[37] But other developments are more certain, and they make for an impressive list. Serious trade began with peoples both to the east and to the west, and it was followed within a generation by serious colonization, especially in the fertile plains of Magna Graeca. Greeks, perhaps traders, adapted the Phoenician script to produce their alphabet. Greek artists borrowed oriental themes and motifs to produce a distinctive, new style, and mythographers systematized traditional tales along oriental lines.[38] These developments alone would be enough to swell any generation with pride, but they were accompanied by three others that, I believe, are even more significant for the widespread reproduction of the *Iliad.*

First, it was in the eighth century that the *polis* emerged generally. The small, isolated settlements of the Dark Ages (in Homer's terms, the *oikoi*) gave way to a new kind of community, whether by the coalescence of *oikoi* ("synoikism") or some other means. A prime characteristic of this new community was the body of "citizens" (variously restricted) who deliberated on communal goals.[39] Second, the religion of the Greeks developed very significant forms. For the first time, Panhellenic sanctuaries at Olympia, Delphi, Delos, and Dodona became active. Mycenaean tombs generally became the sites of hero cults. Most visible of all were the temples that became common at the places around which the emerging *poleis* coalesced.[40] Third, an intense interest in epic poetry seems to have swept the Greek world in the mid to late eighth century, and with it came an interest in "narrative" representational art. The epic influence extended the width and breadth of Greece, from the Ionian east to as far west as Pithecousai off the coast of modern Naples.

It is clear that the defining narrative of the *Iliad* is fully congruent with what would appear to have been ideological developments in the eighth century, whether it caused them or, as I think more probable, reflected and reinforced them. Greeks in the eighth century seem to have made two basic cultural moves: a move to the outside world, to which we can attribute the rise of trade, colonization, writing, and orientalizing art and mythography (and the popularity of the *Odyssey*), and a shift in the basis of power. In the second move we see once again a shift from a hierarchical, probably patriarchal model of power to a model of power based on persuasion and consensus, now in the rise of the full-fledged Greek *polis*.[41]

This shift would have been accompanied by tensions that resulted from the uncertain consensus on which community rested, and Greeks generally resolved these tensions by obscuring them through religious ideology. Seeking an archaeological sign for the new form of organization, Snodgrass can do no better than point to the rise of temples. To justify his choice, he writes, "there was no factor more important in the composition of the state than devotion to common cults." Elsewhere, he recalls Victor Ehrenberg, according to whom "the god became the monarch of a state which had ceased to be monarchical."[42] The eighth century was a seminal period in the development of the religion of the Greeks, in large part because religion was the essential fiction that made the existence of the *polis* possible. Pointedly, the gods most crucial to the process of "polisization" were the gods most active in and familiar from Homer: Zeus, Athena, and Apollo.

The *Iliad* became widely popular in eighth-century Greece because, in mystifying the failure of persuasion, it dramatized the social, religious fiction on which the Greek community had come to be based. It remained popular because its religious fiction retained its hold on Greek political life. As Oswyn Murray notes with regard to *Iliad* 11.807–8, "the rituals and procedures essential for the orderly conduct of mass meetings were well established [in Homer's world], and show remarkable similarities with the highly complex rituals surrounding the only later assemblies whose workings are known in detail, those of democratic Athens."[43] Before Alexander, Greek communities were always communities of persuasion, threatened by the same force of fragmentation that Achilles embodied, and united by the common fiction that the gods were socially supreme. After Alexander, the *Iliad*'s fiction became no longer serviceable, but the poem itself had attained such traditional prominence that new fictions had to be developed for it, the fictions of allegory.[44]

VII

It is impossible to assume that the scholarly consensus on the date of the *Rāmāyaṇa* is correct because there is no scholarly consensus. A distinct minority still clings to the brahminical tradition, according to which Vālmīki, a contemporary of Lord Rāma, lived and worked at the end of the Tretā age. But most find that date, some 869,000 years before the present, considerably too early. It antedates the known appearance of *Homo sapiens* by several hundred thousand years. Still, the majority is a long way from unity. In the last two decades, serious and respected scholars have argued vigorously that the *Rāmāyaṇa* should be dated as far apart as the "pre-Buddhist" era (before the sixth century B.C.E.) and roughly 500 C.E.—a span of over a millennium.[45] In another context, I have tried to strike something of a balance.[46] I have argued that the *Rāmāyaṇa*'s defining narrative arose in the territory of Kośala during the time known as the Śuṅga period (second century B.C.E. to first century C.E.). Since I adopt that date here, I should explain why. What follows is the skeleton of my argument, adapted for readers who may not be Indologists.

Despite a few claims to the contrary, it seems certain that the *Rāmāyaṇa*'s defining narrative dates before the time known as the Kuṣāṇa period, that is, before the end of the first century C.E. One of the strongest reasons for this lies in the work of an accomplished poet of Kośalan origin, Aśvaghoṣa. A brahmin turned Buddhist, Aśvaghoṣa was active in the court of the great

Buddhist king Kaniṣka, who initiated Kuṣāṇa rule in Kośala. One of Aśvaghoṣa's most prominent poems, the *Buddhacarita* ("The Life of the Buddha"), mentions Rāma and Vālmīki by name and contains verses that, Sanskritists have often noted, closely resemble the *Rāmāyaṇa.* So it is likely that the *Rāmāyaṇa* was known to at least one member of Kaniṣka's court, probably more.[47] The question becomes, how much earlier than Aśvaghoṣa shall we place Vālmīki? There is no direct evidence, so we are forced to rely on conjecture.

According to some, the *Rāmāyaṇa* must date much earlier than Aśvaghoṣa. They argue that Vālmīki does not mention Buddhism, therefore his poem must be pre-Buddhist. But in this argument logic slips a little. There is no reason why poets who postdate the Buddha must mention his movement. The critical edition has actually identified a great many additions to the *Rāmāyaṇa* that must be later than the Buddha, and with only a single, pointed exception, none of them mentions the Buddha or Buddhism, either.

In fact, the view that the *Rāmāyaṇa* is pre-Buddhist faces severe difficulties. The *Rāmāyaṇa*'s narrative presupposes a fairly developed civilization: multistoried buildings that (in Northeast, unlike Northwest, India) require burnt brick, goods such as choice jewels and gems that could only have been imported through developed long-distance trade, and the high level of economic prosperity that marks the contrast between the ordinary prosperity of Ayodhyā and the splendid opulence of Laṅkā. Some scholarly and popular descriptions attribute just such features to Northeast India before the Buddha, but those descriptions are anachronisms. They take the cultural climate found in the *jātakas* as accurate descriptions of conditions prior to the Buddha, when in fact those descriptions more accurately reflect the conditions when the *jātakas* were recorded, probably the Śuṅga period. Archaeologists working in Northeast India have established a clear and uniform cultural sequence from very early times to highly developed urban civilizations. The cultural conditions that the *Rāmāyaṇa* presupposes do not appear until sometime during the Maurya period (fourth to third centuries B.C.E.).

But is it possible and necessary to place the *Rāmāyaṇa* as far back as the Maurya period? Some scholars have thought that it is, among them such acknowledged earlier experts as A. B. Keith and Camille Bulcke.[48] Nonetheless, several points speak against that date. A monumental epic such as the *Rāmāyaṇa* cannot have arisen at just any time whatsoever. The cultural atmosphere would have to have met certain requirements. Among them, I would insist on the following: that people be allowed to assemble to listen to poetic recitations, that there be a thriving medium of popular narrative poetry, and that the poet's ideological position not evoke forcible repression. Unfortunately, none of these conditions prevailed during the later Maurya period, the portion of the period most acceptable on cultural grounds.

Historians, European, American, and Indian alike, have tended to romanticize the Mauryas. Especially the emperor Aśoka, who inscribed edicts on rocks, pillars, and cave walls proclaiming the rule of *dharma* or righteousness, has provided a postcolonial world with a tremendously useful mythology. For that reason, the lion-capital from Aśoka's pillar at Sarnath appears on Indian rupee notes of every denomination.[49]

But in the past several decades, two outstanding historians have called that mythology into question. In an epoch-making study, Niharranjan Ray contrasted Maurya monumental art—abstract, impersonal, timeless, imperialistic—with the art of the succeeding Śuṅga period—concrete, personal, narrative, popular. In careful translations of Aśoka's edicts, D. C. Sircar, India's leading epigraphist, revealed an imperial policy that, far from ideal, was actually repressive.[50] Among other things, Aśoka's edicts reminded workers at entrances to his mines that the poor, as well as the rich, could enjoy celestial bliss, if only they worked diligently and disregarded the fruits of their labors.[51] More to the point, they explicitly forbade popular religious assemblies, including those in which poems like the *Rāmāyaṇa* would have been recited. Only one exception was allowed, assemblies that promoted the specific *dharma* and used the distinctly nonnarrative means that Aśoka himself favored.[52]

It is not at all clear to what extent Aśoka's edicts were carried out, and to what extent they were just bluster. S. P. Gupta has argued vigorously—and correctly—that Ray's view of Maurya art is too homogeneous. Even in relative proximity to the Maurya capital, Pāṭaliputra, artists were actively using "non-Maurya" styles on less monumental scales.[53] Presumably, too, people were telling religious stories, brahmins among them, despite the supposedly pervasive presence of Aśoka's *dharma*-ministers (*dhamma-mahamatas*) in every regional center and religious group. Nonetheless, conditions in the late Maurya period would not have been suitable for the production, dissemination, transmission, or preservation of a monumental epic like the *Rāmāyaṇa*. The poem would have violated imperial rescript much more blatantly and publicly than any short story. In addition, it would have celebrated not an isolated backwater but Ayodhyā, a regional center that housed a military garrison and was thus a potential rival to Pāṭaliputra.

Furthermore, as a monumental celebration of brahminical *dharma,* the *Rāmāyaṇa* would have sharply opposed the ideology propagated by imperial ministers and monuments, and it would have done so in a competing monumental style.

To be sure, the preceding negative considerations are only suggestive, but they tend to the conclusion that the *Rāmāyaṇa* was composed after the Mauryas but before Kaniṣka, which is to say, during the Śuṅga period. Several positive indications also point to a Śuṅga date.[54]

First, the Śuṅga period would have provided a suitable artistic climate for a monumental epic like the *Rāmāyaṇa.* Even allowing for greater plurality, Maurya monumental art remains atemporal and abstract; Śuṅga monumental art is, like the *Rāmāyaṇa,* vigorously and plentifully narrative and representational. In Greece, monumental epics arose at a time when representational narrative art flourished (for example, eighth-century vases). It is reasonable to expect that the *Rāmāyaṇa,* too, arose at a time when narrative pervaded monumental art, a time like the Śuṅga.

Second, the Śuṅga period provides appropriate images for Vālmīki to utilize. For example, in the *Rāmāyaṇa*'s world, every king practices brahminism, and every king but Rāma is subject to *kāma,* lust. That would be an odd representation of kings during Maurya times. The Mauryas were notoriously heterodox* and austere. But the Śuṅgas would have given Vālmīki much to allude to. They were disposed to brahminism, and they were, many of them, addicted to sensual pleasures.

Third, only a date in the Śuṅga period makes sense of some archaeological evidence. Digging at sites mentioned in the *Rāmāyaṇa,* B. B. Lal, former director general of the Archaeological Survey of India, made an unexpected discovery. He and his team found that Śṛṅgaverapura, located at a ford of the Ganges about thirty kilometers upstream from the confluence with the Jumna, was in ancient times a major settlement of economic importance.[55] Śṛṅgaverapura is important in the *Rāmāyaṇa,* too. Vālmīki takes pains to emphasize the friendship between Rāma and Guha, the king of Śṛṅgaverapura. In fact, on their first meeting, Guha offers Rāma all his lands. Evidently Vālmīki wanted to underscore the close economic ties between Ayodhyā and Śṛṅgaverapura (in contrast, perhaps, to close ties with nearby Kauśāmbī, which Vālmīki ignores). Significantly, Lal and his coworkers have found coins from Śuṅga Ayodhyā at Śṛṅgaverapura.[56] In

*"Heterodox" refers to religious movements that rejected the authority of the ancient ritual texts called the Veda, "wisdom." The most prominent of these groups are the Buddhists and Jains.

fact, before the end of the Kuṣāṇa era, there is only one period when it makes sense to talk of close economic relations between Śṛṅgaverapura and an independent Ayodhyā. That period is the Śuṅga.

For these reasons, and others that are more technical and obscure, I am convinced that the *Rāmāyaṇa*'s defining narrative dates to the Śuṅga period. As we shall see, that period provides a significant context for Vālmīki's interest in both the tension between *dharma* and *sukha* and in the failure of persuasion.

VIII

The Śuṅga period in India began with a singular event: a coup d'état, somewhere around the year 187 B.C.E., that overthrew the last Maurya emperor, Bṛhadratha, and established his general Puṣyamitra in power. We do not know the precise significance of this event, for we cannot distinguish, in even the roughest terms, between sudden and gradual developments, local and general traits, and partisan and unanimous judgments. But there are indications that in Śuṅga times, the texture of Indian life changed tremendously.

During the Śuṅga period, brahminical ritualists enjoyed considerable, but not exclusive, royal patronage. So far as we can tell, the later Mauryas, kings such as Daśaratha and Sāliśuka, shared the heterodox preferences of their predecessors. But Puṣyamitra was a brahmin, and an aggressive one. According to an uncorroborated Buddhist report, he placed a bounty of one hundred *denarii** on the heads of Buddhist monks. The grammarian Patañjali refers to a sacrifice by Puṣyamitra as still in progress. (Sacrifice was a distinctly brahminical practice, outlawed by Aśoka.) An inscription found in Ayodhyā refers to not one but two horse-sacrifices (*aśvamedhas*) that Puṣyamitra sponsored. Archaeologists have found remains at Kauśāmbī from this period that seem to evidence a grisly practice that literary scholars argued long and hard rarely if ever occurred: a human sacrifice (*puruṣamedha*) on a flying-hawk altar according

*The *denarius* was a Roman coin, so even if the Buddhist legend recalls an actual anti-Buddhist campaign, it cannot have remembered the correct bounty. When Puṣyamitra came to power, Rome was just beginning to extend its domination into the eastern Mediterranean. All *denarii* found in India are imperial coins, which means they date not earlier than about 30 B.C.E.

to the rites of the Taittirīya school of the Black Yajurveda.[57]* Incidentally, the Taittirīyas are the only school of brahmins mentioned by name in the *Rāmāyaṇa* (*Rām.* 2.29.13c).

Along with the shift in favor of brahminical religion came a shift in favor of brahminical language.** As inscriptions attest, Sanskrit began to replace Prakrit for some official purposes. When Patañjali wrote a commentary on the Sanskrit grammarians Pāṇini and Kātyāyana, probably during Puṣyamitra's reign and in Pāṭaliputra, Puṣyamitra's capital, it seems likely that he had other motives besides those of pure scholarship. The preference for brahminical speech eventually led to the development of Buddhist Sanskrit literature (for example, the Mahāyāna *sūtras*) and classical Sanskrit fine letters (*kāvya*). But both developments are too late to consider here.

Besides a shift toward brahminism, the Śuṅga was one of many periods in Indian history when, in contrast to what had preceded, the tendency to centralization gave way to a vigorous regionalism. Rulers at important cities like Ayodhyā (Sāketa), Kauśāmbī, and Vidiśa issued their own coins and presumably enjoyed a degree of political autonomy. Just as important, economic activity became independent of political control. During the Maurya period, the central government seems to have managed the production, transport, and distribution of precious goods: Aśoka's edicts are commonly found at iron and gold mines. But beginning in the Śuṅga period we have specific evidence that significant wealth was in the hands of private merchants.[58]

The same evidence testifies that in Śuṅga times, both within areas of Śuṅga control and outside them, private merchants patronized the arts to an unprecedented degree. Along the trade routes they excavated and decorated caves for monks and nuns, such as the earliest of the famous caves at

*The Yajurveda is one of the four major divisions of the Vedic literature. (The other three are the Ṛgveda, the Sāmaveda, and the Atharvaveda.) A collection of formulas used by the priests who prepared for the sacrifice, the Yajurveda comes in one of two forms: Black, in which the ritual text (*saṃhitā*) and the commentary (*brāhmaṇa*) are mixed, and White, in which they are kept separate. The Taittirīyas were one of several distinct brahminical schools (*śākas*) that transmitted (and later recorded in writing) a tradition of the Black Yajurveda.

**The heterodox schools commonly used the vernacular languages of India at the time, which for convenience here we can call Prakrit. Brahmins were partial to Sanskrit, the "perfect" language more closely related to the language of Vedic ritual. But if we read between the grammatical lines, there are hints that probably in eastern India, brahmins, too, used Prakrit, sometimes even for sacrificial purposes. Vālmīki's language, too, shows clear indications of "prakrit-isms," usages more vernacular than "classical," a point established in a number of technical articles by Nilmadhav Sen (see the bibliography in the first volume of the Goldman et al. translation of the *Rāmāyaṇa*).

Ajanta (Aśoka and his son Daśaratha had excavated caves earlier.) They also contributed immensely to the construction of *stūpas** such as those at Bharhūt and Sāñcī. In comparison with Maurya art, the design of these monuments reflected an increased interest in and proliferation of narrative, as opposed to didactic, modes of discourse.[59]

We would not expect all wealth to be channeled into such noble projects as *stūpas*, *caityas*, and *vihāras*.** There are strong indications that our expectations are correct. Before the Śuṅga era, kings seem to have inclined toward the austere. For example, Candragupta, the founder of the Maurya dynasty, is reputed to have taken the vows of a Jain mendicant. He renounced his life by traditional Jain means, depriving himself of food and eventually water.[60] By contrast, Vasumitra, the fourth Śuṅga ruler of Pāṭaliputra, is remembered as dissolute and overly fond of dramas. According to a later historical play, he was murdered in the midst of his cavorting by a certain Mitradeva. Some speculate that Mitradeva's act of treason actually inaugurated an autonomous Śuṅga dynasty at Ayodhyā, the first Śuṅga dynasty independent of Pāṭaliputra.[61]

The changing texture of life in the Śuṅga periods provides a significant context for Vālmīki's concern with the disjunction between what ought to be and what one ought to do. It also elucidates his concern with the failure of persuasion to negotiate that disjunction.

At least from the time of Aśoka, royal ideology in Northeast India had been an ideology of *dhamma* (Sanskrit, *dharma*). In theory, society was constituted as a community of duty. It flourished when people faithfully performed their prescribed roles and responsibilities without regard for the fruits of their actions.[62] Many Śuṅga rulers, in keeping with the sweeping changes, committed themselves to a distinct version of this ideology, a brahminical rather than a heterodox one; presumably, some of their subjects did, too. For example, the Śuṅga monarch Dhana[deva?] set up an inscription at Ayodhyā that emphasized both his brahminical loyalties (he was "sixth in line from Puṣyamitra, who sponsored two *aśvamedhas*") and an ideology of *dharma* (he styled himself *dharmarāja,* "the king who rules on the basis of *dharma*").[63] Similarly, the grammarian Patañjali, who probably resided at Puṣyamitra's court, also linked brahminism and *dharma.* When pressed for

*A *stūpa* is a mound that (allegedly) contains at its core a relic of Lord Buddha.

**A *caitya,* like a *stūpa,* refers to a funeral mound; but here it refers to certain cave sanctuaries, such as those at Ajanta and Karle, that contain an image of a *stūpa* around which monastics gathered to "worship." A *vihāra* was a cave carved to house mendicants.

reasons to learn and apply the rules of correct Sanskrit, the brahminical language, Patañjali replied with a single word: *dharma*.[64]

But brahminical *dharma* entailed problems, and the Śuṅga period was too pluralistic and decentered to let sleeping problems lie. In particular, it knew two groups who sharply opposed an ideology of brahminical *dharma*.[65] The first has a textual, the second an intertextual relationship with the *Rāmāyaṇa.* Together, they help define a significant context for Vālmīki's concern with the disjunction between what is and what ought to be.

The first group comprised thinkers, whether brahminical or not, who advocated philosophical materialism. Lokāyatas and other materialists denied both the efficacy of moral *dharma* and the imperceptible reality in which brahminism grounded that *dharma.* Their critique actually appears in the *Rāmāyaṇa.* At Citrakūṭa the minister Jābāli urged Rāma to return home, speaking, as Vālmīki says, "words devoid of *dharma*."[66]

> Whoever says, "*Dharma* is better than *artha*
>   [prosperity]," that's who I feel sorry for, no one else.
> Having acquired misery [*duḥkha*] in this world, that
>   person gets nothing but dissolution at death. . . .
>
> Make up your mind, great-minded one, that there is
>   nothing beyond this world.
> Cling to what is visible; put aside what is not.
>   (*Rām.* 2.100.12, 16; my translation)

Besides materialists, a group of more traditional brahmins would have rejected *dharma,* too. I am thinking above all of the Bhārgavas, named for their alleged ancestor Bhṛgu. In antiquity the Bhārgavas dominated the western reaches of the most commonly used trade route, the southern one (*Dakṣiṇa-pātha*), which connected places like Banaras, Ayodhyā, and Kauśāmbī in the northeast to India's west coast. One of that route's two seaports sat at the mouth of the holy river Narmadā, a town known today as Bharuch, from the old Sanskrit name Bhṛgukacchā, "the coast of Bhṛgu." The other port, not quite so old, was Sopara, known in antiquity as Śūrpāraka. (Was the name of Rāvaṇa's sister, Śūrpaṇakhā, "fan-nail," a loose pun?) Among the famous sites at Śūrpāraka was a bathing area (*tīrtha*) dedicated to Rāma, but to Paraśurāma ("Axe-Rāma"), the Rāma of the Bhṛgus, not to Vālmīki's Rāma, the son of Daśaratha.[67]

The existence of a distinctly Bhārgava transmutation of Rāma illustrates the extent to which their convictions fundamentally opposed Vālmīki's. Their Rāma, Axe-Rāma, ran amok, slaughtering high-class nonbrahmins (*kṣatriyas*), until Vālmīki's Rāma, a *kṣatriya,* stopped the rampage (*Rām.* 1.73–75). The distance between the two also appears in the field of literary production. The Bhārgavas were instrumental in producing not the *Rāmāyaṇa* but the other great Indian epic, the *Mahābhārata,* renowned for "telling it like it is," not as it ought to be. As these two examples intimate, one crucial difference between Vālmīki and the Bhārgavas centered on the ideal of *dharma.* Despite Kṛṣṇa's advice on *karma-yoga* in the *Bhagavad-Gītā,* the Bhārgavas seem to have been unwilling to act without regard for the fruits of their actions. Their reluctance accords fully with brahminical tradition. Brahmins had always performed the paradigmatic act, the sacrifice, out of a desire (*kāma*) for rewards (*phalāni,* "fruits").[68]

Together, the materialists and Bhārgavas help define a significant context for Vālmīki's concern with the disjunction between what ought to be and what one ought to do. Both groups promoted goal-oriented, pleasure-seeking action; in the process, they forcefully opposed ancient advocates of brahminical *dharma.* The circumstances of Śuṅga life would have only compounded their critique. The chief advocates of brahminical *dharma* were, of course, the monarchs; unfortunately, the royal example would have lent as much support to *dharma*'s opponents as to its partisans, if not more. To start with, the Śuṅga monarchs were weak and unimpressive, especially in comparison with their heterodox predecessors. Not only had they failed to maintain any centralized political control; they had also ceded a large proportion of their economic privileges to nonroyals.[69] Their collective experience only confirmed Jābāli's lesson: the pursuit of *dharma* leads to misery, nothing more. Worse yet, many Śuṅgas appear to have been hypocrites as well as weaklings. Their ideology may have advanced *dharma,* but their actions served *sukha* instead. Kālidāsa's play about the amorous interests of Puṣyamitra's son Agnimitra (*Mālavikā and Agnimitra*) provides a late but readily accessible example.[70]

It is at least conceivable, then, that during the Śuṅga period, the criticism of materialists and Bhārgavas combined with royal weakness and dissolution to evoke Vālmīki's interest in the tension between *dharma* and *sukha.* But what accounts for the thematic complement to this interest, his attention to the failure of persuasion?

By the second century B.C.E. *dharma* and persuasion were closely linked. Aśoka's Seventh Pillar Edict reads in part: "The advancement of *dhamma* amongst men has been achieved through two means, legislation and persuasion. But of these two, legislation has been less effective, and persuasion more so. . . . Men have increased their adherence to *dhamma* by being persuaded not to injure living beings and not to take life."[71] Aśoka sounds as if he learned from experience to rely on persuasion, but as the conversion of demons in the *jātakas* testifies, that is not entirely true. The propagation of *dharma* by persuasion reflected sound, traditional practice, in Aśoka's case, sound, traditional, Buddhist practice. When the Śuṅgas made *dharma* a brahminical virtue, however, the link between *dharma* and persuasion became problematical.

What made this link problematical was the changed social standing of *dharma*'s exemplars. Aśoka may have propagated *dharma,* but he made no pretense of embodying *dharma*'s highest ideals, at least during his active life. For the adherents of heterodox teachings, the prime embodiments of *dharma* were *śramaṇa*s, renunciants who had given up all interest in pleasure. As a result, among Buddhists and other *śramaṇa*s, the persuasive propagation of *dharma,* action apart from a desire for results, was fully consonant with the social standing of those who embodied the ideal. But brahmins were not renunciants; they were householders and thereby attached to the delights of *artha* and *sukha.* Worse yet, as householders their fundamental professional duty was to persuade, and this professional persuasion conflicted profoundly with the persuasion of *dharma.*

In a masterful study, Romila Thapar has pointed out how, in the middle of the first millennium B.C.E., human communities in the central Ganges basin shifted in structure from lineage-based societies to city-centered territorial states.[72] One result was that the primary occupations of brahmins changed. In a broad sense, brahmins still made their livings in the traditional way: they procured prosperity for their employers by means of speech (*vāc, brahman, mantra*). But by the end of the first millennium, most brahmins could no longer procure prosperity by means of *ritual* speech. There were not enough employers to go around, especially in later Maurya times. Instead, brahmins became *mantrins* or ministers. They instructed public officials on how to achieve what ought to be. In other words, they procured prosperity for their employers by means of sound, practical, goal-oriented persuasion. In this limited sense, Jābāli is exactly what Vālmīki says he is: a true and representative brahmin (*brāhmaṇottamaḥ, Rām.* 2.100.1b).

For brahmins in this position, the ideologies of brahminical *dharma* on which communal life came officially to be based in Śuṅga India presented grave difficulties. To be blunt, it required them to play the fool (a role for which, by the way, they became famous in later Sanskrit drama). At one and the same time, brahmins had to advocate two contradictory positions. On the one hand, they had to advocate a *dharma* of renunciation. On the other, they had to commend a life that neglected this ideal in favor of more traditional notions of what ought to be, *sukha* conceived as prosperity and sensual pleasures. Even worse, they had to give advice that tended to promote the latter ideal. Clearly, one form of brahminical persuasion or the other had to yield. Persuasion became a significant locus in which brahminical practice confronted the disjunction between what is and what ought to be.

Vālmīki's narrative rendered these difficulties less pressing. By means of a compelling if fictional example, it taught that the renunciation of pleasure, prosperity, and results for the sake of *dharma* did not open up an unbridgeable abyss between what ought to be and what one ought to do. To advocate brahminical *dharma* did not abrogate one's professional concerns for the well-being of king and kingdom. Instead, despite initial appearances—the weakness and hypocrisy of the monarchs, the critique of materialists and Bhārgavas—actions performed in accord with *dharma* wonderfully fulfilled the aims that brahminical verbal practice had always pursued.[73] In this way, the *Rāmāyaṇa* provided ancient Indians with a central, mystifying fiction. It made a common life based on brahminical *dharma* tenable. Half a millennium later, it probably helped make that vision of the common life dominant.[74]

IX

In this chapter I have explored how the imagined, literary realities of the *Iliad* and the *Rāmāyaṇa* intersected with the experienced, literal realities in which Homer, Vālmīki, and their audiences lived. I have suggested that both poems performed the same kind of work: the mystification of fundamental threats to social and universal existence, emblematized by the problems that arise when persuasion fails. And I have correlated that mystification with conditions in the worlds that Homer and Vālmīki inhabited, Greece in the eighth century B.C.E. and India during the Śuṅga period (second century B.C.E. to first century C.E.).

Until now, we have discussed the poems' contexts in alternation. How do they compare? If we could date the *Rāmāyaṇa* to the sixth century B.C.E., we might hypothesize, in the historicist manner of a Walter Ruben, that at a certain stage of economic and social development, a strong need to mystify the failure of persuasion provoked the composition of certain kinds of epic poems.[75] As it stands, however, such a unilaterally deterministic relationship between experienced and imagined reality seems unlikely. The structural and dynamic differences between the two contexts are too significant.

In structure, Homer's and Vālmīki's communities varied in size, complexity, and manner of organization. Homer plied his trade in the relatively small settlements of an emergent eighth-century Greece; Vālmīki plied his in the much larger, more established cities of the post-Maurya Gangetic plain. Homer's small-scale settlements were relatively homogeneous, cultivating a shared ideology according to which social reality was sustained by the Olympian gods. Vālmīki's larger city-society was decidedly more pluralistic. It accommodated people who practiced many different ideologies, allowing them to interact and conflict. Homer's settlements determined communal action *via* consensus, presumably the consensus of the leading men. Officially, Vālmīki's cities were governed by a single monarch, in whom authority for communal action resided. In the *Iliad* and the *Rāmāyaṇa,* these structural differences appear most notably, perhaps, in the predominant forms that persuasion assumes. Homer's paradigm of persuasion is the embassy to Achilles. There persuasion is deliberative; it strives to achieve consensus. Vālmīki's paradigms of persuasion are the attempts to dissuade Rāma and Rāvaṇa, for example, Lakṣmaṇa's attempt in *Rāmāyaṇa* 2.20. There persuasion is not deliberative but "ministerial." It strives to give good advice.

Besides structural differences, Homer's and Vālmīki's worlds differed in social movement, too. Both Homer and Vālmīki lived at times of tremendous economic growth. That is clear from the rise in the number and quality of archaeological remains. But the economic upswings were accompanied by different social dynamics. Homer lived in a world emerging from intense social fragmentation. In the so-called Dark Ages, the Greek population had been widely scattered; in most places the largest significant political unit was not much bigger than a well-to-do household. By Homer's day larger settlements (*poleis*) were beginning to coalesce. Vālmīki's world was significantly different. He lived at a time of increasing fragmentation. The previous period had seen the first great attempt at centralization in the Gangetic plain, the rule of the Mauryas. But by Śuṅga times that unifying structure was giving way to decentralization, political regionalism, and economic "privatization."

Clearly, then, Homer's and Vālmīki's worlds were undergoing profound social changes in two very different directions. But the changes share one crucial similarity. In both early Greece and ancient India social flourishing depended on (different kinds of) persuasion. The social changes effectively highlighted the tenuousness of that instrument. They provoked poets to respond by concealing the peril. In narratives whose immense length mirrored the magnitude of the threat, Homer and Vālmīki used a religious ideology—the intervention of the gods, Rāma's defeat of the demons—to mystify it and thereby overcome it. In doing so, they helped make communal life in ancient Greece and India tenable and tolerable.

3

Hiding One's Limitations

I

In *Iliad* 9, Ajax, Phoinix, Odysseus, Achilles, and Patroklos share a proper and pleasant meal, then they converse. But their afterdinner conversation has none of the usual chit-chat. Odysseus offers Achilles a toast, then he offers Agamemnon's gifts.

Achilles wastes no time in replying.

> I will speak to you the way it seems best to me: neither
> do I think the son of Atreus, Agamemnon, will persuade
> me,
> nor the rest of the Danaans. . . .
>
> (*Il.* 9.314–16)

Those who know the poem know full well that that is not all Achilles says. He speaks with great force for over one hundred lines. But the two-plus lines I have quoted are the gist of it. Whatever overtures Odysseus has made, whether on Agamemnon's initiative or his own, Achilles rejects and rejects out of hand. It is a long time before Phoinix can finally think of something to say (*Il.* 9.430–33).

The circumstances of Lakṣmaṇa's speech in *Rāmāyaṇa* 2.20, when he urges his brother not to yield to destiny, are somewhat more spontaneous and passionate. Having learned of his fate, Rāma goes with Lakṣmaṇa to his mother's apartment. A series of quick exchanges follows, after which Rāma tries to pacify his brother. But the latter can hardly contain himself. He bursts forth advising Rāma to resist fate with force.

Like Achilles, Rāma wastes no time in replying. He wipes away a tear, soothes his brother more than once, and speaks: "Know well that I am determined to obey our father's word. That, dear brother, is the true and right path" (*Rām.* 2.20.36; my translation).

Those who know Vālmīki's poem may well have forgotten that these few, simple words are Rāma's entire reply. They are the only reply he needs. He does not emulate the passionate length of Lakṣmaṇa's plea or Achilles' rejoinder. And unlike Achilles' speech, Rāma's firm, calm resolve does not leave those who hear it sitting in stunned silence. Instead, it moves his mother Kausalyā to tears. "I will follow you wherever you go, my son, as a cow follows its calf" (*Rām.* 2.21.6; my translation).

In their own ways, Achilles and Rāma enact the limits of persuasion; Homer and Vālmīki work hard to overcome them. In this chapter I examine how.

First, I analyze the way each poet represents the practice of persuasion. I contend that each poem configures effective verbal activity in distinctive ways, and that these distinctive configurations parallel significant features of Homer's and Vālmīki's societies. But a configuration patterns only because it also excludes. The next step, then, is to show how Achilles and Rāma impersonate forms that the respective configurations of verbal activity exclude. That analysis allows us in turn to characterize more precisely how Homer and Vālmīki mystify the threat of failed persuasion.

Within their literary realities, Homer and Vālmīki imaginatively extended the appropriate configurations of power in ways not possible in the world of ordinary experience. In doing so, they did not erase the limits of those patterns, but they did transpose them to a location from which the threat of social and universal destruction is less immediate and pressing. As a result, I suggest, their poems belong to a distinctive class of religious literature, a class whose members I call *cosmotrophes.*

II

As we already know, Homer's *peithō* is much more versatile than the English verb "to persuade." Its perfect passive, *peithesthai,* "to have been persuaded," characterizes ordinary social interactions. Achilles tells Patroklos to attend to their guests, "and Patroklos was persuaded by his dear companion"—that is, Patroklos obeyed him. The present active, *peithein,* "to persuade," marks an explicit attempt to reestablish social order when it has become strained. When neither passive nor active persuasion works, human community fragments. Friendship (*philotēs*) yields to enmity. The predominant mode of activity shifts from words to deeds. The predominant verb is no longer *peithesthai,* "to have been persuaded," but *machesthai,* "to fight."

In the *Iliad,* Homer depicts persuasion according to specific and consistent patterns. Despite its failure, the speech in which Odysseus offers Agamemnon's gifts is an ideal example. It transcribes the words that the best speaker of the Achaians spoke in the moment of the greatest need. Because the reader may wish to refer to the speech in the discussion that follows, I reproduce it below, picking up where I left off in Chapter 1.

> [Hektor] prays now that the divine Dawn will show most
> quickly,
> since he threatens to shear the uttermost horns from the
> ship-sterns,
> to light the ships themselves with ravening fire, and to
> cut down
> the Achaians themselves as they stir from the smoke
> beside them.
> All this I fear terribly in my heart, lest immortals
> accomplish all these threats, and lest for us it be destiny
> to die here in Troy, far away from horse-pasturing Argos.
> Up, then! if you are minded, late though it be, to rescue
> the afflicted sons of the Achaians from the Trojan
> onslaught.
> It will be an affliction to you hereafter, there will be no
> remedy
> found to heal the evil thing when it has been done. No,
> beforehand

take thought to beat the evil day from the Danaans.
Dear friend, surely thus your father Peleus advised you
that day when he sent you away to Agamemnon from Phthia:
"My child, for the matter of strength, Athena and Hera will give it
if it be their will, but be it yours to hold fast in your bosom
the anger of the proud heart, for consideration is better.
Keep from the bad complication of quarrel, and all the more for this
the Argives will honor you, both their younger men and their elders."
So the old man advised, but you have forgotten. Yet even now
stop, and give way from the anger that hurts the heart. Agamemnon
offers you worthy recompense if you change from your anger.
Come then, if you will, listen to me, while I count off for you
all the gifts in his shelter that Agamemnon has promised:
Seven unfired tripods; ten talents' weight of gold; twenty
shining cauldrons; and twelve horses, strong, race-competitors
who have won prizes in the speed of their feet. That man would not be
poor in possessions, to whom were given all these have won him,
nor be unpossessed of dearly honored gold, were he given
all the prizes Agamemnon's horses won in their speed for him.
He will give you seven women of Lesbos, the work of whose hands
is blameless, whom when you yourself captured strong-founded Lesbos
he chose, and who in their beauty surpass the races of women.

He will give you these, and with them shall go the one he took from you,
the daughter of Briseus. And to all this he will swear a great oath
that he never entered into her bed and never lay with her
as is natural for human people, between men and women.
All these gifts shall be yours at once; but again, if hereafter
the gods grant that we storm and sack the great city of Priam,
you may go to your ship and load it deep as you please with
gold and bronze, when we Achaians divide the war spoils,
and you may choose for yourself twenty of the Trojan women,
who are the loveliest of all after Helen of Argos.
And if we come back to Achaian Argos, pride of the tilled land,
you could be his son-in-law; he would honor you with Orestes,
his growing son, who is brought up there in abundant luxury.
Since, as he has three daughters there in his strong-built castle,
Chrysothemis and Laodike and Iphianassa,
you may lead away the one of these that you like, with no bride-price,
to the house of Peleus; and with the girl he will grant you as dowry
many gifts, such as no man ever gave with his daughter.
He will grant you seven citadels, strongly settled:
Kardamyle and Enope and Hire of the grasses,
Pherai the sacrosanct, and Antheia deep in the meadows,
with Aipeia the lovely, and Pedasos of the vineyards.
All these lie near the sea, at the bottom of sandy Pylos,
and men live among them rich in cattle and rich in sheepflocks,
who will honor you as if you were a god with gifts given
and fulfill your prospering decrees underneath your sceptre.

All this he will bring to pass for you, if you change from
your anger.
But if the son of Atreus is too much hated in your heart,
himself and his gifts, at least take pity on all the other
Achaians, who are afflicted along the host, and will honor
you
as a god. You may win very great glory among them.
For now you might kill Hektor, since he would come very
close to you
with the wicked fury upon him, since he thinks there is
not his equal
among the rest of the Danaans the ships carried hither.
(*Il.* 9.225–306)

In analyzing this and other speeches in the *Iliad,* it is convenient to distinguish four levels on which Homer images rhetorical activity: diction, that is, the use of sounds, words, and phrases in excess of what the poetry requires in order to represent rhetorical effort; the arguments that the speaker makes; how the arguments are elaborated; and the manner in which the speech as a whole is organized. Each area helps reveal the distinctive configuration according to which persuasion operates in Homer's world.[1]

Diction

There are several fine examples of the rhetorical use of diction in Odysseus's speech. Three of them will illustrate the effects nicely. Unfortunately, it is impossible to examine dictional activity without quoting the original. To make these lines accessible to readers who do not know Greek, I have modified them in several ways. An acute accent (´) marks the beginning of each metrical foot; since Homer wrote in a hexameter, there are six accents per line.* Vertical lines in the text (¦) separate, where pertinent, the major units from which the poetic line is constructed (what scholars call *cola*). Significant verbal echoes are printed boldface. When necessary, diagonal brackets enclose important words in both the Greek

*In Greek epic, the foot is a unit of length rather than of stress. All feet are of identical duration and consist of either two long syllables or one long syllable followed by two shorts. A syllable can be long in one of three ways: (1) if it contains a long vowel; (2) if it ends in a consonant cluster; or (3) if it must be long by metrical necessity. The third option, metrical necessity, is allowed only as a matter of last resort.

and English texts, so that readers who do not know Greek can begin to associate phonological effects with the most important meanings.

<haí> ke met' <Árg>eiḗn Helenḗn kallístai eṓsin.
<eí> de ken <Árg>os hikoímeth' Achaḯikon oúthar
  aroúrēs

[<who> after <Arg>ive Helen are the loveliest of all.
And <if> to <Arg>os of the Achaians we return, pride
  of tilled land]

(*Il.* 9.282–83)

The effect of these two simple lines is striking. Odysseus has been summarizing the gifts Agamemnon promises to give at the fall of Troy. Now he wants to shift to the gifts Achilles will receive when they return to the Greek mainland. Homer effects a smooth transition with the help of a simple dictional device. The first foot and a half of the new set of gifts (second line, boldface) echoes the corresponding syllables in the last line of the preceding set (first line, boldface).

nḗa halís **<chrusoú>** ¦ **kai <chálkou> nḗ**ēsásthai

[Your ship deeply with <gold> and <bronze> load.]
(*Il.* 9.279; my translation)

In this line Odysseus describes some of the booty that Agamemnon promises to Achilles when Troy falls. Its effect centers, literally as well as semantically, on the two nouns, "gold and bronze" (*chrusou kai chalkou*). These nouns comprise a unit that, like the promised contents of the ship, is both tightly packed and heavy. The nouns are joined snugly together by alliteration (initial *ch-*) and rhyme (final *-ou*). They consist of five long, slow syllables, so that they are metrically ponderous. On either end, a four-syllable unit brackets the gold and bronze, and each unit begins with *nē-* followed by a vowel. These units—"you may load your ship as deep as you please"—enclose the contents of Achilles' ship in diction, just as the ship to which they refer encloses the contents in real life.

The following two lines are extremely intricate, in fact, so intricate that I have confined most of the discussion to an endnote. But they are still worth reading. They come not from the list of Agamemnon's gifts but from earlier in the speech.

> aútōi toí ¦ meto**písth'** ¦ **<achos> és**setai, ¦ oúde ti mḗchos
> rhéchthentós ¦ kakou **ést'** ¦ **<akos> heú**rein: ¦ álla polú prin
>
> [It will be an <affliction> to you hereafter, there will be no <remedy>
> found to heal the evil thing when it has been done. No, beforehand . . .]
>
> (*Il.* 9.249–50)

In these two lines, metrical and phonetic parallels link the two centers of the argument, affliction (*achos*) and remedy (*akos*). But at the same time, marked contrasts, governed by the single phonetic difference between the two nouns (the consonants *ch* and *k*), emphasize that the two key nouns are really mutually exclusive. Future *achos* (affliction) from present failure to act will preclude any *akos* (remedy).[2]

In all three examples, Homer uses the same basic patterns to image rhetorical effort on the level of diction. He avoids exact verbal repetition, as he does in all of his persuasional speeches.[3] Instead, at important junctures verbal echoes establish relations of both similarity and difference between concepts within a single argument and between various arguments in the speech.

Argument

Homer applies this same pattern at every level of rhetorical effort. For example, at the level of argument he images persuasion in terms of a concern for relations—specifically, social relations—that avoids repetition and opens out onto larger systems.

Odysseus tries two basic argumentative strategies. One strategy was mandated by his mission. He attempts to realign the "systems" of possessions and relations that constitute the standing of the individual *agathos,* his potential reserves, so to speak, of social power. In other words, Odysseus offers Agamemnon's gifts. The hope is that the greater standing Achilles will receive will entice him to return to battle. As we know, that hope is entirely misplaced.

Achilles does not think much of Agamemnon's gifts, even (or especially) the offer to become Agamemnon's son-in-law. In fact, Achilles bluntly says that he hates them (*Il.* 9.378). Perhaps Odysseus anticipates this reaction, for he does not offer the gifts right away. He eases into them by means of a second kind of argument. He invokes relations—friendship, filiality—that still hold firm and so presumably have some power to move Achilles to act.

Odysseus begins with a compliment: that was a nice meal. He immediately uses the compliment to introduce the duties of friendship (*philotēs*). The Trojans are pressing the Achaian ships; if you care for the Achaians at all, you had better act now before it is too late. Then he abruptly changes the subject. With a new vocative, he invokes a relation that is presumably solid for two reasons. First, it is remote from the disputing *aristoi* at Troy; second, it forms (*pace* the stories of Phoinix and Oedipus) one of the surest bonds within the *oikos,* the patterned interactions between father and son. Peleus himself had told Achilles, "Keep from the bad complications of quarrel, and all the more will the Argives honor you for this" (*Il.* 9.257–58). Coming as it does right before the list of Agamemnon's gifts, this fatherly advice establishes a new and more congenial context for those gifts. At least it tries to. Unfortunately, the obligations of filiality have no more effect on Achilles than his fealties to Agamemnon as king.

Elaboration

When Homer's characters elaborate their arguments, they in effect entangle the person addressed in wide nets of relations. To be more specific, they do not repeat individual arguments. Instead, they invariably set them in larger contexts of signification.

One way to do this is by comparing. Odysseus's comparisons are typical in two significant ways. First, they are limited in scope. In speeches that attempt to persuade, gods, women, Helen, Orestes, whatever is a human person or the superior analogue of a human person is a fit object for comparison. Natural objects, such as the sun, the moon, the wind, and the earth, are not. Second, comparisons generally refer to extreme representatives of a class. You will be honored like a god; the seven women Agamemnon will give you exceed the races of women in skill; you may choose the most beautiful after the most beautiful of all, Helen; Agamemnon will treat you like his own son. The idea behind comparison with superlatives seems to be this: if comparison increases an argument's force by setting it within a system of signification, the most forceful comparison is one that invokes the extreme instance of that system.

A second way speakers insert arguments into larger contexts is by recounting. Sometimes Homer's characters recount by telling stories. When Odysseus alludes to Peleus's parting advice to Achilles, he begins to tell a story—almost. Instead, he provides a setting for Peleus's actual words. Odysseus does, however, provide one of the best examples of another way of recounting. He enumerates Agamemnon's gifts. In fact, for a persuasional speech in the *Iliad,* he enumerates at incredible length. As a result, the list of gifts provides an ideal opportunity to observe some of the typical forms of the Homeric list.

On the smallest of scales, Odysseus juxtaposes gifts at random: tripods, gold, cauldrons, horses. But broad, relational systems encompass these juxtapositions and integrate them into an organic whole: now, Agamemnon promises plunder, then women; when Troy falls, he again promises plunder, then women. When the Achaians return home, the gifts and their order change, for one does not plunder one's own property. Agamemnon promises first one of his daughters, a woman in marriage rather than as loot, then entire cities, that is, societies intact rather than destroyed.[4] Individual items in the list are never repeated, and arbitrary juxtaposition is found only among individual members of the same class: Kardamyle, Enope, grassy Hire, Pherai, Antheia, Aipeia, and Pedasos.

Organization

The organization of Odysseus's speech in *Iliad* 9 presents something of a challenge. In general, Homer's speakers avail themselves of two different organizational forms. Either they dispose their speeches according to an overarching parallelism (for example, A–B–A′–B′); or else they organize them according to the model of ring composition, a technique by which one argument is sandwiched between layers of other arguments in an expanding series of concentric circles (for example, A–B–C–B′–A′). Both strategies routinely avoid exact repetition and seek instead to place arguments in an economical system of interrelations.

Odysseus's speech is actually an instance of a lop-sided ring composition. Its rings are not concentric circles but distended ellipses with one focus in common, the list of Agamemnon's gifts. The ring closest to this focus addresses the material reward that Achilles might obtain from all the Achaians (*Il.* 9.252–59; 302–3). The next ring out contains remarks about what must be done: save the ships, since there is no future remedy for harm done now (247–51); act now and you will win great praise (303). The outermost ring appeals most specifically to the situation that demands action: Hektor threatens to cut off the prows and set fire to the ships (229–46); Hektor rages near the ships and boasts that no Achaian is his match (304–6). But these rings are very skewed. Odysseus takes thirty and two-thirds lines to introduce the topics, a mere four and a third to reprise them.

At all four rhetorical levels, diction, argument, elaboration, and organization, Homer images effective verbal activity according to the same broad patterns. First, in the *Iliad* persuasive activity is imaged as *social.* That is, the resources for persuasion only derive from, and the effects of a speech only extend to, human beings and those who are capable of interacting in the manner of human beings, that is, personalized divinities. Second, effective verbal interaction is imaged as *systemic.* Individual occurrences are of little value in isolation. They gain significance only as they combine to form a web of occurrences, in social terms, the core of a society whose fringes are more or less frayed. Third, effective verbal interaction is imaged as *relational.* Persuasion draws its power from interpersonal relations. It also alters persons only insofar as they relate to one another. It cannot of itself create or destroy. Fourth, effective verbal interaction is imaged as *economical.* Repeated applications may result in repeated performances of the same act, but they contribute nothing to the force of an individual argument. When a society operates smoothly, a single act requires no more than a single instance of "having been persuaded." Achilles does not need to ask Patroklos more than once.

III

Like Homer, Vālmīki images effective verbal activity according to distinct and consistent patterns, but his patterns are very different.[5]

In theory, persuasion is not the cornerstone of the *Rāmāyaṇa*'s social order; *dharma* is. When people act according to *dharma,* society flourishes and peace prevails. But *dharma* is too personal, categorical, and nonconsequentialist to be left to operate on its own. Society tries to intervene through persuasion on two occasions in particular: first, when someone is threatening harm by pursuing *sukha* to the exclusion of *dharma,* second, and more interesting, when someone is threatening harm by pursuing *dharma* regardless of its consequences. Lakṣmaṇa's speech to Rāma in *Rāmāyaṇa* 2.20 shows how speakers in the most desperate of circumstances attempt to parry these threats. Once again, I pick up where I left off in Chapter 1.

> A man able to counter fate with manly effort does not give up for all that fate may frustrate his purposes.
>
> No, today the people will see the power of fate and the power of man. Today the disparity between the two will be clearly revealed.
>
> Today they will see fate checked by my power, just as they saw your royal consecration checked by fate.
>
> By my power, I will turn back fate that is running wild, like a careering elephant beyond control of the goad, in a frenzy of rut and might.
>
> Not all the gods who guard the world, Rāma, not the entire three worlds—much less our father—could prevent your consecration today.
>
> Those who conspired to banish you to the wilderness, your majesty, will themselves be exiled to the wilderness for fourteen years.
>
> I shall crush their hopes, Father's and that woman's, of making her son king by overturning your consecration.
>
> The might of fate in aid of one fallen within my mighty grasp will be no match for my terrible power and the sorrow it will work.
>
> Later on, many years from now, my brother, when your sons in turn are protecting the subjects, you can go to live in the forest.
>
> For according to the ways of the royal seers of old, living in the forest is prescribed only after entrusting one's subjects to one's sons, to protect as though they were their very own sons.
>
> If perhaps you are unwilling to assume the kingship without the king's wholehearted support, righteous Rāma, for fear of a revolt against your kingship;
>
> I swear to you, my heroic brother, may I never come to share in the afterworld of heroes if I do not guard the kingship for you as the shore guards the ocean.
>
> Have yourself consecrated with the holy implements; busy yourself with that. I shall be able all on my own to repulse any kings by force.

Not for beauty's sake are these two arms nor is this bow merely to adorn me; this sword is not for the sake of ornament nor are these arrows just for filling a quiver.

All four things exist for subduing my enemies, and I am not very eager that anyone be thought my match.

With my sword held ready, its blade sharp and lustrous as flashing lightning, I count no one my match, be he Indra himself, god of the thunderbolt.

Soon the earth will be impassable, knee-deep in the trunks, flanks, and heads of elephants, horses, and men hacked off by the strokes of my sword.

Like clouds with lightning playing about them, like mountains engulfed in flames, elephants will drop to the ground today under the blows of my sword.

When I stand before them with my bow held ready, with my arm-guards and finger-guards strapped on, how could any of those men fancy himself a man?

Shooting now one man with many, now many men with one, I will ply my arrows in the vitals of men, horses, and elephants.

Today the power of my all-powerful weapons shall prevail to strip the king of his power and make it over to you, my lord.

Today these arms of mine, well-suited for wearing sandalwood cream, sporting bracelets, lavishing wealth, and protecting friends as well, will do their job, Rāma, repulsing those who stand in the way of your consecration.

Just tell me, which of your enemies should I separate this very day from his fame, his loved ones, and his life? Just instruct me what to do to bring the land under your control. I am your servant.

(*Rām.* 2.20.12–35)

Diction

On the level of diction, Vālmīki revels in what Homer shuns: Lakṣmaṇa's speech has an extremely high density of verbal echoes and repetition, both within the verse and between verses.[6] As a result, its texture is rich, detailed, and plush compared with the stark, barren smoothness of Odysseus's speech to Achilles. Three examples will give a good sense of the lushness of this language. Once again I have modified the text with the general reader in mind. A single vertical line (¦) marks the joints between the four *pāda*s (feet) of each verse. Verbal echoes are printed boldface; important words are enclosed in diagonal brackets. A circumflex (ˆ) between two words indicates that the final vowel of one word elides with the initial vowel of the next (an instance of *saṃdhi*); the resulting amalgam counts as a single long syllable.

> **na** <śobhārthāv> imau bāhū ¦ **na dhanur** bhūṣaṇ<āya>
> me ¦
> **naˆasir** ābandhanārth<āya> ¦ **na śarāḥ**
> <stambhahetavaḥ> ¦¦
>
> [These two arms are not <for beauty>; my bow is not
> <for> decoration;
> my sword is not <for> hanging up; my arrows are not
> <for sticking in the ground>.]
> (*Rām.* 2.20.25; my translation)

This verse hammers in Lakṣmaṇa's point with a simple but effective alliterative device. Each *pāda* begins with "not" (*na*) followed in all but the first quarter by a noun that designates a weapon: bow, sword, arrows. A second device gives the verse unity. Sanskrit denotes purpose in several ways. The middle two *pāda*s use a particular inflection of the nouns (the dative case, <*-āya*>). But the first and last *pāda* use a compound in apposition to Lakṣmaṇa's arms and arrows (<*śobhārthāv*>, <*stambhahetavaḥ*>). The careful placement of these two compounds—they are virtually the first and last words of this passage—encloses the verse and makes it a distinct unit.

> drakṣyanti tv adya daivasya ¦ <**pauruṣaṃ**>
> <**puruṣasya**> ca ¦
> daiva-mānuṣayor adya ¦ <**vyaktā**> <**vyaktir**>
> bhaviśyati ¦¦
>
> [Today everyone will see the <manliness> of fate and
> <of man>;

the <difference> between fate and humanity will today
be <manifest>.]

(*Rām.* 2.20.13; my translation)

This verse makes the same point twice: choose to resist, and everyone will see immediately that a hero is more powerful than fate. It also employs the same kind of wordplay twice. The second half of each line juxtaposes two words from the same root: the manliness (*pauruṣaṃ*) of man (*puruṣasya,* literally, a male) and the difference (*vyaktir*) that is manifest (*vyaktā*).[7] In context, the verbal texture of the verse is even richer. In the preceding and subsequent verses, several prominent words appear over and over again: fate (*daiva*), man (*puruṣa*), today (*adya*), and forms of the verb "to see" (√*dṛś,* in this verse the first word, *drakṣyanti*). Unity derives from the same device used in verse 25. The two more or less synonymous lines are marked off and tied together by future verbs at either end: they will see (*drakṣyanti*) and it will be (*bhaviśyati*).

adya me 'stra**prabhāvasya** ¦ **prabhāvaḥ**
prabhaviṣyati ¦
rājñaś ca^**aprabhutāṃ** kartuṃ ¦ **prabhutvaṃ** ca tava
prabho ¦¦

[Today will appear the power of me, possessor of
powerful weapons,
to make the king powerless and you powerful, oh
powerful one.]

(*Rām.* 2.20.32)

Even my inelegant translation cannot entirely capture the verbal repetition found in this remarkable verse, which is quite unlike anything found in Homer. Its force derives almost entirely from repeating the same verb root (√*bhū* + *pra-*). The first line contains three words built from the form *prabh(ā/a)v-;* the second contains three words built from the form *-prabhu-*. My translation renders most of these forms with the English word "power" and its adjectives, "powerful" and "powerless," but not the verb. I have had to render *prabhaviṣyati* as "will appear," even though it, too, derives from the same root.[8] This verse offers virtually no argument; it is nothing more than naked assertion. Still, the impact of Lakṣmaṇa's wordplay is almost irresistible. The powerful repetitions in his speech overwhelm the ear, just as his powerful actions will overwhelm whoever interrupts Rāma's inauguration.

At the level of diction, then, Vālmīki pursues a rhetorical strategy at odds with the strategy found in Homer, one that begins and ends with repetition. The dictional repetitions in Vālmīki's speeches do not serve to relate different arguments or even different parts of the same argument. They function instead to bolster the force of single statements. In fact, in the last example dictional repetition *is* the force of the statement.[9]

Argument

Vālmīki follows the same rhetorical strategy on other levels of rhetorical activity, too: he deploys persuasive forces by repeating what are basically isolated *individua.* Thus, Vālmīki's arguments do not share Homer's concern for social relations and their systemic encumbrances. Not once does Lakṣmaṇa plead, "Consider the fate of your friends." Instead, he concentrates on the natures of isolated personae and the implications of those natures for action.

In trying to dissuade Rāma, Lakṣmaṇa articulates three basic arguments. First, he argues that a person as heroic as Rāma should not succumb to fate. (He is countering a speech in which Rāma had cited fate to support his decision.) In addition, a person like Rāma should be able to see that Daśaratha and Kaikeyī are only feigning *dharma* to further their own selfish purposes. Next, Lakṣmaṇa insists that, with his martial support, Rāma's inauguration is unstoppable. Daśaratha and Kaikeyī will themselves be banished to the wilderness; then "at the end of a thousand years' rule," Rāma can take to the forest, if he still wishes. Finally, Lakṣmaṇa gives repeated evidence of his own prowess, what he can and wants to do.

These arguments are quite unlike Odysseus's appeals to *philotēs,* friendship: they make no attempt to obligate Rāma by means of relationships. At the same time, Lakṣmaṇa does not try to entice Rāma by adducing pleasures in excess of those he should already enjoy. Instead, he centers his attention on the privilege and power of the isolated virtuous person. He reminds Rāma that certain obligatory privileges derive from who and what Rāma is. He also points out that certain consequences will inevitably accompany the manifestation of Rāma's nature and his own.

Elaboration

Because Vālmīki's basic rhetorical strategy differs from Homer's, he employs the same basic elaborative techniques—comparing and recounting—

to construct quite different argumentative arrays. Unlike speakers in the *Iliad,* those in the *Rāmāyaṇa* generally elaborate as a way to add force to individual, isolated arguments. They often do so in conjunction with extreme reiteration, and without Homer's awareness for what does and does not belong to human society.

Lakṣmaṇa can hardly avoid the kinds of comparisons that are typical in Homer, comparisons with humans or, in the case of the gods, humanoids. In verse 21, for example, he invokes the paradigm of the ancient royal sages. But in this speech, and in the *Rāmāyaṇa* generally, the more common comparison is a kind almost entirely absent from persuasional speeches in the *Iliad:* comparison with nature. Lakṣmaṇa swears he will conquer fate, though it rage like a rutting elephant (v. 15). He will protect the kingdom the way the shore encircles the ocean (v. 23). The brilliance of his sword gleams like lightning (v. 27). These comparisons differ from Homer's in another way, too. Odysseus compares with the preeminent representatives of a class: Helen, Orestes, the best of women. Lakṣmaṇa's comparisons are, so to speak, generic. They only cite what is a typical element in a set: an elephant, lightning, the seashore. The shift from human or humanoid objects to natural objects, and from preeminent instances to generic ones, parallels a shift in rhetorical purpose. Lakṣmaṇa's comparisons endeavor not to entangle Rāma in a net of social relations but to convey some idea of the force or power of the object at hand.

Vālmīki's speeches also differ from Homer's in the way they recount. An obvious example is the omnipresent list. In the *Rāmāyaṇa,* smaller lists almost seem Homeric: they are constructed according to a careful economy in which relations of meaning and sound lend dignity, fullness, and completeness. But as lists grow, Vālmīki freely abandons any economy or system. His lists persuade not by relating parts to each other but by protracted repetition. As a result, the lists provide a mirror image of Agamemnon's gifts. On the smallest of scales, Odysseus merely juxtaposes elements whereas Vālmīki's speakers relate them. On larger scales, Odysseus relates and Vālmīki's speakers juxtapose.

Perhaps the best example in *Rāmāyaṇa* 2.20 is the last argument, in which Lakṣmaṇa boasts at length of his abilities. A verse like number 25 clearly intends a relation between Lakṣmaṇa's arms, bow, sword, and arrows. His arms and bow propel his sword and arrows and cause them to kill. But in the speech as a whole, this minor series is engulfed in the torrent of Lakṣmaṇa's physical attributes. Like those who encounter them in real life, the audience finds Lakṣmaṇa's martial virtues difficult to resist.

Organization

By now it should come as no surprise that in organizing speeches Vālmīki pursues a strategy that is repetitive and additive, not cumulative and systemic.

Lakṣmaṇa presents Rāma with three distinct blocks of material, followed by a final verse that is unique in both meter and meaning. The first block (vv. 5–12) groups together all the verses—they are much more individually distinct than any of Homer's verses[10]—that assert the incompatibility of Rāma's heroic nature and fate. The third block (vv. 24–34) groups together verses that relate Lakṣmaṇa's immense prowess. The second block (vv. 13–23) is more complex. Its verses insist that Rāma's inauguration continue. But they also bridge the first and third groups by enunciating two further, contrapuntal themes. The one is a contrast between present rule and future forest-dwelling, the other a contrast between the weakness of fate and Lakṣmaṇa's own strength. Finally, the last verse (v. 35), outside all three blocks, virtually collapses into desperation: just tell me what you want me to do, and I'll do it.

In the *Iliad,* rhetorical arguments are arranged harmoniously, like blended stops on an organ or the lines of a geometric vase. But in the *Rāmāyaṇa,* persuasiveness resides in the individual expression. Organization does not supplement the power of individual arguments by inserting them into broader webs of argumentative relations. Instead, it loosely corrals different expressions of the same argument together. This arrangement enables each individual argument to exercise its persuasive power to the fullest.

Lakṣmaṇa's speech is entirely typical of the kinds of persuasive speeches that Vālmīki constructs. At every level of rhetorical activity, Vālmīki's characters adopt the same general strategy. First, effective verbal interaction is *natural.* It employs resources and seeks to employ persuasive effects well beyond the limits of human or humanoid society. Vālmīki knows no sharp distinction between human and animal (monkeys, bears, and people all address one another) or between nonpersonal nature and personal identity (people and their actions resemble elephants, lightning, the seashore). Second, effective verbal interaction is *individuated.*[11] It is applied by individua to individua in isolated "spurts." Appropriately, the magnitude of the desired effect derives more from quantity than from extent. The more units a speaker employs, the greater the rhetorical force. Third, effective verbal interaction is more than relational; it is *generative and destructive.* It effects and affects actualization. Under the best of circumstances, words can address a person's being directly. They call beings or particular forms of being into existence. They can also destroy them. Finally, effective verbal interaction is *repetitive.* Repeated invocations for the same aim increase an individual's stores until power is released. Even ascetics did not fail to notice this lesson of the paradigmatic generative act: in the performance of austerities (*tapas*) repetition and endurance are essential.[12]

IV

For Homer the practice of persuasion is social, systemic, relational, and economical. For Vālmīki it is natural, individuated, repetitive, and generative-destructive. These configurations recur on the level of social relations. They do so because in the *Iliad* and the *Rāmāyaṇa,* the practice of persuasion and social relations are two facets of the same cultural reality, social and universal order. Persuasion represents that order in motion (as event); social relations represent it at rest (as structure).

In both the *Iliad* and the *Rāmāyaṇa,* the principal goal of persuasion is to maintain social order and harmony. In pursuing this goal, it replicates the patterns that characterize order and harmony. It attempts to apply or "reactualize" the power that is latent when society operates harmoniously and in good order. For example, in the *Iliad* persuasion attempts to reactualize the relations of kinship and friendship that govern ordinary social interactions (recall *peithesthai,* "to obey"). It fashions words, arguments, and metaphors that, like Homeric society, are social, systemic, relational, and economic. In the *Rāmāyaṇa dharma* (quite literally, "that which sustains") maintains order and harmony. In Vālmīki's speeches words, arguments, and metaphors are fashioned after the image of *dharma.* They are individuated, honored by repetition, and able to effect the creation and destruction not just of human society but of the universe as a whole.[13]

Like every configuration, these configurations of effective verbal activity or, if you will, social power impose limits. They create order by excluding as fragmentary and chaotic whatever lies outside the order they define. For example, Homer's configuration of persuasive activity excludes words, arguments, and images that, like some of the most powerful words in the *Rāmāyaṇa,* are natural, individuated, repetitive, and do not address social relations. In the *Iliad,* words, arguments, and images of these sorts do not share in the power to persuade. Vālmīki's configuration marks different limits. It tends to exclude words, arguments, and images that, like the most powerful speeches in the *Iliad,* preclude repetition and introduce expansive systems of functional social relations. In the *Rāmāyaṇa,* these words, arguments, and images do not share in the power to persuade.

But neither the *Iliad* nor the *Rāmāyaṇa* shows much interest in problems posed by speeches that violate the configurations of effective verbal action. With few if any exceptions, the persuasive rhetoric that these two poems present generally conforms to the configurations outlined.[14] Homer and Vālmīki concentrate instead on problematic persons. In Achilles and Rāma, the words excluded from persuasion become flesh. When the forms that are imaged in speech as powerless to persuade appear in action, they reveal the ultimate powerlessness of persuasion itself.

In the *Iliad* social incoherence resides where rhetorical incoherence resides: in the individual who dares to break out of the economical web of social relations that constitute the human community. In most cases, the actual incoherence is minimal, and order is easily restored. For example, Thersites' daring is little more than folly. It places him in a position that he cannot possibly sustain. When he steps out of line, Odysseus has no trouble whacking him back.

But Homeric values unavoidably create cases where incoherence is not minimal and ordinary mechanisms cannot restore calm. Homer's characters value, in fact, desperately need, persons who can maximize their own position within the social economy, who can call on and affect ever more extensive relational systems. The demands of systemic economy only amplify the tendency for power to concentrate. There is and can be only one true *aristos* for every dwelling unit (*oikos*). More to the point, there can be, as Agamemnon recognizes, only one lord (*anax*), only one most regal (*basileutatos*), only one "best man" (*aristos*) of all the Achaians (see *Il.* 1.91, 286–91, 2.82, 9.160–61; cf. 2.204–6, 9.69).

With courage and determination Homer's society marches, without looking right or left, into the no man's land of structural incoherence. If the "best of all the Achaians" is willing to apply his abilities for the common good, fine. But what if he is not? The paradigm of Thersites no longer helps. Odysseus can hardly whack Achilles across the back. He may, of course, try, but more than likely Achilles would respond by sending Odysseus's mighty soul spinning to Hades. Instead, Odysseus must approach Achilles as he does the more kingly of Agamemnon's stampeders. He must stand beside him and try to restrain him with gentle words (*Il.* 2.188–89). But Achilles is better by far than any of those earlier turncoats. More powerful and more independent, he stands absolutely beyond everything Homer's speakers routinely use to give their words force. Odysseus can call on no higher, human social relationship to constrain him. Homer's lesson is as unfortunate as it is clear. For all that Achilles is necessary for survival, human persuasion cannot move him.

The case of the *Rāmāyaṇa* is more complex. The purpose of persuasion remains the same, to achieve social thriving. But the practice of persuasion is quite different. To achieve social thriving, Vālmīki's speakers resort to a practice that calls on distinctly intrapersonal resources. They seek to realize a social and systemic end by means of a practice that indulges the natural, individuated, repetitive, and creative-destructive. The resulting tension between purpose and practice creates a rift between what ought to be (the social ends) and what one ought to do (the persuasional means, fashioned in the image of *dharma*). As a result, the *Rāmāyaṇa* enacts two different occasions in which forms that fail to persuade in speech reveal, in social action, the powerlessness of persuasion.

On the one hand, a being may pursue the interpersonal goals of *sukha, artha,* and *kāma* (pleasure, prosperity, and desire) to the exclusion of the demands of *dharma* (duty). In more analytical terms, success in constituting ever larger systems of social relations for one's own pleasure may override all nonconsequentialist demands. The paradigm for such behavior is Rāvaṇa—or, in experienced reality, the Śuṅga king Mitradeva. On the other hand, devotion to the demands of duty may leave a being dreadfully subject to manipulation when that being is inserted, as all beings inevitably are, into social relations. All that is needed is a person clever and mean enough to manipulate the demands of duty to his or her own personal advantage. The paradigm for this predicament is Rāma—or again in experienced reality, those brahmins who, following *dharma,* found it difficult to oppose the rule of the dissolute.

Because Vālmīki's ideology makes *dharma* the root of human association and flourishing, the second occasion, the one exemplified by Rāma, is actually the more perplexing. It requires that the being on whom society depends act in a way that disregards society. A lament by Daśaratha captures the systematic, transpersonal nature of these difficulties nicely. He has been caught, the king moans, in a net of *dharma,* more literally, the "bind of *dharma*" (*dharma-bandhaḥ; Rām.* 2.12.16; see also 98.47; also *satyapāśa,* "trap or noose of truth," 247*, 816*).* The phrase denotes,

The Baroda critical edition identifies passages excised from the text but present in the critical apparatus with successive numbers followed by asterisks, for example 247 or 816*.

first and more obviously, Kaikeyī's ability to manipulate the requirements of *dharma* so that father and son must do her will. But at a second and more subtle level, it suggests that Kaikeyī's machinations (and later, Rāvaṇa's advances) systematically bind *dharma* itself.[15] They prevent the full realization of Rāma's virtues.

As a result, the second problematic represents the fundamental paradox of Vālmīki's society. Harmony and order, not just in society but in the universe as a whole, are created and sustained by a force that is individuated, repetitive, and intrapersonal. Vālmīki's narrative begins with a disturbing revelation: the means to maintain harmony are inconsistent with the end.

At the end of Chapter 1, we contrasted the values, settings, emotions, and social activities in terms of which Homer and Vālmīki formulated the problem of persuasion. Note that these differences correspond to the configurations of effective verbal activity that operate in each poem. Homer's virtue, as exemplified by Achilles, is consequentialist; it adjudicates actions in terms of effects within an economic system of social relations. Vālmīki's virtue is categorical; it adjudicates actions as isolable, repeatable quantities according to their nature, not their results. Furthermore, Homer sets his tale within the social system of the Achaian camp. The problem of failed persuasion highlights the strain within this system, as Achilles retires to its edge. But as Homer presents it, the problematic never exceeds the social; Achilles threatens to pack his bags, but he never actually leaves for home. Vālmīki's setting presents a distinct contrast. The *Rāmāyaṇa* begins in the city of Ayodhyā, but its central problematic quickly requires Rāma to abandon civilized society altogether. As the story unfolds, Rāma penetrates ever more deeply the isolated realm in which brahminical Indians had always encountered the primal forces of generation and destruction, the forest.

Again, in presenting the problem of failed persuasion, Homer depicts Achilles as furiously antagonistic. This emotional state, directed against those who would infringe his rights to property, reflects his social and relational claims on his fellow Achaians. In presenting the same problem, Vālmīki depicts Rāma as painfully an-agonistic. He refuses to act on social and relational claims, and so gives manifest expression to an atomizing, retiring attitude of withdrawal and renunciation. Finally, Achilles acts to avoid pain or to inflict it on others. As a hero, he must seek to appropriate and enjoy the most extensive possible webs of social relation. By contrast, Rāma acts to avoid all pleasure that would compromise his virtue. As a good hero, he must demonstrate that the individuated nature responsible for his very existence stands removed from all social pressures.

V

Contemporary, postmodern sensibilities favor the chaotic and fragmentary. They find it a useful tool with which to oppose overbearing, systemic order. Homer and Vālmīki, however, preferred order and integration. They sang mammoth poems to mystify the threats of chaos and fragmentation that arose when persuasion failed. We can now offer an analysis of that mystification. In briefest form, it runs as follows. Through the devices of imaginative narration, Homer and Vālmīki extended the configurations of effective verbal activity in ways that are not available in the worlds of experienced, physical reality. In doing so, they transposed the limits of those configurations to locations from which they no longer posed significant threats.

In the *Iliad* persuasion finds its limit in the supremely powerful individual. Achilles occupies the apex of the economical relations that constitute Homer's society. Consequently, he stands outside the constraints of those relations. To resolve this problem, Homer inserts Achilles, along with Achaian society more generally, into an even broader set of relations that is available in imagined but not in experienced reality. He recounts the deeds of persons who are hidden from ordinary perception, the ghosts and the gods. Especially the latter are superior to all mortals in the way that the *agathoi* are superior to the masses. They exceed mortals in virtue (*aretē*), strength (*biē*), and the material marks of status (*timē*) (*Il.* 9.498).

Two features make the projection of this broader system strikingly effective. First, it provides a mechanism to check the tensions that result when an *aristos* becomes enraged. The ghosts and especially the gods constitute a system that can allegedly constrain even Achilles himself. As the poem proceeds, that system performs its constraining function amazingly well. Achilles rants and raves; in blind fury he attacks even the lesser immortals (*Il.* 20–21). But he would never dream of attacking Zeus or Athena or Apollo. Second, although the broader system does not, indeed, cannot, completely eliminate the limits marked by the supremely powerful individual, it can and does do something almost as important. It transposes the threatening, powerful individual from human to divine society. In doing so, it makes the threat more remote.

At the beginning of *Iliad* 8, Zeus challenges the Olympians to a contest, a game of celestial tug-of-war. If the rest dare to play, Zeus boasts, he will pull up all the gods and goddesses, together with earth and sea, tie them up, and leave them dangling from the peak of Olympos (*Il.* 8.19–27). Such a taunt is uncomfortably reminiscent of Achilles' antisocial behavior. In fact, Zeus speaks it in support of that behavior. But unlike the paradigmatic placability of Apollo at the opening of the poem, Homer never actually depicts the supreme all-father completely violating social constraints. Consider, for example, what happens when it is time for Zeus's son Sarpedon to die (*Il.* 16). The sorrowing father expresses his desire to contravene destiny, but Hera dissuades him. It would, she says, disrupt the order of society (*Il.* 16.440–57). What would have happened had Zeus become enraged and Hera's persuasion failed? Homer does not say. He leaves Zeus a little ambiguous. Transposed to the realm of the heavens, the threat that the most powerful individual will ignore persuasion and choose to violate the demands of social order is apparently too remote and imaginary for Homer's audiences to have cared.

Thus, Homer resolved the threat of failure implicit in a persuasive practice that was systemic, social, relational, and economical by imaginatively projecting systems of social relations to a realm beyond the human. Vālmīki provided an imagined resolution to a similar threat by extending a configuration that was natural, individuated, repetitive, and generative-destructive. But he did not project that configuration onto the sky.

Suppose for a moment that Vālmīki had chosen to celebrate a supremely virtuous individual who also happened to be, quite openly, a celestial divinity. What would he have gained? Not a solution to the conflict between what ought to be and what one ought to do. A wholly virtuous god would presumably face the same difficulties as a wholly virtuous human being. The only difference is that a narrative about a wholly virtuous deity would be significantly weaker. It would articulate an imagined problematic severely dissociated from the experiences of its audiences. Appropriately, then, the gods play almost no active role in Vālmīki's story. (On Rāma's later divinity, see Chapter 4.)

But Vālmīki did vigorously use the device of imaginative projection for one purpose: not to resolve but develop the threat. Kaikeyī exemplifies the demands of *sukha* within human community, but she marks only the beginning. With the *rākṣasas* and above all Rāvaṇa, Vālmīki projects the same demands onto a superhuman plane. In doing so, he amplifies, virtually to infinity, the social, systemic threat implicit in the configuration on which human association in the *Rāmāyaṇa* rests. Then he resolves it through a device more consistent with that configuration than projection: imaginative concentration.

As Vālmīki imagines him, Rāma is an individuated embodiment of *dharma* more perfect and more powerful than any we could encounter in the world of literal experience. He is the bearer of *dharma* (*dharmabhṛt*), whose very being is *dharma* (*dharmātma*), in complete control of sensory experience (*jitendriya*). As in Homer, two features make this imaginative device effective. First, the concentration of *dharma* provides a mechanism that effectively resolves the tensions between *dharma* and *sukha.* Initially, Rāma appears helpless before the human machinations of *sukha;* in the end, however, he destroys *dharma*'s most potent enemies. The resolution may come slowly, almost painfully, but it does come, and it comes inevitably: even for first-time readers the *Rāmāyaṇa* contains very few surprises. Second, in the *Rāmāyaṇa* as in the *Iliad,* imaginative concentration does not and cannot entirely eliminate the limits marked by the exile of virtue, but it effects a close second-best. It makes those limits so remote that they are almost unthinkable.

After Rāma kills Rāvaṇa, something unsettling happens. Having struggled for so long to rescue Sītā, Rāma tries to renounce her.[16] Throughout the poem, Vālmīki's logic has been clear: *dharma* and *sukha* must not be confused. At the end, the binds of *dharma* threaten to ensnare us one more time. I rescued you, Rāma tells Sītā, not from any desire for the pleasure of your company but from a desire to fulfill *dharma;* you are free to go. But the renunciatory, categorical virtue that we so admired at the beginning of the poem has spent its force. The audience rebels; the gods cry out; the ordeal fire itself attests to Sītā's purity. We can hardly accuse Rāma of violating *dharma.* We ourselves have demanded that he take Sītā back. By the end of the *Rāmāyaṇa*'s narrative, the threat that derives from failed persuasion has become so remote that the poet cannot even bring himself to portray it.

This, then, is how the poetic work of mystification proceeds: in ways unavailable in the worlds of quotidian experience, the poets imaginatively extend the configurations of effective verbal activity. Homer projects onto the heavens a configuration that is social, systemic, economic, and relational. Vālmīki concentrates in a single, supreme human being a configuration that is natural, individuated, repetitive, and generative-destructive. In both cases, the poets transposed the limits implicit in the configurations to locations from which they no longer posed serious threats. Audiences do not seem to have cared about whether Zeus might act like Achilles. They react with sometimes vehement anger when Rāma suggests that *dharma* requires him to renounce Sītā.

At the end of Chapter 1, we contrasted the ways in which Homer and Vālmīki resolved the problematic of failed persuasion. One contrast concerned the instruments through which Homer and Vālmīki achieved that resolution: the ghosts and the gods, the manifestation of Rāma's supreme virtue. The preceding discussion has related those instruments to the configurations of verbal activity that operate in each poem. It remains to observe that the same relationship pertains in the case of the other elements contrasted in Chapter 1, too, the moods and the results.

The profound but fitful calm that descends in the last two books of the *Iliad* images the restoration of the total, economic system of social relations that Achilles' affliction has disrupted. But as we know, that calm will last only as long as the truce between the two sides. The divine guarantors ensure only that order will not unravel completely. They do nothing to eliminate the struggle by which various heroes seek to control ever more extensive relational systems. The *Rāmāyaṇa* presents different moods and results. The initial, profound an-agonism gives way first to Rāma's deep, antagonistic emotions, then to everyone's immense joy. These emotions reflect the manifestation of *dharma*'s interior power. First *dharma* erupts forcefully into the world of appearances; then it establishes a glorious congruence between what ought to be and what ought to be done that evokes joyous celebration. Just how long that new and wondrous world will endure is difficult to say. Rāma's *dharma* is so pure and vital that we are inclined to ascribe to it a duration of quite some time. Indian audiences have traditionally had the same inclination. They fixed the length of Rāma's brilliant *rājya* at sixteen thousand years.

VI

Historians of religions in the hermeneutical tradition have analyzed several kinds of narratives. Two have been important in discussions of the *Iliad* and the *Rāmāyaṇa*. The first is cosmogony, accounts of the origin of the world; the second is hagiography or, better, sacred biography.

In Mircea Eliade's widely influential account, cosmogony is the paradigmatic myth. It recounts the time before time, the sacred instant before the beginning of profane duration, the holy time when the universe came to be.

Everything was fresh then; everything was pure and brimming with life. These features make cosmogony the paradigm for all other myths, because other myths reprise the action of creation on a smaller scale. They also make cosmogony the paradigm for life, because in order to be meaningful and true, human actions replicate actions performed in the sacred moment of creation. Cosmogony makes ritual meaningful, too. Rituals transport participants back to the sacred instant of initial creation, renewing them and recreating their world. Charles Long has insightfully extended Eliade's views by developing a taxonomy of the five or six primary symbols that cosmogonies utilize: creation from nothing, from chaos, through the intercourse of world parents, from the cosmic egg, through emergence, or by the actions of an earth diver.[17]

Sacred biography is a somewhat different kind of narrative. It usually recounts the lives of founders of religious traditions or extremely devout practitioners. This choice of subject alters both the time of the story and the manner of its presentation. Sacred biographies relate the deeds of people in historical time, not the primal acts of deities or ancestors in a mythical, pretemporal time. They also tend to rehearse entire lives, from birth to death, giving special attention to occasions when subjects received their religious missions and exercised special powers. But there are some ways in which sacred biographies resemble cosmogonies. They often provide moral paradigms. The *hadith* of the prophet Muhammad are a good example, although they are only biographical fragments. In recording the words and deeds of the prophet, they teach the ideal response to God's revelation. Events in a sacred biography may also become the subject of ritual reproduction. Think of some celebrations of the Christian eucharist.[18]

The point here is not to engage critically any specific theory of cosmogonies or sacred biographies. Instead, I want to observe the difficulty that those who have taken cosmogony or sacred biography as their primary paradigms for religious narratives have had in seeing either the *Iliad* or the *Rāmāyaṇa* as religious works. (I should emphasize here that I am speaking specifically of Vālmīki's *Rāmāyaṇa*). That difficulty evinces, I think, a certain poverty of conception.

Eliade believed (mistakenly) that all cultural forms initially grew from religious roots. Literature provides a specific example. In Eliade's eyes, it separated itself from mythology in antiquity, but unconsciously uses mythic themes even today. Postulates such as these colored Eliade's view of Greek epics, among other works. As he saw it, the epics recounted stories of the gods, but they were literary adaptations, not genuine religious productions.

As a result, the *Iliad* was postreligious. Hermann Jacobi, one of the first European scholars of high quality to write on the *Rāmāyaṇa,* thought the other way around. As he saw it, the "original" *Rāmāyaṇa* underwent a process of sacralization, not secularization. Initially, the *Rāmāyaṇa* was prereligious. During the first millennium C.E., however, devotional movements arose in India, and the *Rāmāyaṇa* suffered a devotional redaction. Rāma became identified with the god Viṣṇu, and what had once been a secular poem became a blatantly religious one. Recently, Robert Goldman, the general editor of the ongoing Princeton translation of the Baroda critical edition of the *Rāmāyaṇa,* has updated Jacobi's judgments.[19]

These judgments are not, however, beyond suspicion. Although Eliade's *Iliad* is postreligious and Jacobi and Goldman's *Rāmāyaṇa* is prereligious, most general surveys of Greek and Indian religions, operating perhaps with a better intuitive grasp of what counts as religion, have discussed both poems seriously. If one adopts a sufficiently broad notion of religion and religious literature, that practice can be justified.

In effect, Eliade and Goldman think of religions as sets of meanings. Narratives are religious if their meanings are religious. Eliade favors cosmogonies, because those narratives mirror most directly his general account of religion as hierophany, an eruption of the Sacred into the profane through meanings and symbols. Jacobi and Goldman apply a limited notion of sacred biography to the *Rāmāyaṇa.* The poem is religious to the extent that it recounts the deeds of god incarnate. Both approaches are unnecessarily constricting. Bound by their spell, we would overlook a way in which both the *Iliad* and the *Rāmāyaṇa* are profoundly religious: not in what they mean but in what they do. To be specific, they mystify perils of ultimate destruction that arise when persuasion, the ordinary force of social and universal order, fails.

This recognition leads us to postulate a new class of religious literature. When hermeneutically oriented historians of religions have studied accounts of the world as it is—as distinct from its coming into or going out of existence (cosmogony, eschatology)—they have usually restricted their attention to didactic or speculative descriptions. That is, they have talked about cosmologies, even when these cosmologies are inextricably embedded in narrative contexts. The *Iliad* and the *Rāmāyaṇa,* however, are clearly not cosmologies. They belong to a different class of religious literature, *cosmotrophes,* from the Greek verb *trephein,* "to sustain or nurture." The *Iliad* and the *Rāmāyaṇa* are cosmotrophes because they sustain or nurture life in the world of experienced, literal reality, and they illustrate a principal device by which cosmotrophes act, mystification. They resolve significant problematics in the world of experience through solutions that are only immediately available in the world of imagined, literary reality.[20]

Current ideas in literary criticism, like current ideas in the history of religions, tend to favor the cosmogonic to the detriment of the cosmotrophic. That is, it has become common to speak of poems and other literary works as creating or constructing worlds or realities, worlds or realities that critics can then reconstruct and deconstruct.[21] But to apply such language to Homer and Vālmīki would actually obscure their fundamental work. It would do so because in three very important respects, Homer, Vālmīki, and their early audiences did not create or construct worlds or realities, they inherited them.

In the traditions of formulaic poetry Homer and Vālmīki inherited the elements that constituted their worlds: verbal expressions, names and characters, motifs, symbols, and themes (anger caused by affliction, renunciation as a manifestation of virtue, the failure of persuasion). But Homer and Vālmīki inherited more than disconnected elements. They inherited patterns according to which the formulaic elements were arrayed, such as the patterns of effective verbal activity that have occupied this chapter. They also inherited limitations that the elements and patterns entailed. In other words, they inherited their worlds neither as scattered fragments nor as coherent totalities but as problematic pluralities. They composed their narratives in part to address some of those problems, to render the worlds they already knew livable and reliable.

We noted at the end of Chapter 1 how Homer and Vālmīki approached this task differently. The *Iliad* presents a structural solution to a dynamic problem, the *Rāmāyaṇa* a dynamic solution to a structural problem. These two different approaches to the work of cosmotrophy actually reflect the configurations whose limitations the narratives hide.

In the *Iliad,* limitations threaten to disrupt the systemic structures of human interrelationship that persuasion routinely dramatizes and on which human society routinely depends. Accordingly, the poem recounts a dynamic series of non-acts and acts that progressively unravel increasingly larger segments of the social fabric. The solution comes when the ghosts and gods intervene to stop the unraveling and patch the pieces back together. They restore the economical system of relations that constitutes Homer's society—at least for the time being.

In the *Rāmāyaṇa,* however, it is the limitations, not the solution, that are structured and systemic. Vālmīki casts the nets of *dharma* quickly and with devastating force. Then he lets us watch as slowly but inevitably Rāma cuts his way loose. The poem recounts the progressive manifestation in the world of appearances of an individuated nature, such as we all share, on which the thriving or withering of the entire universe depends. When Rāvaṇa is slain, Sītā recovered, and the kingdom obtained, Rāma and his subjects emerge unencumbered and free.

As cosmotrophes, the *Iliad* and the *Rāmāyaṇa* worked to hide the limitations implicit in the configurations according to which social order in Homer's and Vālmīki's worlds was disposed. In doing so, they worked to ensure the continuation of those configurations. In Chapter 4 I discuss some ways in which they succeeded.

4

Texts, Meanings, and Social Acts

As long as mountains stand and rivers flow, the tale of the *Rāmāyaṇa* will enjoy universal fame.
—*Rām.* 1.2.35; my translation

I

No one knows who wrote the beginning of the *Rāmāyaṇa,* but whoever did had no reservations about the poem's future. Its glory would be eternal. Homer's admirers, too, have ascribed to his poems immortal divinity. Presumably, such claims to eternity aim to place the *Iliad* and the *Rāmāyaṇa* outside time, but they can also have the opposite effect. They can remind us that no poetic work, at least no influential poetic work, is a momentary occurrence. In one sense, the words *Iliad* and *Rāmāyaṇa* name complex series of events that have taken place for the last two thousand years and more.

In the preceding chapters I have suggested that in their contexts of origination the *Iliad* and the *Rāmāyaṇa* were cosmotrophes. They mystified the apparent limits of human association that appeared when persuasion failed. They did so by imaginatively and convincingly removing those limits in ways that are not actually available in the world of experienced, literal reality. In that way they made life tenable and tolerable.

This chapter concentrates on only a single aspect of the events that the terms *Iliad* and *Rāmāyaṇa* name: the configurations whose limits the poems mystified. It suggests that in significant ways these configurations have continued to characterize the events of the poems to the present day. That topic is complex and tangled. For the sake of convenience, I will take up three broad areas of poetic activity in turn: the reproduction of the poems as texts, as meanings, and as social acts. I will conclude with more general remarks on the directions of European and Indian scholarship.

I can hardly pretend to recount a complete history of these topics here. A single chapter can do no more than identify certain trends and movements. So what follows is not comprehensive but deliberately selective and suggestive.

II

The textual histories of the *Iliad* and the *Rāmāyaṇa* differ remarkably. If we want brief labels, we can refer to the texts of the poems as "closed" and "open," or as "fixed" and "fluid." But these adjectives are not entirely fortunate. For one thing, they refer rather indiscriminately to two separate aspects of textual reproduction, namely, the ongoing production of the texts of the poem itself, and the simultaneous production of other literary works. The first is the work of textual scholars, the second that of artists. But in both cases, the distinctive traits are the same: artists and scholars interested in the *Iliad* have generally tried to reproduce it; those interested in the *Rāmāyaṇa* have repeatedly tried to reperform it.

Textual artists in the Hellenic and Hellenistic worlds adopted a rather peculiar attitude to the *Iliad*'s defining narrative. They more or less ignored it. I do not mean that they never attended recitations of the *Iliad,* or that they never talked about the poem. As a standard fixture in all Greek education, the *Iliad* provided a topic for centuries-long conversations. By Hellenistic times it enjoyed all the privileges to which classical status entitled it, including the scholarly attention given to a recognized model for poetic imitation. But however much Greek poets talked about, studied, criticized, or imitated the *Iliad,* they rarely reproduced its defining narrative.

The failure to reuse the *Iliad*'s defining narrative probably does not seem odd today. Americans and Europeans, at least, take it for granted that authors will produce (or pretend to produce) new defining narratives, not reproduce used ones. But the treatment of the *Iliad*'s defining narrative by

Greek poets contrasts sharply with the same poets' treatment of other themes. For example, both Aeschylus and Sophocles made full use of the stories about the three generations of ancient Thebes: Laius and Jocasta, Oedipus, and the children of Oedipus and Jocasta. Today only the *Seven against Thebes* survives to represent Aeschylus's Theban efforts; his *Laios* and *Oidipous* have been lost. But several plays on these subjects are among Sophocles' best: *Oedipus Rex, Oedipus at Colonus,* and *Antigone.*

Even more to the point is the rich use to which the three best-known tragedians put materials from the Trojan cycle. Perhaps a full third of Sophocles' plays (he is said to have written 123) were based on the Trojan cycle.[1] Aeschylus, Sophocles, and Euripides each wrote a *Philoctetes.** All three also wrote plays or trilogies on the story of Telephus, a story in which Achilles figures prominently.** But only Aeschylus wrote an Achilles-trilogy that reused the defining narrative of the *Iliad.* In this act he stands virtually alone in Greek literature. Even so, Aeschylus's trilogy did not dwell on Achilles' angry withdrawal from battle but only presented his return, or so scholars suppose from the titles of the plays: *Myrmidons, Nereids,* and *Phryges* (also known as *The Ransom of Hektor*). The plays themselves are lost.[2]

By and large, ancient Greek textual artists did not reformulate the defining narrative of the *Iliad.*[3] Instead, they developed a whole cycle of poems about the other events of the Trojan War into which they could insert Homer's epics: the *Cypria,* the *Iliad,* the *Aithiopis,* the *Ilias parva* (the *Little Iliad*), the *Iliu persis* (the *Destruction of Troy*), and the *Nostoi* (*Homecomings*), followed by the *Odyssey* and the *Telegony.* The ancient Greeks also formulated a complete, detailed biography for Achilles, from his natal dip in the Stygian stream to his death from an arrow in his vulnerable heel. Thanks to Homer, Achilles' biography even continued beyond his death. When Odysseus conjured up the spirits of the dead in order to consult with Teiresias, Achilles put in a postmortem appearance, uttering the famous sentiment that he would rather live as a poor man's slave on earth than rule as a shade over all the dead (*Od.* 11.489–91).[4]

*The title character, Philoctetes, possessed the bow of Herakles. On the way to Troy he contracted an odious disease and was abandoned on an island (according to the *Iliad,* on Lemnos). At Troy, Odysseus takes Helenus, a Trojan prophet, captive. He learns that Troy cannot be taken without the bow of Herakles, and so, in Sophocles' play, Odysseus and Neoptolemus return to the island to try to retrieve the bow, by fair means or foul.

**Telephus, the son of Herakles and Auge, was king of Mysia. He was wounded by Achilles, then, guided by an oracle of Apollo, sought out Achilles to heal him.

Contrary to customary practice, then, Greek poets did not repeat the defining narrative of the *Iliad.* Once this plot was articulated, its power was spent. Instead, they set both the poem and its hero into a grand, systemic context. The same reluctance to reperform the *Iliad* has continued to typify its treatment to the present day. The *Odyssey* has inspired many works, including one of the masterpieces of twentieth century fiction, James Joyce's *Ulysses.*[5] But with some unnotable exceptions, such as the *Iliad latine* of (perhaps) Italicus Baebius or, in the twentieth century, John Cowper Powys's *Homer and the Aether,* the *Iliad*'s defining narrative has provided little opportunity for creative writing. Even many educators have preferred to praise the story without having students read it. Like Livius Andronicus, who first translated the *Odyssey* into Latin but ignored the *Iliad,* they find the tales of the *Odyssey* and the Trojan cycle more attractive. The result is that people who have never read the *Iliad* presume that its subject is the Trojan war and that it contains incidents such as the judgment of Paris, the abduction of Helen, and the ruse of the Trojan horse.

At times, however, the *Iliad* has attracted the efforts of major literary talents, such as Alexander Pope and John Dryden. Strikingly, these artists, justly renowned for their own work, have generally not tried to reperform or retell the *Iliad* but to reproduce it. As we usually say, they have translated it.[6] Commenting on Alexander Pope's *Iliad,* the irascible Richard Bentley voiced the major criterion by which their efforts have been and continue to be judged: "It is a pretty poem, Mr. Pope, . . . [but] you must not call it Homer."[7] Samuel Taylor Coleridge passed a similar judgment on George Chapman's Homer, celebrated by Keats in a famous ode: "It will give you small idea of Homer."[8] Needless to say, these judgments are overly strict. Bentley's misgivings aside, most people would never dream of calling Pope's production anything but Homer—not Homer himself, perhaps, but certainly Homer translated.

The emphasis on accurate reproduction reached a high point in the nineteenth century with Matthew Arnold's perceptive but feisty essay "On Translating Homer."[9] Arnold condemns as "not Homer" almost every translation he cites, with the exception of one or two fragmentary renderings. He advises the prospective translator of Homer—Arnold would prefer, he says, a truly gifted poet like Gladstone, but he knows a truly gifted person will never have the time to translate all of Homer—he advises a translator to note four stylistic points: "Homer is rapid in his movement, Homer is plain in his words and style, Homer is simple in his ideas, Homer is noble in his manner."[10] Translators who emulate these characteristics will, according to Arnold, translate Homer well. They will evoke in those who read their translations the effect of the original on those who know Greek.

Ancient textual scholars also realized early what textual artists seem always to have known:[11] there could really be only one *Iliad,* just as in the world of the *Iliad* there could really be only one Achilles. How the *Iliad* came to be written is a mystery, but the apparent flexibility of oral recitation seems to indicate that the interval between final composition and inscription was not large. Otherwise, the poem would have changed before it was written down. More important, the texts seem to have been inscribed under a kind of spell. Inscription started the Greeks on a race, completed after several centuries, in pursuit of what we would now call the "correct" text, that is, a single, authoritative text. Rhapsodes continued to recite the *Iliad*—in competitions and, at least from the time of Solon, *seriatim,* not repetitively[12]—and the Greeks came to judge their performances not on the basis of who could produce the most stunning (version of the) *Iliad* but on the basis of who could best render the single, set text. Thus, the "city-texts" were born: one best hero, one best poem, one best reciter, at least within the confines of the *polis,* the largest, coherent political unit. The collapse, or better, the supersession of the *polis* and the spread of Greek-like culture throughout the eastern Mediterranean world made the city-texts less satisfactory. Perhaps it was felt that political universality should be matched by textual universality. In any case, that was the need scholars at Alexandria addressed. They began to establish normative, single texts for most authors. First and most continuously, they worked on the text of Homer, which attracted the best minds (Zenodotus, Aristophanes, Aristarchus) as well as those not so good (for example, Rhianus of Crete).[13] Working from "city-texts" as well as texts ascribed to single individuals, these scholars canonized an *Iliad* that underlies the *Iliad* today. For scholars as for artists, the textual myth stated that, once performed, the *Iliad* could only be preserved, not performed again. Practice generally followed the myth.

III

Those who know India—and those who may recall the beginning of Chapter 1—will have recognized already how different the textual history of the *Rāmāyaṇa* is. The ancient Indians did not insert the *Rāmāyaṇa,* a supreme bearer of individuated power, into an economical system of poems. They could hardly avoid the sorts of questions that the Greeks asked about events that happened before and after the story. How was Rāma born? What was his childhood like? How did he and Sītā come to be married? How did Rāvaṇa acquire his boon? How did he become so evil? What happened after Rāma returned to Ayodhyā? But the ancient Indians disposed the answers to these questions differently. They did not use them to formulate an Ayodhyan cycle, the way, for example, the Kṛṣṇa stories of the *Bhāgavata-purāṇa* complement the figure of Kṛṣṇa in the *Mahābhārata.* Instead, ancient Indians integrated the material directly into the *Rāmāyaṇa* itself as its first and last books.

At the same time, a supreme manifestation of the kind of power that the *Rāmāyaṇa* realizes could hardly be performed once, then merely preserved. It demanded repeated performances, first in Sanskrit, then in all the vernacular languages. As a result, unlike the *Iliad,* the *Rāmāyaṇa* has been responsible for some of the best works in Indian literature. Certain vernacular *Ramayan*s* are regional favorites today: in the north the Hindi *Ramcaritmanas* of Tulsi Das, in the south Kamban's Tamil *Ramayan.* But from the prominence of these two we should not underestimate the diversity of *Ramayan*s in any region. Gujarat in western India has hardly been a center of Rāma devotionalism. Nevertheless, up to the year 1933, P. C. Divanji was able to identify at least 105 authors who had written poems on *Rāmāyaṇa* themes in Gujarati. Of the 105, 42 had produced full translations or complete retellings of the poem.[14]

It is difficult to exaggerate the extent to which these *Ramayan*s reperform rather than reproduce the poem. They are not the somewhat free translations familiar from Alexander Pope, who supplements a word for word rendering of the Greek *Iliad* with English elegance and wit. They also go far beyond the somewhat inventive efforts of Powys's *Homer and the Aether,* which adds an extra narrative voice, the Aether, to doctor up the poem in ways that Powys felt necessary. The extent of the alterations appears in exemplary fashion in Tulsi's mammoth *Ramcaritmanas.*

Like Powys, Tulsi includes narrative levels that Vālmīki lacks, although he may not have been the first to introduce them. For example, toward the beginning of the poem the god Śiva and his consort Pārvatī converse, as they do in the earlier *Adhyātma-rāmāyaṇa.* In the course of the conversa-

*I reserve the spelling *Rāmāyaṇa* for Sanskrit renderings of the tale. When referring to vernacular poems, I spell the title *Ramayan.*

tion, they address many of the difficulties Vālmīki's narrative had traditionally raised. But Tulsi performs a great deal more cosmetic surgery on the *Rāmāyaṇa* than Powys did on the *Iliad.* For example, in Tulsi's version mother Sītā is not actually abducted by Rāvaṇa. Instead, Rāma in his prescience secretly entrusts Sītā to Agni, the god of fire, before Rāvaṇa appears. As a result, Rāvaṇa actually abducts only an image of Sītā, and Tulsi can dispense with the rather lame explanation that Sītā must enter the ordeal fire to prove her purity. Instead, the fire is the instrument by which the image-Sītā is destroyed and the real Sītā reappears.

Furthermore, Tulsi does considerably more than spice a rough translation or summary paraphrase with a few additions of his own. At the beginning of the *Ramcaritmanas* the reader may wonder if the story is ever going to begin—not the story of Rāma's exile but the story of Rāma's boyhood, which expands the defining narrative in the received version of Vālmīki. The story of Rāma's youth does finally begin, about one sixth of the way through the entire poem. Tulsi also displays relatively little interest in the *Rāmāyaṇa*'s defining narrative. By far the two longest books are the first two, the *Bāla-kāṇḍa* (the book of Rāma's boyhood deeds) and the *Ayodhyā-kāṇḍa* (the book that describes Rāma's exile from Ayodhyā). After that Tulsi seems to run out of steam.[15] Furthermore, although Tulsi is putatively telling the *Rāmāyaṇa,* he occasionally concentrates so much on commentary and reflections that every now and then readers are forced to recall for themselves the actual events of the story. The poet has forgotten to tell his tale, or perhaps he has assumed—properly—that his audience already knew it.

Unlike the *Iliad,* then, the *Rāmāyaṇa* has provided an opportunity for repeated and free reperformances. The disposition to reperform as well as preserve the *Rāmāyaṇa* motivated India's textual scholars, too. Consider the Baroda critical edition. The editors of that edition have managed to excise over 5,000 verses from the poem, almost a fourth of the traditional total of 24,000.[16] Lakṣmaṇa's speech to Rāma, familiar from Chapters 1 and 3, illustrates the extent of the textual omissions, additions, and variations possible. In the critical edition the speech occupies thirty and a half verses (2.20.5c–35); in the so-called Southern Recension it occupies thirty-five and a half (2.23.5c–40), an increase of about 18 percent.[17] What is more, the critical edition notes fifty variant full lines (about 80 percent of the edited speech) that are found in some version of Vālmīki as either additions to or substitutions for the lines given in the critical text. The speech in which Odysseus offers Agamemnon's gifts to Achilles provides a sharp contrast. The critical apparatus for this speech, which runs a full eighty-two lines, does not note a single variation or addition that occupies a complete hexameter. The longest single variant replaces only four feet, and it is found in only one of the poem's twenty-four families of manuscripts (see the critical apparatus to 9.250 in the Oxford Classical Texts edition).

In assessing the *Rāmāyaṇa*'s textual plurality, it is especially important to note the function of the additions. In general, the added verses do not appreciably alter the narrative. Instead, they extend descriptions, amplify speeches, detail battles further—that is, they attempt to reperform the text of the *Rāmāyaṇa* in a way that realizes yet more forcefully what the poem itself was trying to achieve. For example, all of the Southern Recension's additions to Lakṣmaṇa's speech come before, within, and after the critical edition's ninth verse. The following reproduces the pertinent portion of the speech in its fuller version. The lines printed boldface are found only in the Southern Recension.

> Don't you know . . . that there are cunning people who wear the guise of righteousness?
>
> **They have acted very skillfully, eager to seize their own advantage through guile. For if they had not conspired before now, Rāghava, then long before now she would have raised the matter of the boon and he would have granted it.**[18]
>
> What all people find hateful has begun: the inauguration of somebody besides you.
>
> **I can't bear it, hero. Please forgive me.**
>
> I hate this *dharma* that has changed your plans and confused your mind.
>
> **How can you, who are skilled in action, do this reprehensible, most undharmic thing that our father has spoken, enslaved to Kaikeyī's wishes?**
>
> **Don't you see that the inauguration is being interrupted improperly?**
>
> **That's what grieves me, and why I hate your concern for *dharma*.**

The whole world despises this concern of yours for *dharma.*

How could you even dream (*manasā api*) of doing what those two desire, who always act out of desire.

Those two enemies, always hostile, are parents in name only.

(*Rām.* 2.20.8cd, 503*, 9ab, 504*, 9c–f, 507*; all but 8cd and 503* are my translation)

Such wholesale variation in the received texts usually strikes European tastes as illicit tampering and careless transmission. But in one sense, the function of the *śloka*s that the critical editors excised is sound, even if their attestation in the manuscripts is not. They reperform the *Rāmāyaṇa* in order to realize yet more fully what the "genuine" verses were trying to manifest.[19] As far as the epics are concerned, and here the contrast with *śruti** is sharp,[20] the phantom of the authoritative text, as close to the original as possible, first stalked the Indian subcontinent when European scholars arrived. As a result, the production of the *Rāmāyaṇa*'s critical edition, like that of the *Mahābhārata,* marks a significant new stage in the textual history of the poem, a stage that is entirely in keeping with the contemporary Indian pursuit of modern technology and economic development.[21] The widespread reluctance to accept the *Rāmāyaṇa*'s critical edition (that of the *Mahābhārata* has been widely proclaimed) may partly display a discomfort with the disruption of patterns implicit in the texture of the poem itself. It resembles the ambivalent feelings many Indians have about adopting "Western" technology, even when that technology happens to come from Japan.[22]

IV

The history of the reproduction of the *Rāmāyaṇa* as meaning has resembled the history of the poem's texts in at least one important respect: it has been a history of fuller elaboration. In fact, the two histories are intimately

*Literally, "what has been heard," from the root √*śru,* "to hear." *Śruti* refers specifically to the eternal, unchanging, and indeed unchangeable revelation heard in the beginning of time by the *ṛṣi*s and recorded in the Vedic Samhitās and Brāhmaṇas.

related, because one of the most influential ways of interpreting the *Rāmāyaṇa* has been to retell it.

For centuries interpretations of the poem have routinely begun with a single, important question: is it conceivable that Rāma, the supreme bearer of virtue and power, the destroyer of evil, was just a human being? Many modern scholars are uncomfortable with notions of divine incarnation. According to them, Rāma was initially a secular hero, the *Rāmāyaṇa* a secular poem. In maintaining their position, they ignore—or in rather bald instances of circular reasoning, excise—the few hints found in *Rāmāyaṇa* 2–6 that a being of Rāma's caliber cannot be merely human; he must have some share in the divine.[23] But Vālmīki only provides tantalizing hints. In his poem, the question of Rāma's identity puzzles even Rāma himself. "So far as I know, I'm a human being, Rāma, Daśaratha's son. Tell me, Lord [Brahmā], who am I, whose am I, and where have I come from?" (*Rām.* 6.105.10; my translation). At the same time, a solely human Rāma has satisfied most Indians about as much as a solely human Jesus has satisfied most Christians, which is to say not at all. The question is, if Rāma is more than human, what else is he?

The first and last books of Vālmīki's *Rāmāyaṇa,* the *Bāla-* and *Uttarakāṇḍas,* established the parameters within which this answer had to be given. They tell how one day the gods came to Lord Viṣṇu to solicit help against the demon Rāvaṇa. By means of intense austerities this demon, before he was a demon, had earned a boon from Brahmā the creator. But even in those most ancient of days absolute power corrupted absolutely. Rāvaṇa requested a fateful invincibility before all the mighty creatures of the universe. Brahmā had no choice. He granted the request, and Rāvaṇa became a demon. But Rāvaṇa had made a fatal error. He did not think enough of human beings to include them in his request. So to rid the world of terror in the form of Rāvaṇa, Viṣṇu descended to earth as the four sons of the righteous king Daśaratha. Work done, he returned to his own celestial abode (*Rām.* 1.14–15; 7.100).

Compositions of several different kinds elaborated these indications into a full-scale mythology: the compendia of myths and legends known as *Purāṇas* ("Tales of the Old Days"), the Vaiṣṇava commentaries on the *Vālmīki-Rāmāyaṇa,* and the reperformances of the poems. According to the most prominent mythological tradition, Rāma was one element in a series whose elements were related only because they were—and still are—taken as repeated manifestations of the same, divine, preservative force. Rāma joined the likes of Lords Kṛṣṇa and Buddha, a fish, a turtle, a boar, a dwarf, a man-lion, and a rampaging brahmin who killed *kṣatriyas* with an axe. That is to say, Daśaratha's son became the seventh of the ten canonical *avatāras** of Viṣṇu. His activities were alleged to have ended one age, the Tretā yuga, and ushered in the next, the Dvāpara yuga. Sītā became Viṣṇu's consort Śrī. Lakṣmaṇa became Ādiśeṣa, the cosmic serpent on which Viṣṇu reclines in sleep between the ages of the universe.

But although some people enjoy mythology, others prefer a less narrative, more abstract mode of thought. The philosophically inclined have read the *Rāmāyaṇa* in more subtle fashions. For them, not human phenomenalities but philosophical realities were at work in the poem. The content and the quality of the philosophical interpretations varied with the convictions and abilities of their authors. For present purposes, one poem can illustrate the general trend.

The *Adhyātma-rāmāyaṇa* (Sanskrit, fourteenth century [?]), a portion of the *Brahmāṇḍa-purāṇa,* introduced an overarching, at times overbearing, Advaita (nondualist) metaphysics into the narrative of the *Rāmāyaṇa.* Its primary vehicle for doing so was the composition of speeches, not the ministerial speeches familiar from Vālmīki, but didactic ones. In this poem, speakers ceaselessly and tirelessly proclaim Rāma's identity at every turn. A question addressed by the goddess Pārvatī to her consort, Mahādeva (Śiva), provides the occasion for the entire narrative: people worship Rāma as the unmanifest *brahman,*** devoid of alteration and unaffected by the world of appearances; so how could Vālmīki describe him as a human being apparently unaware of his own supreme stature (*Adhyātma-rām.* 1.1.10–15)? To answer this question, Śiva recites a precept, then tells the Rāma-tale to prove it: "Rāma is the highest self [*parātmā*] which does not derive from nature [*prakṛti*], pure

**Avatāra,* from the verb $\sqrt{}$*tṝ* + *ava-,* literally means "descent," but is often translated "incarnation." There are distinct differences between Hindu notions of descent and Christian notions of incarnation. Hindus would never locate "the fullness of Godhead" in the terrestrial figure, nor have they distinguished between a god—or a person of the Godhead—who remains transcendent, and a god or person who comes to earth in human vesture. Strikingly, Hindus have never experienced the need to try to formulate precise and universally agreed upon metaphysical notions of precisely what "incarnation" means (contrast the christological controversies in the early Christian councils and later).

**In Vedāntic thought the *brahman,* originally a ritual utterance, was the metaphysical force that generated and sustained the universe, "reality," if you will. Śaṅkarācarya (eighth century), the founder of the nondualist (*advaita*) Vedānta, distinguished between the *nirguṇa brahman,* or *parabrahman,* which was beyond qualities altogether, and the lesser *saguṇa brahman,* which possessed qualities and thus appeared to human beings as God.

bliss, one, the highest person [*puruṣottama*]" (*Adhyātma-rām.* 1.1.17cd). As the poem proceeds, speaker after speaker repeats the same lesson, starting with the instructions Sītā gives Hanumān before the action begins. "Know that Rāma is the ultimate *brahman,* being, consciousness, and bliss, devoid of duality, Being itself, free from all attributes and inaccessible to the senses" (*Adhyātma-rām.* 1.1.32).[24]

The *Adhyātma-rāmāyaṇa*'s pervasive nondualism mandated some changes in the narrative.[25] For example, as the ultimate *brahman,* Rāma could not be responsible for the events of the poem. Sītā herself was, in her nature as *Prakṛti* and as Rāma's power over appearances (*Yoga-māyā*).* The poem also contains much less genuine conflict and confrontation than Vālmīki's version. Mantharā and Kaikeyī do not act out of greed but on divine instruction. Sītā is not really abducted; only an apparent Sītā is. Most striking of all, Rāvaṇa attacks Rāma not out of physical lust and ambition but out of a desire for salvation. He knows that if he fights Rāma, he will focus his attention on Rāma without distraction. It only stands to reason that anyone who thinks only of God reaps great rewards.

The *Adhyātma-rāmāyaṇa*'s depiction of Rāvaṇa reflects a transformation in the reception of Rāma implicit in many of the preceding accounts. From being a subject of narrative, Rāma became as well a subject of intense veneration and devotion. In the *Adhyātma-rāmāyaṇa* this transformation appears as soon as Pārvatī asks Śiva the question that sets the poem in motion. She comments: "Firm devotion to lord Rāmacandra is renowned as the ship that sails on the essence of all existence" (*Adhyātma-rām.* 1.1.10cd). In a meticulous study of the sacred town Ayodhyā, Rāma's supposed capital, Hans Bakker has elaborated a chronological sequence for that transformation. The pilgrimage rituals that take place in Ayodhyā today began early in the second millennium C.E., which is when the cults of Rāma seem to have arisen in India generally.[26] By the fifteenth century worshipers known as Rāmānandīs were addressing Rāma as the one, supreme God. That in turn opened the door for a different rendering of the *Rāmāyaṇa,* one that focused not so much on philosophical didacticism as on the responses of a devotee to Rāma as God. The most prominent example is the massive *Ramcaritmanas* of the Hindi poet Tulsi Das, discussed earlier.

**Prakṛti:* "nature"; in dualistic schools, the active feminine (as distinct from the inert masculine) principle that is responsible for the generation of the world of appearances. *Yoga-māyā:* Rāma's ability to act in the world of appearances.

Both the *Adhyātma-rāmāyaṇa* and the *Ramcaritmanas* render the story of Rāma in a way that interprets Vālmīki's characters symbolically. In a strict sense, however, neither of them reads the *Rāmāyaṇa*'s narrative allegorically. That is, neither version renders a hidden, metaphysical or devotional truth concealed in the naked events of the story, as distinct from its characters. A general scarcity of narrative allegory should not be unexpected. After all, the *Rāmāyaṇa* is a poem in which character takes precedence over plot. But occasionally the *Rāmāyaṇa* has become a vehicle for full-scale narrative allegories, too. A rather recent example is the version of the Rāma story told by the Gujarati Advaitin saint Vasudevananda Saraswati (late nineteenth century).

According to Vasudevananda, Rāma, as the god Viṣṇu, is really the *parabrahman* (the ultimate reality), which is reflected in the *buddhi* (intellect) and further in the *ahaṃkāra* (the ego, under the three *guṇas* of *sattva, rajas,* and *tamas*) as the *jīvātman,* a living person (namely, the human Rāma). The reflected *jīvātman* forgets its true nature and wanders in *saṃsāra* (that is, the Daṇḍaka forest), lamenting the spiritual experience which it has lost (namely, Sītā). Through the grace of a guru, the *jīva* achieves discrimination (*viveka,* namely Hanumān), and with the help of the *sattvāhaṃkāra* (namely, Vibhīṣaṇa), this discrimination makes it possible for the *jīvātman* to find and be reunited with its spiritual experience (Sītā) and thus to return to the realm of pure bliss (*parabrahman*).[27]

When I first learned of Vasudevananda's interpretations, my reaction was one of amused tolerance. After all, the categories in which Vasudevananda formulates his account seem completely removed from Vālmīki's concerns. Europeans and those of European cultural descent have at times reacted even more extremely to interpretations of the *Rāmāyaṇa.* They have expressed perplexity and even disgust over the divinization of Rāma and the allegorization of his tale. But we should recognize that distinctive dynamics of appropriation are operating here. Just as Indian textual scholars did not and could not merely preserve but had also to reperform the *Rāmāyaṇa,* so too interpreters could not simply reproduce the apparent meaning of the poem's text. The poem itself posed a much more profound task: to make explicit the deeper meanings implicit in the characters and, to a lesser extent, the events of the narrative. The true profundity of these meanings could only be realized through repeated and varied attempts to express the true, hidden nature of Rāma. In other words, divinization and symbolic interpretation were not just entirely acceptable as means of interpreting the *Rāmāyaṇa.* They were inevitable.

V

Allegory and worship have played significant roles in the history of the *Iliad*'s meanings, too, but with some important differences. Achilles could never be worshiped as God (capital G), and readings of the defining narrative, unlike readings of isolated, incidental features, have tended to emphasize the systemic, the literal, and the historical.

According to some, the admirable Rāma had to wait more than a thousand years before receiving a cult. But from very early times, Achilles was worshiped, though usually as a hero, not a god. Since many scholars suppose that heroic epic was a prime cause in the rise of hero-worship in eighth-century Greece,[28] it is not entirely surprising that a central epic hero should become an object of cult. But unlike the case with the *Rāmāyaṇa* and Rāma, it is difficult to ascertain how much the *Iliad*'s defining narrative contributed to Achilles' heroization. It seems to have contributed virtually nothing to the most important cult, Achilles as "ruler of the Black Sea."[29] Achilles' mythical instruction in the arts of healing by the centaur Cheiron certainly could not have harmed his heroic reputation. But if Walter Burkert is correct that "from about 700 . . . the cult of the common heroes of the land becomes the expression of group solidarity,"[30] there may have been sufficient cause to establish for Achilles an apotropaic cult, as other peoples have done for the angry dead.

The veneration of Achilles survived into the Hellenistic and Roman periods. According to Plutarch, Alexander of Macedon anointed Achilles' gravestone at Troy. Then, following ancient custom, he ran naked around it and garlanded it. The observant traveler Pausanias creates a less picturesque image, but one that is more geographically expansive. He leaves the impression that in the mid-second century C.E. minor temples, altars, and cenotaphs dedicated to Achilles were scattered in mainland Greece—scattered very sparsely, perhaps, but scattered nonetheless. At them Achilles, whose denial of *timē* during his lifetime created so much misery for the Achaians, received *timai,* perpetual honors, from the observant (2.1.8). Undeterred by Alexander's experiences in Troia, Pausanias visited Achilles' tomb at Elis in the northwestern Peloponnesus, where, he says, on a specified day at sundown Elean women wailed Achilles' fate.[31]

Two centuries after Pausanias, the rituals of Achilles became illegal, at least insofar as they were memorials of Achilles. They have never been revived. As a result, in the history of the interpretation of the *Iliad*'s defining narrative, and of Homer generally, the more potent trend has not been heroization but allegorical interpretation. Just how prevalent Homeric allegories were in the pre-Hellenistic era is debated, but everyone seems to agree that at least Theagenes of Rhegium (fl. ca. 525 B.C.E.) and Metrodorus of Lampsacus (mid fifth century B.C.E.) advanced them.[32] Later, Stoics such as Crates and Neoplatonists such as Porphyry composed detailed Homeric allegories. Medieval Europeans did not, for the simple reason that they did not know Greek, so they could not read Homer. But in the fifteenth century Western Europeans finally learned enough Greek to make Homer more than just a name, and once again physical and moral allegories proved useful. They did not yield to literal, historical perspectives until well into the eighteenth century.

Thus, allegory has had a venerable career in Homeric interpretation, but relations between allegorical interpretation and the *Iliad*'s defining narrative have almost always been strained.[33] In general allegorists much preferred the *Odyssey,* with its far-flung voyages and strange cast of characters, to the *Iliad,* filled as it is with the tedious repetition of battle. Proclus's treatment of the *Iliad* is instructive. Finding no allegory in Achilles' truly dreadful mistreatment of Hektor's corpse, Proclus appealed to history. Achilles' barbarity, he suggested, reflected the brutality of his time.[34] On those relatively infrequent occasions when allegorists did turn their attention to the *Iliad,* they concentrated on isolated incidents and descriptions: the shield of Achilles, the battle of the gods (*Il.* 20 and 21), and specific gods or goddesses as personifying the forces of nature. Quite unlike, say, Vasudevananda's allegorical retelling of the *Rāmāyaṇa* or even the *Adhyātma-rāmāyāṇa*'s discourses on the concealed (or not so concealed) identity of Rāma, allegorists interpreting the *Iliad* generally ignored both its defining narrative and Achilles, its central figure.[35] Furthermore, unlike Indians, who generally turned to allegory to realize potentials that were latent in the *Rāmāyaṇa*'s narrative, Greeks and, much later, Western Europeans turned to allegory largely for cosmetic reasons. They sought to remove unsightly features that Homer had left annoyingly visible, most notably, the gods. In antiquity Greeks like Theagenes used allegory to defend Homer and his gods against the systematic charges of rationalists like Xenophanes and, later, Plato. In a Christian world, Renaissance humanists and some of Homer's later partisans found that allegory could help them justify the preeminence in which they held a poet who turned out, when they could finally read him, to have been incredibly pagan.[36]

The deliberate effect of allegorization, then, was to exclude the *Iliad*'s narrative. The reason was simple. The crux of that narrative, the persuasion and behavior of the gods, violated first philosophical and then theological norms. When theology's power finally waned, the *Iliad*'s fictions became more tolerable, its narrative revived, and allegory was generally abandoned and even ridiculed.[37] As Howard Clarke writes, "Ultimately, the allegories, even when made to work, could not be made to satisfy. . . . Neither the physical nor the moral allegories seemed worthy of the poems they were meant to illuminate but in fact fragmented. In the *Odyssey* the allegorists belabored the obvious; in the *Iliad* they ignored it. It did not help readers much to be told that Circe, Calypso, and Polyphemus were a bad lot; it helped them even less to be told nothing about Achilles, his pride or his fate."[38]

The recovery of the *Iliad*'s narrative did more than bury Homeric allegories. It replaced them as the primary topic of conversations about the *Iliad*'s meanings. Scholars tried to make systematic sense of the narrative in terms of internal coherence and external correspondence. They sought to remove logical inconsistencies and thereby establish Homer's original, consistent narrative. They also sought to construct a rational account of the world in which Homer sang, and thereby to determine whether and to what extent Homer's poetry could count as history.

The ancients already knew that the *Iliad* bristles with inconsistencies and repetitions, but beginning in the late eighteenth century these curiosities evoked a new public response. The Roman critic Horace had been willing to excuse Homer for nodding every now then, especially in such a lengthy tale.[39] Alexander Pope, who knew Homer with the intimacy of a translator, was even more generous. He exonerated Homer from all blame: "Those oft are Stratagems which Errors seem, Nor is it Homer Nods, but We that Dream."[40] But in 1795 Friedrich August Wolf's *Prolegomena ad Homerum* asked "the Homeric question," and the warm tolerance of a unitarian summer gave way to a stormy analytical winter.[41]

Homeric inconsistencies and repetitions touched off a mighty battle between the analysts on one side and the unitarians on the other. The analysts acted as if Homer was—in fact, as if every poet were—a perfect systematician. They insisted that inconsistencies of any sort had to derive from the interference of later hands. To prove their point, they constructed any number of ur-*Iliads*, along with scenarios to explain how Homer's original eventually ended up as the *Iliad* we know. The unitarians took the opposite position. They were convinced that each and every inconsistency in the *Iliad* could and should be explained solely on the basis of Homeric—that is to say, human—fallibility. The analysts, they decided, built houses on sand, and analytical reconstructions of the poem were something akin to blasphemy.

With the end of World War II, the great Homeric battles seemed to subside. Milman Parry's notions of oral-formulaic poetry became widely known, and they seemed to declare the battle a draw.[42] The analysts were right that Homeric epic contained layers from several different periods, but they were wrong to conceive of these layers as separate lays. Instead, they were elements of the poetic vocabulary, sets of formulas that accumulated over a period of time and thus preserved the features of different pasts. The unitarians were right, too. The *Iliad* and the *Odyssey* were composed by one, perhaps two monumental poets. But they were wrong if they attributed any wholesale, inventive genius to those poets. In the process of oral recitation, these poets assembled disparate formulaic elements into a poem, with the result that the finished products were not always consistent. At present it is difficult to say whether Parry's notions had effected a treaty or only a truce. The longer people look at his notions of "oral" and "formulaic," the less they are able to describe what they see.

The analysts and unitarians had fought over the answer to "the" Homeric question. But another Homeric question frequently exercised scholarly imagination in the nineteenth and twentieth centuries, and it raised another issue of systematic consistency: How commensurate is the story of the *Iliad* with other, "factual" stories that modern scholars want to tell about the ancient world? The presumed answer was, not very—until a free-thinking entrepreneur named Heinrich Schliemann started digging at Hissarlik, Turkey. He discovered the site of ancient Troy, then proceeded to the Greek mainland, where he unearthed at ancient Mycenae cyclopean walls, beehive tombs, and a gold death mask that his unfaltering faith attributed to Agamemnon. Of course, Schliemann probably did not discover Agamemnon's death mask, and he certainly did not prove that the events of the *Iliad* actually occurred. But he did reveal what few at the time seem seriously to have expected: that the world inhabited by Homer's heroes was not pure poetic fancy. And that discovery posed a riddle.

If Homer's worlds are not pure poetic fabrication, how historical are they? This question has absorbed tremendous scholarly energy. Parry's notions of a conservative, oral-formulaic medium gave an aura of feasibility to the popular hope that Homer's heroes actually lived in the Mycenaean age, a world replete with silver-studded swords, boar's-tooth helmets, and figure-eight shields. All of these features appear in the *Iliad,* and all of them disappear from the archaeological record with the demise of the great Mycenaean citadels. Unfortunately, Homer also includes later features, so a Mycenaean Homer, like a historical one, has generally been confined to popular fancy. M. I. Finley has argued that "the world of Odysseus" was actually the world one to two centuries before Homer's time, the world of the tenth to ninth centuries B.C.E. Some agree, but to my mind, the most secure position is that claimed by Anthony Snodgrass. He has argued that Homer's world is a composite, assembled from bits and pieces of several different periods.[43]

The history of the interpretation of the *Iliad* contrasts sharply with the history of the *Rāmāyaṇa*'s interpretation, and in a way reminiscent of the contrast between the histories of the two poetic texts. Interpreters of the *Rāmāyaṇa* have favored repeated manifestation. They have sought to supplement a literal reading of Vālmīki with symbolism and allegory, often by reperforming the poem itself. But interpreters of the *Iliad*'s narrative have preferred economical systems of meaning. Those who have pursued Homeric symbolism and allegory have tended to neglect the defining narrative. Those who have been attentive to the narrative have attempted to make systematic sense of it. Equally sharp contrasts characterize the history of the *Iliad* and the *Rāmāyaṇa* as social acts. The *Iliad* has tended to perform acts that are social and relational. But the *Rāmāyaṇa* has also included acts that transcend society to create and destroy on a universal scale.

VI

As we have already seen, it is difficult to situate the *Iliad* in its original context. Presumably the poem was first sung by professional reciters, sponsored by elite patrons, and enjoyed by audiences that were at least semi-popular. But more specific information is available for later times. It reveals that in ancient Greece, then Western Europe, the *Iliad* became a cultural tool used to further social and national ambitions. Such a tool was too powerful to circulate freely. In both Greece and Europe it was entrusted to professional scholars for safekeeping.

Education in ancient Greece was never so formally codified as the *smṛti*s* would have us believe it was in ancient India. Nonetheless, the *Iliad* was an important pedagogical tool from very early on. The rhapsodes

*Literally, something that is remembered, from the verb √*smṛ*, to remember. In one sense, *smṛti* comprises all sacred writings but the Veda, which is *śruti*, revelation. Here I use the term more technically, to refer specifically to the tractates on *dharma* (*dharma-śāstra*s), the most famous of which is the *Laws of Manu* (*Manu-smṛti*).

claimed, at least some of them did, that every practical skill one needed to know could be learned from Homer. The sophists, too, found that teaching Homer was useful. From Xenophon's *Symposium* we learn why. The participants in that dialogue tell each other what they value most about themselves. Niceratus relates how his father, Nicias, made him memorize the whole of the *Iliad* and *Odyssey.* The reason? To make him a virtuous man. In other words, Homer was an essential tool for "finishing" upper-class youth in Greek antiquity. Even Plato credited Homer with educating Greece; that was why he banned Homeric poetry from the ideal state.[44]

Ancient Greeks found Homer useful for politics as well as pedagogy. Cities vied with one another by introducing competitive recitations of Homer into their festivals. The most famous were the recitations during the Panathenaia, Athens's celebration of itself. The poems were also useful in "international" politics. To Herodotus's way of thinking, the campaign that pitted Achaians against Trojans foreshadowed the war between the Greek *poleis* and the great kings of Persia. A century later, Isocrates conscripted Homer for his anti-Persian panhellenism.

> I think that even the poetry of Homer has won a greater renown because he has nobly glorified the men who fought against the barbarians, and that on this account our ancestors determined to give his art a place of honor in our musical contests and in the education of our youth, in order that we, hearing his verses over and over again, may learn by heart the enmity which stands from of old between us and them, and that we, admiring the valour of those who were in the war against Troy, may conceive a passion for like deeds. (*Panegyric* 159)

If we can trust Plutarch, Isocrates' Homeric vision inspired Alexander of Macedon. The young Alexander is alleged to have slept with a copy of the *Iliad*—and a dagger—under his pillow. When he first breached Asia Minor, he visited the site of Troy, sacrificing to Athena and pouring a libation at Achilles' grave (Plutarch *Alexander* 15). On this passage, J. R. Hamilton comments with insight, "Alexander was well aware of the value of propaganda."[45]

The conquests of Alexander transformed more than the political map of the ancient world. They transformed the institutions of knowledge, too, and the way Homer was used. Before Alexander a general, cultivated paideutic, instilled by private tutors, had been common. In fact, Alexander's tutor had been Aristotle himself, who is said to have re-edited the text of Homer specifically for the benefit of his noble pupil.[46] After Alexander, a more confined, specialized learning, inspired by Aristotelianism, became prevalent. The leading scholars worked at institutions established and maintained by imperial patrons. In this new setting, the archaic and artificial language of Homer's poems and their divergent texts provided the challenges, the prime examples, and perhaps even the immediate impetus to sophisticated schools of literary criticism and linguistic philosophy.

What would motivate such intense scholarly efforts? Rudolf Pfeiffer has written about Callimachus's cataloging: "Only the most passionate desire to save the complete literary heritage of the past from oblivion and to make it a permanent and fruitful possession for all ages could have provided strength and patience for this immense effort."[47] Pfeiffer may be partly right. Passionate desire was certainly there, but the passions he describes are a little too pure. The competition between Alexandrian scholars and those working at a place like Pergamon on linguistic theory and the text of Homer suggest a panoply of institutional and political motives that are not unknown today. As we know, even within Alexandria the passion for scholarship was not untainted by "baser" instincts. Callimachus, Pfeiffer's well-known cataloguer and epigrammatist, pronounced long poems dead; his pupil Apollonius of Rhodes proceeded to write one.

The rise of Rome inaugurated a moratorium on the use of the *Iliad* for social and national ambitions, a moratorium that lasted more than fifteen hundred years. Rome needed a new mythology commensurate with its imperial ambitions and abilities. Vergil's masterful *Aeneid* answered that need by recounting the valiant struggles of *pius* Aeneas, the noble Trojan ancestor of Rome. The old equivalence, Greek is to Persian as Achaian is to Trojan, was replaced by a new one, Roman is to Greek as Trojan is to Achaian. Pro-Roman, and thus pro-Trojan, loyalties dominated the Latin-speaking world throughout the Middle Ages and beyond. The accounts of the Trojan campaign most popular in the Middle Ages, the writings of Dares and Dictys, are good examples.[48]

The Renaissance rejected the medieval synthesis and returned to ancient models, but its impact on Homer was limited. It made him presentable, but it did not make him popular. Homer's style and loyalties still counted against him. Julius Caesar Scaliger's "Seven Books on Poetics" spoke for many: he preferred Vergil's polished hexameters to Homer's rustic ones, and Vergil's Trojan loyalties to Homer's Greek leanings.[49] In the France of Louis XIV, Homer was blamed as much as praised. The "moderns" pointed to the rough archaism of Homer's writing and the provincial superstition of his thought as typifying the worst antiquity had to offer.

Finally, in the eighteenth century, the wheel of Homer's fortune completed its revolution. Two European nations arose, one earlier and more unified than the other, that discovered in Homer's Greek a useful weapon against the previously dominant Latin culture. In England Homer entered into intimate relations with the ambitions and ethos of the landed aristocracy. In Germany he made major contributions to the nationalist campaign of *Bildung,* superiority through cultural refinement.

The Italians and French had blamed Homer's poetry for its rough and rugged manner. At first the English followed them. Then they learned how to turn Homer's defects into virtues. For example, Robert Wood rejected Vergil's refinement as artifice and praised instead "Homer's original genius." He meant Homer's alleged ability to reproduce what was given by nature at the time of composition.[50] At the same time Wood recorded an incident that nicely illustrates the alliance between Homeric paradigms and English aristocratic values.[51] I quote Matthew Arnold's account.

> In 1762, at the end of the Seven Years' War, [Wood] was directed to wait upon the President of the Council, Lord Granville, a few days before he died, with the preliminary articles of the Treaty of Paris. "I found him," he continues, "so languid, that I proposed postponing my business for another time; but he insisted that I should stay, saying, it could not prolong his life to neglect his duty; and repeating the following passage out of Sarpedon's speech, he dwelled with particular emphasis on the third line, which recalled to his mind the distinguishing part he had taken in public affairs:
>
> ["Man, supposing you and I, escaping this battle,
> would be able to live on forever, ageless, immortal,
> so neither would I myself go on fighting in the foremost
> nor would I urge you into the fighting where men win glory.
> But now, seeing that the spirits of death stand close about us
> in their thousands, no man can turn aside nor escape them,
> let us go.
> (*Il.* 12.322–28, Lattimore trans.)]

> His Lordship repeated the last word [*iomen,* "let us go"] several times with a calm and determinate resignation; and, after a serious pause of some minutes, he desired to hear the Treaty read, to which he listened with great attention, and recovered spirits enough to declare the approbation of a dying statesman "on the most glorious war, and most honorable peace this nation ever saw."[52]

"I quote this story," Arnold remarks, ". . . because it is interesting as exhibiting the English aristocracy at its very height of culture, lofty spirit, and greatness, towards the middle of the 18th century."[53]

With the growing success of the industrial revolution, the hegemony of the English aristocracy waned. So did the preeminence of its classical curriculum. Two other courses of study came to dominate English pedagogy: the polishing curriculum of the nonaristocratic monied classes, based on English studies, and the vocational education needed by industrial workers. But every now and then one still hears, even in the twentieth century, faint echoes of an outmoded British pride.

> I am tempted to go so far as to say that we Britishers have appreciated Homer more than any other race in the world; and I think a person has only to read a little of Chaucer and Spenser to see why. The truth is we are the most unphilosophical race in the world. We are also, second only to the Saxons and Bavarians of Germany, the fondest of fairy tales in the world. We are certainly the fondest of old ballads and old popular sayings for their own sake. We are the most obstinate in hanging on to old local traditions for their own sake; and finally we are the least cultivated, least concerned with what is called intellectuality, of all the races in the world. Then again we have appreciated the Jews, and done justice to the Jews, beyond all other western peoples; and if, compared with the Germans, our lack of metaphysical and psychological power is deplorable, and compared with the French, our lack of civilised receptivity and subtle appreciation of the nuances of human life is almost comical, no Europeans have given themselves up with a more impassioned and, I might say, a more childlike abandonment to delight in simple beauty for its own sake than English travellers have done when visiting Italy or Greece.
>
> All these qualities, both positive and negative, when joined together, tend to strengthen my conviction, quite apart from the num-

> ber of famous translations of the *Iliad* that have been made in this country . . . that there is something about our attitude to Homer that comes nearer to the attitude of the immortal Aether, to whom I have presumed to give a human consciousness, than that of any other nation.[54]

The words are those of a very old John Cowper Powys.

For Germany, the *Iliad* became one of the most important events in international cultural competitions. Beginning with Wolf's *Prolegomena* in 1795, no nation competed more effectively. Ever since the peace of Westphalia was concluded in 1648, the compelling issue for Germans had been the creation of a state and identity in central Europe that could vie for autonomy, prestige, and influence with other European nation-states, especially France. In the late eighteenth century, a "new humanism" came to their aid. Intended to replace the old Latin humanism, which sought to develop eloquence and debating skills, this humanism aimed considerably higher. Its goal was nothing less than, as Herder put it, a *Bildung zur Humanität,* a nurturing of the total, cultured person.[55] Its models were decidedly Greek: Homer, Sophocles, Herodotus, and Plato.

More than those of any other nation, the institutions of Germany's new humanism provided the material and personnel with which to address Homeric questions. Friedrich August Wolf not only asked "the Homeric question." He helped lead the institutionalization of the new humanism. He was instrumental both in inventing the pedagogical method known as the seminar and in creating the German gymnasium. As for his question about Homer's text, British, French, and other scholars contributed some answers, but from Wolf at the end of the eighteenth century to Ulrich von Wilamowitz-Moellendorf at the beginning of the twentieth, German classicists contributed the most important ones. Their subtle analyses of inconsistencies and careful attempts to reconstruct the genesis of the poem are exemplary, if now largely out of date. It was a German, too, although a nonresident German, who decided to try to dig up Troy.

Seventy-six years after Wolf's *Prolegomena,* Germany's cultural ambitions found their political counterpart with unification in 1871. But the second *Reich* soon ended disastrously with the abdication of Wilhelm II (November 1918) and the subsequent Treaty of Versailles. Before 1945, Germany found genuine prominence not on the field of battle but in the fields of scholarship. On those fields, Homerists led the charge.

VII

I cannot sketch a history of the social action of the *Rāmāyaṇa* such as I have just done for the *Iliad*. The dates, sources, and movements in the history of both Indian literature and cultural scholarship have not yet been determined with sufficient accuracy or consensus.[56] But the prospects are not entirely hopeless. The *Rāmāyaṇa* in India today provides a rich field of remarkable data, and these data contrast sharply with the social action of the *Iliad*. To speak generally, although the *Rāmāyaṇa* is and seems always to have been a tool to further and negotiate social ambitions, it has also always been something more. The *Rāmāyaṇa* has been a speech act in the strongest sense of the word. In the vocabulary used earlier, the *Rāmāyaṇa* is analogous to *mantra* as ritual act. It directly alters those who hear it.

As I indicated in Chapter 2, Indians have used the *Rāmāyaṇa* for purposes of political legitimation from the second century C.E., maybe earlier, right up to the present. At the time of writing, prominent organizations like the Bharatiya Janata Party (the right-wing "Indian People's Party"), the Vishwa Hindu Parishad (All Hindu Conference), and the Rastriya Svayamsevak Sangh (The National Volunteer Corps) have invoked Rāma's name to advance a form of anti-Muslim Hindu nationalism. To date, the biggest event in this movement has been the destruction on December 6, 1992, of the Babri Masjid, a mosque built in the 1520s on a site that is now alleged to have been Rāma's birthplace. Curiously, sophisticated observers are discussing whether the events we have been witnessing represent genuine tradition or whether they are not in fact a pseudo-tradition constructed since Indian independence in 1947.

There is no disputing that Indians have used the *Rāmāyaṇa* for baldly political purposes, but they have used it to accomplish other purposes, too. One of Vālmīki's own *phalaśrutis** claims:

> The deeds of Rāma are purifying, cleansing, meritorious,
> and equal to the Vedas.
> Whoever recites them is freed of all evils.
>
> By reciting the life-giving story of the *Rāmāyaṇa*, a man
> rejoices in heaven with
> his sons, grandsons, and servants.

*Verses that traditionally appear at the end of Indian religious poems and recount the good results (*phala*) that will accrue to the person who hears the poems.

> Reciting the *Rāmāyaṇa,* a brahmin attains the speech of a
> bull,
> a warrior becomes lord of the earth,
> a merchant becomes rich from trade,
> even a servant [*śūdra*] becomes great.
> (*Rām.* 1.1.77–79; my translation)

The tasks to which these verses allude are entirely foreign to the *Iliad.*[57] And even when the *Rāmāyaṇa* has performed social tasks similar to those performed by the *Iliad,* it has often performed them differently.

An example of this "difference in identity" is the *Rāmāyaṇa*'s role in pedagogy and learning. The language of the *Rāmāyaṇa* is not difficult Sanskrit. In its challenge it resembles the simpler Greek of, say, Hellenistic *koinē,* so that the study of the *Rāmāyaṇa,* like that of the *Purāṇas,* has never been important in sophisticated Sanskrit pedagogy. Traditionally, the poem has been read only at the beginning stages of instruction, as an easy exercise for students. As a result, it provides no equivalent to the rich traditions of sophisticated, scholarly thought that one finds in Vedic, grammatical, philosophical, and poetic studies—or, for that matter, in the ancient study of the *Iliad.* Commentaries on the *Rāmāyaṇa* are plentiful, but unlike the commentaries on Homer, they were written in specifically religious contexts to meet religious, not scholarly, needs.

The *Rāmāyaṇa* has been more of a popular poem than an academic one. Especially in vernacular renderings, it has exerted and continues to exert its effects in other ways besides pedagogy: first, as a general paradigm for action, and second, as a morally effective act.

The *Rāmāyaṇa* provides paradigms for both personal and social action. On the one hand, the characters of the poem—Rāma, Sītā, Lakṣmaṇa, Hanumān, Bharata, Kausalyā, and many others—have defined and continue to define the roles people assume at all levels of Indian society: husband, wife, brother, mother, friend, and so on. In fact, the *Rāmāyaṇa*'s paradigms have probably been more influential in practice than the abstract expositions that scholars, Indian as well as European and American, so often rely on, such as the *Manu-smṛti* (the well-known *Laws of Manu*).[58] On the other hand, the *Rāmāyaṇa* has articulated what no society can attain, but at the same time what no society can ever live without, an image of utopia. For example, at the beginning of his poem Vālmīki describes *Rāma-rājya,* the utopian reign of Rāma:

> His people are pleased and joyful, contented, well-fed, and righteous. They are also free from physical and mental afflictions and the danger of famine.
>
> Nowhere in his realm do men experience the death of a son. Women are never widowed and remain always faithful to their husbands.
>
> Just as in the Golden Age, there is no danger whatever of fire or wind, and no creatures are lost in floods.
>
> He performs hundreds of Horse Sacrifices involving vast quantities of gold. And, in accordance with custom, he donates tens and hundreds of millions of cows to the learned.
>
> Rāghava [i.e., Rāma] is establishing hundreds of royal lines and has set the four social orders each to its own work in the world.
>
> (*Rām.* 1.1.71–75)

The *Rāmāyaṇa* even provides some of the tools needed to realize its universal dreams. For example, it has provided a large proportion of the populus in central North India with that indispensable prerequisite of personal and social identity, names. It has also provided imprecations, blessings, and curses, starting with a way to say "hello"—"Rām Rām."

But for North Americans and Europeans schooled in Homer, perhaps the most striking feature of the *Rāmāyaṇa*'s activity is not the paradigms it provides but the moral act that the poem itself is. Reading or reciting the *Ramayan* (most people use a vernacular version today) imparts tremendous spiritual benefits. The most serious devotees of Lord Rāma recite the poem daily, perhaps most frequently in morning devotions. For example, in central Uttar Pradesh some people recite successive portions of the poem from beginning to end, others read favorite passages, and, most interesting of all, at least a few refrain from doing anything in the morning until they have read the particularly auspicious and relatively short *Sundara-kāṇḍa* of Tulsi's *Ramcaritmanas* all the way through.

Another way to acquire benefit from the poem is to listen to it or, if time is short, to pay for a recitation. The contexts, formats, and occasions of such activities are limited only by the basic structures of Indian social life itself. The *Rāmāyaṇa* is recited or performed in private residences, in temples, in clubs, in open areas in the center of villages, on stage, almost anywhere a recitation or performance is possible. The formats encompass virtually every artistic medium and genre, popular and sophisticated. And these events occur on almost every kind of occasion: days of regular or irregular interest to a single person or family (an anniversary, say, or an illness), at regular, short-term intervals (for example, every Sunday morning), during annual festivals or certain seasons (Navaratri, Ramanavami, in the summer heat that precedes the monsoon), or irregularly as a community gathers the resources. In July 1989, for example, people of Indian descent living in New Jersey sponsored a series of performances by the popular Gujarati Rāmāyaṇī Morari Bapu. In August or September 1993 persons with $2500 to spare could hear Morari Bapu recite Ram Katha, the story of Rāma, during a ten-day cruise aboard the luxury liner Cunard Princess.[59]

A third and particularly moving way to receive spiritual benefits from the poem is pilgrimage. At Ayodhyā religious tourists worship God at any number of temples, including the fort from which the monkey general Hanumān ruled India as Rāma's vice-gerent (Hanuman-garhi), a palace that once belonged to Sītā and in whose courtyard are enshrined the slippers Rāma entrusted to Bharata during the fourteen years of exile (Kanaka-bhavan), and, most notorious of all, the site where, some allege, Rāma himself was born, the long-disputed site of Babur's mosque. Famous *Rāmāyaṇa* sites, such as Ayodhyā, Citrakūṭa, Bharadvāja's āśrama (a park in Allahabad), Nāsik, and Rāmeśvaram, attract large numbers of visitors. Even those that are less well known and accessible, such as Śṛṅgaverapura, still welcome a small trickle.

To my mind, what especially distinguishes these practices is the manner by which their benefits accrue. That manner is the point of a well-known legend. Before the sage Vālmīki was a sage, he was a poor man, and he worked to support his family by means of an unfortunate occupation: he was what Indians call a "dacoit," a highwayman or armed robber. One day he accosted a group of brahmins who were traveling in the vicinity. Distressed at Vālmīki's fate, they convinced him to change jobs. "Go home and ask your family," they instructed him, "whether they are willing to be born in hell along with you; after all, they have been living off the fruits of your sins." Without exception, Vālmīki's relatives declined his generous offer. The now distraught dacoit returned to the priests and asked them how he might redeem himself. They gave him careful instructions. "Remain here and recite continuously two sacred syllables, 'ma' and 'rā,' until we return." So diligent was the dacoit's practice that an anthill (*valmīka*) grew up around him, from which he received the name Vālmīki. After a thousand divine years the priests returned and Vālmīki became a sage. Then he recognized what had saved him. He had been chanting the name Rāma.[60]

As the legend shows, the *Rāmāyaṇa*'s spiritual benefits do not derive from understanding its words. The poem is itself a powerful act which works its effects apart from human understanding. This seemingly magical view of poetic action is not confined to the uneducated and superstitious, as North American and European readers might suppose. It is found among very educated people, too. When the editorial group at work on the *Rāmāyaṇa*'s critical edition came to the *Yuddha-kāṇḍa,* one editor gave his colleagues a warning. As an account of battles, the *Yuddha-kāṇḍa* is particularly inauspicious, so members of the editorial team should take care to offset its ill-effects. He recommended that they begin each day with a recitation from the auspicious *Sundara-kāṇḍa.*

The former director of the Oriental Institute, Baroda, who told me of this warning, A. N. Jani, recounted another incident to underscore how important the precaution was. The other great Indian epic, the *Mahābhārata,* is preeminently a battle poem, so it is just as inauspicious as the *Yuddha-kāṇḍa.* But V. S. Sukthankar, the first editor of the *Mahābhārata*'s critical edition, had been trained in Europe. He did not have much patience for what he considered silly superstitions. As a result, Jani said, Sukthankar took no similar precautions while editing the *Mahābhārata.* The poor, incredulous man died prematurely.[61]

VIII

In formulating a proposal to remake ethnography, the anthropologist Renato Rosaldo has addressed the manner in which we address other cultures and our own.

> In presenting culture as a subject for anlaysis and critique, the ethnographic perspective develops an interplay between making the familiar strange and the strange familiar. . . . Social descriptions by, of, and for members of a particular culture require a relative emphasis on defamiliarization, so they will appear—as they in fact are—humanly made, and not given in nature. . . . Social descriptions about cultures distant from both the writer and the reader require a

> relative emphasis on familiarization, so they will appear—as they also in fact are—sharply distinct in their differences, yet recognizably human in their resemblances.[62]

The present study has not pursued this program. It has not sought to defamiliarize the familiar (presumably the *Iliad*) and to familiarize the strange (presumably the *Rāmāyaṇa*). Instead, it has sought to give equal, parallel, and comparative treatment to both epics. But it may have some of the effects that Rosaldo envisions.

This chapter has suggested that the textual, interpretive, and social histories of the *Iliad* and the *Rāmāyaṇa* have tended in specific directions, and that these directions derive neither from natural common sense (in the case of the *Iliad* for Americans) nor from a peculiarly exotic disposition (in the case of the *Rāmāyaṇa*) but from culturally determined configurations that are extremely important in each poem. The *Iliad* has tended toward forms that are social, systemic, relational, and economical. The *Rāmāyaṇa* has tended toward forms that are natural, individuated, repetitive, creative, and as A. N. Jani's account illustrates so well, destructive.

Textual scholars and artists have worked assiduously to preserve the *Iliad* and translate accurately not just the meanings of the words but even the reactions that those words evoke in modern scholars of Greek, since the reactions of ancient Greeks themselves are beyond recovery. Only rarely have scholars or artists sought to reperform the *Iliad.* By contrast, reperformance is precisely what textual scholars and artists seem always to have done for the *Rāmāyaṇa.* The text of Vālmīki's poem has been growing for at least two thousand years, each successive version striving to realize more fully the poem at which Vālmīki aimed.[63] More than that, artists have constantly reperformed the *Rāmāyaṇa,* not just in India but throughout South and Southeast Asia, in virtually every language, genre, and medium available. The seeming boundlessness of their efforts defies any attempt at comprehensive treatment.

The interpretation of the two poems has followed similar patterns. The *Iliad*'s narrative has generally resisted the addition of meaning through allegories. When allegory prevailed, and had to prevail, in the interpretation of Greek literature in Western Europe, the *Iliad*'s narrative receded from view. But because it did, an allegorical *Iliad* could never fully satisfy. When the narrative regained prominence, the allegories disappeared, to be replaced by a systematic concern with internal coherence and external correspondence. The history of the *Rāmāyaṇa*'s interpretation has been quite different. Interpreters have consistently and repeatedly tried to express the full but hidden meaning of the *Rāmāyaṇa,* and to do so they have left the literal meaning of Vālmīki's text behind. At times these interpreters have provided allegorical renderings of the events of the narrative. But since the meaning of the narrative centers on the character of the being that it manifests ("Is there anyone at all who is . . . ?"), interpreters have been intent on answering one question above all: "Who shall we say Rāma was?"

Finally, as a complex series of social acts, the *Iliad* has tended to further the ambitions of the upper classes (or strata) and of nations. In antiquity it formed the educational foundation of the Greek upper crusts. It also served to promote the prominence of city against city, Greeks against Persians, then the various Greek dynasts against one another. The *Iliad* remained wholly out of fashion so long as it seemed to favor the wrong side, the enemies of Rome's ancestors. But in modern times it became useful once again. It was associated with the economic and educational elites and the national aspirations of both England and Germany. The *Rāmāyaṇa,* too, has clearly been open to political manipulation. Recent events in India surrounding the controversy over Rāma's birthplace show that only too clearly. But in addition to furthering political and social ambition, the poem has performed acts that render the classification "social activity" hopelessly narrow and ethnocentric. The recitation of the *Rāmāyaṇa* affects not just society but the universe as a whole, creating good *karman* with all its attendant benefits: health and pleasure, wealth, political harmony, and ultimate release.

The result of this analysis may approximate Rosaldo's program of familiarization and defamiliarization, but perhaps these are not the best terms. On the one hand, it is ultimately unsatisfying continually to defamiliarize one's own culture while familiarizing oneself with all others. On the other, as Rosaldo recognizes, moments of familiarization and defamiliarization attend our treatments of both poems. It may be better, then, to speak instead of a particular moment of deabsolutization or decolonization. In a global context of tremendous economic disparity, it is tempting for Indians as well as Americans and Europeans to value supremely one form of scholarship, that attendant on the *Iliad,* and at the same time to denigrate another form, that traditionally attendant on the *Rāmāyaṇa.* The present analysis makes that disparate evaluation unjustified.

I may still prefer to write scholarship that is systematic, historical, and social. Obviously, this book is structured in accord with canons of just that sort. But the book also leads in a higher, deabsolutizing direction. The kind of scholarship in which this book engages is neither universally compelling nor universally binding. Instead, it is congruent with the particular practices of persuasion in which Homer and his characters engage. To be more precise, it is congruent with practices whose tolerability and tenability ultimately derived not from truth but from mystifications such as those that the *Iliad* advanced.

This observation, however, is somewhat broad and ill-defined. In Chapter 5 I develop a more specific critical moment by applying the results of our investigations to the academic endeavor that is my particular concern, the academic study of religions.

5

Beyond Dialogue, Violence, and Meaning

I began this book by noting what I called a certain "dynamic of decolonization." The colonialist and countercolonialist agendas that once prompted comparisons of Greek and Indian classics are gradually spending their force. As a result, different agendas must be found for such comparisons today. One of mine, I suggested, was to redress the disparity in cultural status that a disparity in economic status between North and South has tended to foster.

Some readers, I expect, will have found my investigations extremely irreverent. In claiming that the religious work of the *Iliad* and the *Rāmāyaṇa* is mystification, I risk being seen as degrading cultural values that people of both European and Indian provenance cherish. Indeed, my position as a European American writing about the *Rāmāyaṇa* is particularly precarious. I want to stress, therefore, that my aim has not been to degrade either culture. It has been in part to further, in however limited a manner, a sense of common dignity and humanity between the inhabitants of the Southern and Northern hemispheres, and more specifically between those who cherish Indian and Greek classics. Both groups of peoples share significant cultural affinities. Both have faced similar, severe threats, and both have responded in much the same way.

But this book began with more specific agendas, too, and it is to these agendas, having to do with the academic study of religions, that my final chapter returns. As I noted in the introduction, Jerome McGann has suggested a specific, overarching purpose for studying poetic works: to perform a social and ideological analysis that, taking poems as "culturally alienated products," confronts "readers with ideological differentials that help to define the limits and special functions of . . . current ideological practices."[1] Taking up that suggestion, in the present chapter I seek to identify some limits, emerging from the preceding investigations, of several current practices in the academic study of religions. My eventual concern will be with the history of religions, the discipline with which I began. But as I noted in the introduction, our investigations also articulate with two other recent, significant practices in the academic study of religions. I begin by taking up these practices in turn: first, interreligious-interideological dialogue, then the academic celebration of religious violence.

I

Advocates of interreligious dialogue often separate two elements that the *Iliad* and the *Rāmāyaṇa* emphatically join together, the failure of persuasion and the threat of ultimate disaster.

As we saw in the introduction, persuasion poses a theoretical problem for those who advocate interreligious dialogue. Apparently it poses a practical problem, too. Each contributor to *Death or Dialogue?,* for example, writes a response to the major contributions made by others. Curiously, each begins with a similar, almost formulaic emphasis that shies away from intellectual engagement and persuasion. Once again, Leonard Swidler's opening provides a nice illustration.

> I have come to this "Dialogue on Dialogue" with what I think is a dialogic attitude, that is, I came *primarily* to learn from my partners. At the same time, I presumed they came with a similar attitude, and therefore I have also written down my understanding of interreligious, interideological dialogue as one essential part in this learning conversation. I will leave it to them to decide whether or not

> they have learned anything so far in this encounter, but for my part I can say that I have indeed learned a great deal—and look forward to learning still more in our conversation.[2]

To say the least, this style of conversation is incredibly polite. But why engage in it? One can imagine a variety of reasons. A dialogue in Swidler's sense might be a pleasant, neighborly conversation between persons who happen to be curious about one another's convictions and practices. It might also be, as non-Christians have often suspected, a particularly slippery and underhanded way for Christians to go about winning converts. But recent proponents have tended to imagine dialogue in apocalyptic terms. All four contributors to Swidler's "dialogue on dialogue" expect the procedure to rectify the most pressing problems of our day. Paul Knitter identifies these problems concisely—but with staggering reach—as physical suffering, socioeconomic oppression (including discrimination on the basis of race and gender), the threat of nuclear holocaust, and ecological disaster (27–30). In a different context, Hans Küng presents a different apocalyptic vision. "There will be no peace," he insists, "among peoples of this world without peace among the world religions." For that reason, he says, "ecumenical dialogue . . . has now taken on the character of an urgent desideratum for world politics."[3]

The expectations with which Küng, Knitter, Swidler, and others approach interreligious dialogue differ markedly from the visions of the *Iliad* and the *Rāmāyaṇa.* As the dialoguers do, the epics concern themselves with severe threats to social well-being. They depict these threats in fashions that we still find compelling, but their depictions seem incommensurable with the analysis of human well-being that advocates of interreligious dialogue presume.

In the epics, threats arise not when communication fails, but when persuasion fails. In fact, it is difficult to see what substantial contribution dialogue in, say, Swidler's sense would make to the poems. It is not only unrealistic to imagine Agamemnon and Achilles, Rāma and Kaikeyī, or Rāvaṇa and Sītā sitting down for a dialogue, because it is completely out of keeping with their characters; it is also trivial. A more fundamental issue is involved here. The problems that Homer and Vālmīki rehearse are not at heart failures to communicate; they are not failures that can be rectified by the kind of dialogue Swidler and others envision. They are instead conflicts of moral conviction and interests. Juxtaposed to the claims made for interreligious dialogue, they recall a criticism that Perry Anderson made of

Isaiah Berlin. Accusing Berlin of failing to make a necessary distinction between interests and understanding, Anderson reminds us that "the Allies and the Axis had no difficulty following each other's communiqués."[4] These ideological differentials between the *Iliad* and *Rāmāyaṇa* on the one hand and interreligious-interideological dialogue on the other, invite us to consider dialogue's possible limits.

To begin with, the thematic of failed persuasion in the *Iliad* and the *Rāmāyaṇa* would appear to illuminate a major flaw in the notion of dialogue embedded, for example, in Swidler's introduction. Instead of recognizing the complexity of human communication and interaction, this conception offers a simplistic, binary model. Typically, Swidler erects an image of the dialogic enterprise on a set of contraries: dialogue and monologue, dialogue and death. He does so even though he knows full well, as he says in his independent chapter, that there are many different kinds of communication between persons. But given this plurality, is dialogue really the only salutary form of discourse? Can all other possible forms of communication and conversation be collapsed into monologue or, worse yet, death? Were Homer and Vālmīki simply wrong in locating significant social benefit in persuasion? Were they wrong to fear significant social disruption from its failure? Have audiences been wrong to be moved by narratives in which the thematic of failed persuasion is so heavily implicated? The answer to all these questions is, I think, no.

The simplistic, binary model of human communication and interaction on which the dialogic model is based has unfortunate consequences. For one thing, it encourages an image of dialogue that is singularly uninspiring, if not entirely uninteresting. In fact, it virtually ignores what the best religious dialogues have always been, in Asia as well as in Europe. From Plato through Yehuda ha Levi to David Hume, to mention only three prominent European examples, dialogue about religious topics has been an exercise in mutual persuasion that sought sustainable religious "truths." The most profound Indian sages, such as Śaṅkarācarya, systematizer of Advaita Vedānta, and Rāmānuja, systematizer of Viśiṣṭādvaita, gained renown for being able to defeat all comers in debate. To be sure, advocates of dialogue frequently claim that we live in a unique age, one that demands "something new under the sun." But their own practice belies their words. Even those contributors to *Death or Dialogue?* who do not allow themselves to say that persuasion is the one element which makes dialogue interesting write as if it were. After the brief, conciliatory opening formulas of the responses, they very quickly turn to criticizing other views and defending their own.

Set beside the narrative concerns of the *Iliad* and the *Rāmāyaṇa,* however, the binary model of human communication and interaction with which Swidler and others operate has a consequence that is even more unfortunate. Because Homer and Vālmīki imply that social thriving derives from persuasion, not dialogue, they lead us to ask whether the method of interreligious-interideological dialogue is commensurate with the goals that it pursues. So far as I can see, it is not. Dialogue cannot bear the burden of heavy expectations that its partisans heap upon it.

How and why should dialogue be capable of resolving the panoply of problems that Knitter identifies: physical suffering, socioeconomic oppression, nuclear proliferation, ecological disaster? To be somewhat more modest, how and why should interreligious dialogue alone be capable of resolving even religiously entwined conflicts like those in Northern Ireland, Palestine, and India? Nowhere do the interlocutors in *Death or Dialogue?* consider such questions in detail. Nowhere does Hans Küng give us any reason to believe that his hopes for world peace through dialogue are realistic. There is good reason to lament this lack.

The issues that Knitter and Küng identify have prompted those who deal with them on a daily basis to respond with many different kinds of words and actions. On the surface, it would appear that such words and actions are also at least necessary, if not sufficient, to resolving the major crises currently facing the human and natural worlds. If interreligious dialogue holds out more hope than medicine, political agitation, diplomacy, ecological research, and the myriad other goal-directed ways in which human beings have addressed and continue to address the problems that they face, those who advocate dialogue ought at least provide compelling reasons why. One suspects, however, that in addressing these extreme crises, interreligious dialogue may play no more than a decidedly minor role. Once again a comment of Perry Anderson's comes to mind, this one aimed at Jürgen Habermas's dialogic notion of intersubjectivity: "If such solutions typically deliver less than they promise, the reason lies in their starting-point: the nuclear 'dialogue' between two persons is a domestic, not a civic model."[5] If correct, Anderson's diagnosis would only confirm a position to which our investigations of the *Iliad* and the *Rāmāyaṇa* point. Among other things, those who expect dialogue to solve the world's problems fail to grapple seriously with the need for persuasion, especially civic and social persuasion. That is one reason, if only one, why the repeated disclaimer in Swidler's introduction to *Death or Dialogue?,* "This statement is not overdramatization," rings false.

To be sure, if interreligious-interideological dialogue has little hope of meeting the grand expectations that its most enthusiastic proponents have for it, that does not imply that dialogue has no social value whatever. It simply invites us to reassess what that value might be and to ask about the ideological purposes the advocates of dialogue have been serving. Their claims seem questionable on two counts. Dialogue is not the only salutary form of human communication, and it will not lead in a straight line to world peace, ecological balance, physical wellness, social and economic equality, or the other hyperinflated aims that many of its champions advance.

II

At the end of his recently translated *Theory of Religion,* Georges Bataille writes some disparaging words about advocates of interreligious dialogue or, to be more precise, about those "who are alarmed about the lack of harmony" in religion.

> The spirit farthest removed from the virility necessary for joining *violence and consciousness* is the spirit of "synthesis." The endeavor to sum up that which separate religious possibilities have revealed, and to make their shared content the principle of a human life raised to universality, seems unassailable despite its insipid results, but for anyone *to whom human life is an experience to be carried as far as possible,* the *universal sum* is necessarily that of the religious sensibility of the time.[6]

For those who have read the earlier parts of Bataille's book, this comment comes as no surprise. He begins his thinking by referring to a basic biological, animalistic act, eating. Animalistic eating, he says, characterizes relations of immanence with the environment, even if they differ from the complete immanence of a stone. Human consciousness introduces the moment of transcendence. In Bataille's abstract, Hegelian logic, the tension between these two poles, immanence and transcendence, provides the impetus for the development of sacrifice, festivals, and more generally of religion. "The basic problem of religion," Bataille writes, "is given in this fatal misunderstanding of sacrifice. Man is the being that has lost, and even rejected, that which he obscurely is, a vague intimacy."[7] Predictably,

Bataille envisions a resolution of the tensions; equally predictably, that resolution is somewhat fitful. "When clear consciousness regains intimacy, it will do so in darkness, and then it will have reached the highest degree of distinct clarity, but it will so fully realize the possibility of man, or of being, that it will rediscover the night of the animal intimate with the world—*into which it will enter.*"[8]

The double emphasis on violence and consciousness leaves little room for such practices as interreligious dialogue. Indeed, one supposes that if Bataille were alive, he would emphatically reject many other ideological practices that have recently been current, starting with animal rights and vegetarianism. But Bataille's abstract schematism, intentionally devoid of ethnographic and historical examples, preserves all the defects of his Hegelian model. Indeed, it is difficult to discern how one might apply these ideas in detail to any specific ethnographic or historical material. Naturally, I have the *Iliad* and the *Rāmāyaṇa* most particularly in mind.

Bataille's fundamental themes—violence, sacrifice, a coming to consciousness—are René Girard's themes, too. But important differences separate the two thinkers. Bataille reflects on individuals in relation to their environment; Girard reflects on life in society. Bataille is relentlessly abstract and "logical" (in a Hegelian sense); Girard is relentlessly ethnographic—or at least literary-critical. For these reasons, Girard's celebration of violence seems closer to the *Iliad* and the *Rāmāyaṇa.*

As we saw in the introduction, Girard develops a theory or hypothesis (he calls it both) that focuses on ritual killing. Sacrifice, he says, is society's way of avoiding a runaway cycle of vengeance. It redirects violence onto a victim whose position is integral enough to satisfy the demands of violence, but marginal enough that it provokes no violent response. Girard is not shy about drawing the implications of his views. Not only does he claim that this insight makes possible for the first time a genuine science of religion; he further claims that it elucidates "all the great institutions of mankind, both secular and religious." In terms well-suited to the present investigations: "The endless diversity of myths and rituals derives from the fact that they all seek to recollect and reproduce something they never succeed in comprehending. There is only one generative event, only one way to grasp its truth: by means of my hypothesis."[9]

This claim challenges us to seek Girard's ideas in the *Rāmāyaṇa* and the *Iliad.* To Girard's credit, our search is not entirely futile. In the *Rāmāyaṇa,* Rāma's voluntary exile is sacrificial (in the manner of a sacred king), even if Rāma does not die. His retirement precludes the disastrous proliferation of violence and untruth that might have arisen had Rāma followed, say, Lakṣmaṇa's advice. Similarly, Rāvaṇa's death redirects aggressive impulses that might have led after exile to a destruction of society and a dissolution of the worlds. The latter is, in fact, the frightful scenario that the *Mahābhārata* enacts.

Girard's notions would seem to fit the *Iliad* even more snugly, for Homer narrates cycles of affliction and anger, and his poem climaxes when, day after day, Achilles disfigures Hektor's corpse in a vain effort to avenge the loss of Patroklos, his dearest companion. Despite these resemblances, however, it is doubtful that Girard identifies the event that generates either poem. Because Greek examples are so prominent in his own exposition, the *Iliad* provides the more effective counter.

Several points speak against reading the *Iliad* in terms of Girard's sacrificial crisis. The poem may present an escalating spiral of violence and affliction, but this spiral includes only a single instance of retributive murder, Achilles' killing of Hektor. The first major turn of the spiral results, we have seen, not from retributive action but from nonaction, Achilles' refusal to fight. Patroklos dies as an unintended victim of that refusal, not an intended one. Furthermore, when Homer's crisis reaches truly horrific proportions, it does so not because the cycle of wrath and affliction continues to spin without stop, but precisely because the cycle stops. Priam cannot kill Achilles and redeem Hektor's corpse. If he could, the wheel of human events would simply continue to revolve. Most important of all, although Homer eventually articulates the escalating spiral of affliction and wrath by means of violence, he does not resolve it through violence. Resolution and a temporary calm come not from Girard's violence but from words, the words of Patroklos's ghost, then those of the king of the gods. Unlike Girard, then, Homer assigns persuasion a notable social role, and that is a role we ignore only at our peril. For the contrast between words and deeds is well developed in Homer's vocabulary and thought, even if it is a contrast that Girard's theory entirely fails to include.

This critical observation leads to some more general comments. To the extent that Girard's analysis succeeds, it does so largely by a sleight of hand. Girard can single-mindedly champion the management of violence in society by violent ritual only because, from the very beginning, he has arbitrarily excluded any other means from consideration. Girard proposes a rather suspicious but very convenient divide between "primitive" and "civilized" societies. Primitive societies, he says, manage the violence of vengeance by sacrifice, civilized ones manage it by judicial procedures.[10] Invocations of ethnography aside, this implausibly sharp distinction probably owes more to Girard's imagination than to any actual observation of "primitive societies," for Girard has previously observed: "Vengeance is a vicious circle whose effect on primitive societies can only be surmised."[11]

One problem with Girard's distinction should be immediately apparent: it is not sufficiently inclusive. On these terms Homer's and Vālmīki's imagined worlds are neither primitive nor civilized. Once in place, however, Girard's distinction operates most effectively. It justifies a procedure that simply ignores other social institutions that manage violence. It also explains why societies that do not sacrifice, such as Europe and North America today, manage to survive. As Girard writes, "For us the circle [of violence] has been broken. We owe our good fortune to one of our social institutions above all: our judicial system."[12]

Viewed in this light, Girard's selective use of Greek tragedy is suspicious and disturbing. There can be few more profound explorations of the aporias of vengeance than Aeschylus's *Oresteia.* That is why I referred to the trilogy when I explicated Girard's views in the introduction. But if the index to *Violence and the Sacred* is correct, Girard himself mentions Aeschylus on only a single page, and then only as part of a litany: "Aeschylus, Sophocles, and Euripides."[13] In sharp contrast, Girard mentions Sophocles and Euripides frequently and discusses their work extensively. Chapter 3, "Oedipus and the Surrogate Victim," is largely devoted to the *Oedipus Rex,* and chapter 5, "Dionysos," gives similar attention to *The Bacchae.* Like Girard's special definition of "civilized society," then, his failure to consider Aeschylus makes it all too easy for him to claim to be discovering "the unity of all rites" and, even more, the source of "all the great institutions of mankind, both secular and religious." Despite such totalistic aspirations, Girard's vision is not very comprehensive. It fails to consider seriously other religious practices and human institutions that manage violence. The overall effect is to make Girard's "primitives" no more than stereotypes. They neither talk nor think. They simply act, and act in a most savage way: they kill uncontrollably for revenge. This heavy-handed procedure misses, among other mechanisms, the very mechanism for controlling vengeance that the first great Greek tragedy was written to celebrate, the procedures of the Athenian law courts rooted in the practice of juridical persuasion. As Oswyn Murray puts it, these procedures are in essence also the Homeric institutions of formal persuasion, and they are unimaginable except as a gift of the gods.[14]

Girard deserves credit, I think, and gratitude for drawing close attention to the role of violence in religion and human society.[15] But he is wrong if he thinks that sacrificial violence is the only mechanism by which societies maintain order. He is also wrong if he thinks that sacrificial violence alone provides an adequate foundation for an entire science of religion.

III

One discipline in particular has aspired to create a scientific or scholarly, as distinct from a theological, study of religions. In some languages, it is simply called the "science of religions" (for example, in German *Religionswissenschaft*). In English the more common phrase has been the one used in the subtitle of this series: the history of religions. As the introduction notes and the series title implies, this discipline has largely been constituted as a variety of hermeneutics. It has imagined religions as sets of meanings; as a result, it has envisioned its task as the recovery, decipherment, translation, or significant classification of those meanings.[16] The preceding investigations of the *Iliad* and the *Rāmāyaṇa* suggest, however, that a different orientation may be preferable for the history of religions. As I said at the beginning, the orientation I have in mind is historical. It envisions the history of religions as a principled investigation of events.

Perhaps the greatest practitioner of the hermeneutical history of religions was the Rumanian-born comparativist, Mircea Eliade. At least Eliade was certainly the most prominent of that discipline's recent systematizers. Perhaps Eliade's most basic project sought to construct a metanarrative that would render every manifestation of the Sacred intelligible. He sought to do so by constructing a comprehensive morphology of the symbols through which the Sacred manifested itself. This general program was articulated with amazing scope in Eliade's magisterial *Traité d'histoire des religions,* translated into English as *Patterns in Comparative Religion.*[17] It later became the subject of many popular restatements.

As one might expect, an era such as our own, which tends to abnegate as a matter of principle the possibility of comprehensive metanarratives, has found Eliade's morphology wanting. Two critics with very different academic perspectives illustrate this criticism well. Taking his lead from analytical philosophy and symbolic anthropology, Jonathan Z. Smith has shown time and again how Eliade misreads and misrepresents data in the interests of his own theories.[18] From the different perspective of a history centered in philology and suspicious of theoretical abstractions, Kurt Rudolph has vigorously criticized Eliade's morphology for being not truly empirical history but a hidden, universalizing, essentially Neoplatonist theology.[19]

In effect, Eliade himself invited these sorts of criticism. In the introduction to his early classic, *Patterns in Comparative Religion,* he explicitly embraced a normative rather than empirical notion of Christianity—or any religion, for that matter. "Imagine a Buddhist," he invited his readers, "trying to understand Christianity . . . [from studying] the religious life of some European village."

> No doubt the first thing our Buddhist observer would note would be a distinct difference between the religious life of the peasants and the theological, moral and mystical ideas of the village priest. . . . The modalities of the sacred revealed by Christianity are in fact more truly preserved in the tradition represented by the priest (however strongly coloured by history and theology) than in the beliefs of the villagers. What the observer is interested in is not the one moment in the history of Christianity, or one part of Christendom, but the Christian religion as such.[20]

It is certainly questionable that the priest represents "the Christian religion as such," even granting that such a mysterious quiddity exists. But in a later article, Eliade seems to justify interpretations that are entirely arbitrary.

> The historian of religions is especially grateful to Freud for proving that images and symbols communicate their "messages" even if the conscious mind remains unaware of this fact. The historian is now free to conduct his hermeneutical work upon a symbol without having to ask himself how many individuals in a certain society and at a given historical moment understood all the meanings and implications of that symbol.[21]

Such blatant disregard for empirical evidence in principle only seems designed to lead to disaster in practice.

Another current of criticism takes Eliade to task not for developing a metanarrative but, it seems, for developing the wrong kind of metanarrative. Since his death in 1986, the specter of a possible fascist past has haunted Eliade's memory, as it has haunted so many others of his generation. Rumors have circulated, for example, that Eliade collaborated with the

Rumanian Iron Guard in the 1930s. Although Eliade's right-wing inclinations seem certain, the extent of his fascism remains an open but significant question.

More incisive, because more integral to Eliade's entire intellectual venture, is a somewhat different version of moral criticism advanced by Eliade's former colleague, Charles H. Long.[22] Traditionally, Long reminds us, the history of religions has been seen as a child of the Enlightenment. It has presumed scholars who are objective observers, capable of discerning the truth by applying reason to the data of sensory experience. These scholars may not be able to discern much that is substantive about religious truths, the kinds of issues that philosophers of religion generally address. But they can certainly interpret religions as human phenomena.

Long insists that this neutral, objective face is an empty facade. The history of religions has never been written from a position of moral or political neutrality. Instead, scholarship has been a signification of the conquered by the conquerors, of the oppressed by the oppressors, and as such is implicated in an obscured discourse of power. It is the task of the present to deconstruct such discourses, and in this task the oppressed have a major, indeed, a privileged role, for "those who have lived in the cultures of the oppressed know something about freedom that the oppressors will never know." Long frequently addresses his critique not at historians of religions but at "theologians of transparence," as distinct from "opaque theologians" or, as one would more commonly say today, theologians of color. But scholars of the history of religions, and Eliade in particular, are equally vulnerable to this criticism. By the conclusion of "Primitive/Civilized: The Locus of a Problem," Long has effectively erased the line between primitive and civilized, as a result eliminated a fundamental component of "Eliade's notion of primitive ontology," and called for a demythologization of the history of religions.[23]

Although I am generally sympathetic to Long's loyalties, I do have some hesitations. His position risks reducing complex scholarly motivations, actions, and convictions to a single, simplistic history of colonialism that is more reminiscent of caricature than of portraiture. At the same time, the notion that any group of people, colonizing or colonized, enjoys a hermeneutical or epistemological privilege can ultimately justify nothing but intellectual laziness and domination. So far as I can see, all human beings are equally limited, although we are all limited in different ways.

The point I want to draw attention to, however, is that Eliade, Smith, and Long represent three different, hermeneutical approaches to the history of religions. Eliade focuses on the universal meaning of the symbols through which the Sacred manifests itself. Smith adopts an objectivist posture in order to analyze culturally specific meanings and codes. (In that way he reminds us of the anthropology of Clifford Geertz.) Long attends to undeniable social and cultural differentials among interpreters, assigning not just a moral but at times an epistemological superiority to those who are relatively disadvantaged.

Each scholar's work has enjoyed significant acclaim, and I have no wish to diminish the undeniable value to which this acclaim attests. I do want to suggest, however, that the *Iliad* and the *Rāmāyaṇa,* as we have come to know them here, point to certain limits in a hermeneutical approach to the history of religions. Let me summarize points already made at greater length. Academics have long recognized that from the hermeneutical point of view, these poems are not religious. The meanings they convey are not particularly religious and neither, for that matter, are the practices of persuasion on which this book concentrates. Yet the *Iliad* and the *Rāmāyaṇa* have struck many as profoundly religious poems. What makes them so, I have suggested, is the work they perform: not their specific meanings but how they render and use those meanings. The *Iliad* and the *Rāmāyaṇa* mystify fundamental aporias in the world of experience by providing compelling, satisfying, indeed, foundational solutions that are nevertheless available only in the world of imagined reality.

In advancing this analysis, I propose, even in the case of such a hermeneutical topic as the study of sacred texts, a shift from a history of religions conceived as hermeneutics to one conceived more broadly as history. By history I do not mean the methodologically defined history, rooted in philology, that Kurt Rudolph has so tirelessly championed.[24] I mean a conceptually defined history, one that sees its central task not as the elucidation or translation of meaning or meanings but one whose task is the principled investigation of events, including, to be sure, events of meaning. This approach would begin not with the question, "What do religious people mean?" It would begin with the questions, "What is happening in religion? What are religious people doing?" Questions of meaning would arise in that broader context.

A local study such as this cannot begin to develop a full, theoretical account of any discipline, but it can suggest fragments that a fuller, theoretical exposition might take up and transform. In that spirit, I advance four fragments that a history of religions formulated as the investigation of events may later find useful.

1. As a set of events, religion aims to promote human thriving. It may not always succeed. Indeed, it has been common knowledge at least from the time of Lucretius that religion actually creates a great deal of suffering and misery.[25] But like Agamemnon, who sacrificed his daughter Iphigenia or, as Lucretius has it, Iphianassa, religious people have created suffering in the service of a supposedly higher ideal of human well-being.

The example of the *Iliad* and the *Rāmāyaṇa* suggests that religion promotes human thriving in a particular way: it enables people to tolerate problematic situations and overcome threats. To that extent, we may call religion a tool for survival. But we should do so with caution. We cannot thereby directly insert religion into human evolutionary history. To make a case for religion in human evolution, one would need to demonstrate how religion or better yet, specific religious tools, selectively adapted human beings or specific human communities to compete successfully in a given environment with other organisms exploiting the same resources. Faced with the difficulty of making that case, I am inclined to think that Smith—and Eliade before him—are probably right. Taxonomy—Eliade thought in terms of morphology—must precede genealogy.

2. The example of the *Iliad* and the *Rāmāyaṇa* suggests that religion enables human thriving in at least one significant manner. That manner is imaginative manipulation. In other words, religion enables people to tolerate problematic situations and overcome threats in the world of experienced, lived reality by offering solutions that are, strictly speaking, available only in the world of imagined reality. But religion elides the difference between these two realities, and people receive the solutions as compelling in the world of lived reality, too. As a result, the products of the religious imagination provide a frame through which to understand past experiences and expectations with which to approach future ones. In this sense, mystification is a significant dimension of religious practice.

The present book has concentrated on the religious mystifications of two epic poems, but imaginative manipulation is by no means confined to literature or even to words. Jonathan Z. Smith's article, "The Bare Facts of Ritual," illustrates imaginative manipulation at work on the level of deeds. Smith's concern in the article is with the ceremonialism of bear hunting. He suggests that in ritual, hunters enact a perfect or ideal hunt. To quote him, "There is a 'gnostic' dimension to ritual. It provides the means for demonstrating that we know what ought to have been done, what ought to have taken place. But, by the fact that it is ritual action rather than everyday action, it demonstrates that we know 'what is the case.' Ritual provides an occasion for reflection and rationalization on the fact that what ought to have been done was not done, what ought to have taken place did not occur."[26] Smith has, of course, his own case to make. But in my terms, the enactment of a hunt in a ritual world of imagined reality redresses problematics that arise during hunting in the world of experienced reality.

3. The example of the *Iliad* and the *Rāmāyaṇa* also suggests that religion can engage in at least two distinct forms of imaginative manipulation. One form I have called cosmotrophic. The cosmotrophic imagination works to sustain and support. It resolves the difficulties people confront in the world of experienced, lived reality by postulating an imaginative solution that is commensurate or compatible with that world. The solution sustains the world and supports its structures. Both the *Iliad* and the *Rāmāyaṇa* provide examples of the cosmotrophic imagination.

Cosmotrophy as one form of imaginative manipulation implies, however, at least one other form, one that the denotation cosmotrophy excludes. Let us call it the soteric imagination. If the cosmotrophic imagination sustains and supports the present orders of existence, the soteric imagination overturns and negates them. It resolves the difficulties people confront in the world of experienced, lived reality by postulating an imaginative solution that refuses the difficulties and rescues people from them. The so-called religions of salvation, religions such as Christianity and Pure Land Buddhism, provide good examples of the soteric imagination.

It has been customary for historians of religions to speak of cosmogonies and cosmologies, accounts of how the world came to be and of how it is organized. The primacy of both concepts derives from attaching primary significance to the meanings that such accounts convey. But perhaps that misses the crucial question. In a history of religions conceived as the principled investigation of events, the more pertinent question might concern whether a given cosmogony or cosmology is advanced for cosmotrophic or soteric ends. Since this speculation falls well outside the parameters of the present study, I do no more here than raise the question.

4. Finally, the example of the *Iliad* and the *Rāmāyaṇa* suggests that there are at least two significant, formal variants of the cosmotrophic imagination. The operative variables in these variants are agents, structures, and events.

In one variant, the difficulties posed in the world of experienced, lived reality are structural. An agent overcomes these difficulties by imaginatively postulating a series of events that satisfactorily redresses them. The *Rāmāyaṇa* exemplifies this variant. The difficulties are the nets of *dharma;*

the agent is the poet Vālmīki (whatever we mean by that name); and the series of events is the progressive, steady manifestation of Rāma's virtues with whose enumeration the poem began.

In another variant, the difficulties posed in the world of lived reality are dynamic; they result from a series of events. In this variant, an agent overcomes the difficulties by imaginatively postulating a structure that satisfactorily keeps the series of events in check. The *Iliad* exemplifies this variant. The difficulties are the cycles of wrath and affliction that eventually lead to Achilles' uncontrollable rage; the agent is the poet Homer (whatever we mean by that name); and the structure is the society of the ghosts and especially the gods.

I should note once again that I mean these four, numbered points as fragmentary suggestions, nothing more. I make no claims about their general applicability, their universal adequacy, or their eventual significance. In listing them, I intend only to sketch out some of the possible implications from the study at hand for a future history of religions conceived as history.

IV

In 1930 the German historian of religions Joachim Wach published an article on the then-new "science of religion" in the German encyclopedia, *Die Religion in Geschichte und Gegenwart* (s.v. "Religionswissenschaft").[27] He discussed this science's object in terms reminiscent of some age-old rhetorical procedures. "The aim of this science is to investigate, to understand, and to present," Wach wrote tersely and programmatically.[28] But his commentary on these three aims is curious. On understanding Wach wrote a very full gloss. That is not surprising, for he was in the midst of composing his lengthy three-volume study of hermeneutics, *Das Verstehen.*[29] Investigation received less attention, but Wach did note several critical methods by which scholars proceed, ethnographical when studying a religion that is practiced today, archaeological, historical, and philological when current information is no longer available. About presentation, however, Wach had very little to say. He merely commented that the rhetorical means must be appropriate to both the subject under consideration and the audience being addressed.

This half-column of text actually reveals a great deal about Wach's own intellectual practice. In Isaiah Berlin's terms, he was always more fox than hedgehog. He engaged in little if any genuine religio-historical investigation, preferring instead to range over the entire territory of religion in search of a comprehensive understanding. Even more striking, however, is his scant regard for the arts of communication, what I prefer to think of as the arts of persuasion. This indifference finds perhaps an inevitable reflex in Wach's works themselves. Their prose is extremely dull, a defect that Wach's obsession with typology and dry, descriptive taxonomies only exacerbates.

It is probably petty to lament that Wach wrote boring books about a subject as interesting as religion. For one thing, most of the books I have in mind were written in English, which was not Wach's native language. For another, scholars usually write and read books for reasons other than entertainment. But Wach's brief remarks deserve our attention here because in one sense they are symptoms of a failure that is more than personal. I do not mean, of course, that historians of religions have been routinely boring. The works of engaging and witty writers like Mircea Eliade and Wendy Doniger quickly dispel that notion. What I mean is that the history of religions owes its existence to the exclusion of a certain kind of persuasion, and in that regard, our investigation of the *Iliad* and the *Rāmāyaṇa* eventually raises questions about its own investigation.

We can detect the exclusion of persuasion close to its origins in the writings of the Scottish philosopher David Hume. In the introduction to his *Natural History of Religion,* Hume distinguishes two topics "of the utmost importance" in thinking about religion, "that concerning its foundation in reason, and that concerning its origin in human nature."[30] Hume's *Dialogues Concerning Natural Religion* take up the former question; his *Natural History* takes up the latter.

To modern sensibilities, the *Dialogues*—mostly a conversation between a pious Christian (Demea), a rational theist (Cleanthes), and a thorough skeptic (Philo)—seem designed to demolish a proposition that the *Natural History* accepted as "most obvious": "The whole frame of nature bespeaks an intelligent author; and no rational enquirer can, after serious reflection, suspend his belief a moment with regard to the primary principles of genuine Theism and Religion." True, disclaimers fill the *Dialogues;* true, too, at the close of the volume Pamphilus, who allegedly reports the discussions, grants the laurel of victory to Cleanthes, not Philo. But the paragraph that pronounces this judgment limps in comparison with Philo's vigorous, skeptical conclusion.

Whether Philo is the true protagonist of the *Dialogues* is not of particular interest here. What is of interest is a sharp distinction that Hume—or better, Philo—makes in developing the skeptical position. In words that anticipate Schleiermacher's *Speeches,* Demea suggests religion is not a matter of reason but of feeling. Philo ironically agrees.

> The best and indeed the only method of bringing everyone to a due sense of religion is by just representations of the misery and wickedness of men. And for that purpose a talent of eloquence and strong imagery is more requisite than that of reasoning and argument. For is it necessary to prove, what everyone feels within himself? It is only necessary to make us feel it, if possible, more intimately and sensibly.[31]

Cleanthes later echoes the same distinction. "I have been apt to suspect the frequent repetition of the word, infinite, which we meet with in all theological writers, to savour more of panegyric than of philosophy" (113).

The distinction here between philosophy and rhetoric appears to have been something of a commonplace among Hume's near-contemporaries. Rhetoric is emotive, philosophy rational. Rhetoric is entertaining, but not particularly truthful; philosophy is justifiably persuasive.[32] In Philo's skeptical view, this distinction correlates with the two questions that stand at the beginning of the *Natural History.* The question about nature's intelligent author, which the *Natural History* says is so obvious that it requires no discussion whatsoever, appears in the *Dialogues* as so obscure that it precludes any genuine philosophical insight. As Philo says of the design of the universe, "All that belongs to human understanding, in this deep ignorance and obscurity, is to be sceptical, or at least cautious; and not to admit of any hypothesis, whatever; much less, of any which is supported by no appearance of probability."[33] In other words, Philo's skepticism leads to a philosophical silence that assigns the truths of religion to an emotive, rhetorical realm. But it still permits one sort of rational, philosophical inquiry into religion, the inquiry of natural history. As Hume conceived it, that inquiry investigated "what those [first religious] principles are, which give rise to the original belief, and what those accidents and causes are, which direct its operation" (*Natural History,* 21). Hume identified polytheism, not monotheism, with the first principles of religion. In doing so, he scandalized many of his contemporaries and anticipated an argument that would exercise scholars of religions over a hundred years later.

Not all who have thought about the "natural history of religion" have followed Philo and maintained a principled silence about religious truth. The most important alternative arose in 1799, when a young preacher named Friedrich Schleiermacher published five widely read speeches under the title *On Religion.* These speeches implored his cultivated friends not to reject religion. To make this plea, Schleiermacher argued that religion was neither metaphysics nor morals but a feeling or intuition of wholeness with the universe.[34] Inspired in part by Schleiermacher, later historians of religions like Rudolf Otto sought to identify the valid experiential essence behind all empirical religious phenomena.[35]

Some historians of religions, then, have violated Philo's recommended skeptical silence about religious truth, but that is hardly prevailing practice today. So far as I can tell, most contemporary historians of religions follow Philo's advice, even if Hume's terms are somewhat antiquated. They routinely place questions of religious truth to one side, in professional practice if not in personal life, justifying this practice under many rubrics. The old slogan was phenomenological "bracketing." Others have distinguished accounts as insider and outsider, first and third person, cognitive and behavioral, emic and etic, experience-near and experience-distant, biographical and autobiographical. The crux of the matter, however, is perhaps expressed most straightforwardly in the terminology of persuasion. At its broadest and simplest, the history of religions is a discourse about religion—some insist it is about religion*s*—that refuses every attempt to persuade about religious truth.

This characterization prompts me to end my book not with a conclusion in the strict sense of the term but with an extension. That is, in closing I want very briefly to direct toward the enterprise of the book itself some of the themes I have applied to the *Iliad* and the *Rāmāyaṇa.* In one significant respect, the religio-historical enterprise parallels Homer's and Vālmīki's: it is a form of discourse evoked when persuasion fails.[36] For the theologically minded, like Otto and his soulmates, the history of religions arises when the persuasion of traditional, confessional apologetics fails. For the rest of us, it arises when, for whatever reasons, the persuasion of theologians (or buddhologists or what have you) fails to attract our efforts. We very much want to reflect and talk and write about religions, but we do so without wanting to engage in religious persuasion ourselves. As a result, theology and the history of religions have increasingly diverged ever since their divorce became finalized with the appearance of Joachim Wach's declaration of independence, *Religionswissenschaft: Prolegomena zu ihrer wissenschafts-*

theoretischen Grundlegung, with the rise of neo-orthodox or dialectical theology, and with the death of the last liberal theologians, scholars like Rudolf Otto and Heinrich Frick.

In recent years, some have questioned the necessity and wisdom of this great divorce. For example, Wilfred Cantwell Smith has wanted to reconcile religious truth with the study of history. As he puts it, "Once we recognize . . . that God has spoken to men and women and children, historically . . . in differing times and places, differing languages, differing moods and modes, the historian's task becomes recognizably theological, and the theologian's, recognizably historical."[37] Taking quite a different approach, Frank Reynolds, David Tracy, and their collaborators have seen philosophy as a potential bridge between the two disciplines.[38] But as we have seen, Homer and Vālmīki found in the failure of persuasion a problematic that they could not easily eliminate. And to my tastes, the efforts to reconcile the history of religions with theology are also too facile. In part this reflects the state of my personal convictions. If I still practice the religion in which I was raised, I do so in a somewhat Kierkegaardian fashion: not because of but despite the kinds of things I want to say academically. In part, too, my hesitations about reconciling the history of religions and theology reflect a certain political solution to the problems of living, thinking, and writing about religions in a religiously plural society, better yet, in a religiously plural world.

What, then, do we make of a discipline such as the history of religions, a discipline that inhabits the space that remains when theological persuasion fails? Jonathan Z. Smith has emphasized that "religion" is not a given in nature but a product of the imagination. "Religion is solely the creation of the scholar's study. It is created for the scholar's analytic purposes by his imaginative acts of comparison and generalization."[39] If Smith is correct, our question becomes, what kind of imaginative actions does the historian of religions perform? Our encounter with the *Iliad* and the *Rāmāyaṇa* leads to questions about our own practice. Could it be that the history of religions, too, is a kind of cosmotrophe, but a cosmotrophe of a second order? Is it an act of the imagination by which we sustain our confidence that the world in which we live coheres, is tolerable, and will persist, even when those practices that had been charged with sustaining our confidence in the world fail any more to persuade?

Clearly, these questions and their implications extend well beyond what can be established on the basis of an investigation of the *Iliad* and the *Rāmāyaṇa.* They require separate and extensive investigation on their own.

Notes

Introduction

1. Unless otherwise noted, when I speak of the *Rāmāyaṇa* I am referring to the *Rāmāyaṇa* of Vālmīki. I have used the text of the standard critical edition, *The Vālmīki-Rāmāyaṇa, Critically Edited for the First Time,* ed. G. H. Bhatt et al., 7 vols. (Vadodara, India: The Oriental Institute, M.S. University of Baroda, 1958–75). Unless otherwise indicated the translation cited, at least for those volumes that have already appeared, is *The Rāmāyaṇa of Vālmīki: An Epic of Ancient India,* trans. Robert P. Goldman et al., 4 vols. to date (Princeton, N.J.: Princeton University Press, 1984–). Volumes 2 and 3 were translated by Sheldon Pollock.

For the *Iliad,* I have used the edition in the Oxford Classical Texts series: *Homeri Opera,* vols. 1–2, ed. David B. Monro and Thomas W. Allen, 3d ed. (1920; reprint, Oxford: Clarendon Press, 1969, 1971). Although the recent translation by Robert Fagles, published by Penguin, has received much attention, I have routinely cited the older translation by Richmond Lattimore, because the numbering of his lines corresponds to that of the Greek text. Thus, unless otherwise indicated, the translation cited is his: *The Iliad of Homer,* trans. Richmond Lattimore (Chicago: University of Chicago Press, 1951).

For the sake of readability and accessibility I have deliberately avoided any single system of transcribing Greek names. An inflexible insistence on Greek forms produces almost affected results: Aias and *Ilias* instead of Ajax and *Iliad.* But so would an equally inflexible insistence on Latin forms: Hercules for Herakles, or worse yet, Ulysses for Odysseus. In general I have preserved Greek names, but in their more familiar Latin spellings.

2. If nothing else, the following collections provide at least an overwhelming sense of this diversity: V. Raghavan, ed., *The Ramayana Tradition in Asia: Papers Presented at the International Seminar on the Ramayana Tradition in Asia, New Delhi, December, 1975* (New Delhi: Sahitya Akademi, 1975), and *Ramayana, Mahabharata, and Bhagavata Writers,* Cultural Leaders of India Series (New Delhi: Government of India, 1978); K. R. Srinivasa Iyengar, ed., *Asian Variations in Ramayana. Papers Presented at the International Seminar on Variations in Ramayana in Asia: Their Cultural, Social, and Anthropological Significance (New Delhi, January 1981)* (New Delhi: Sahitya Akademi, 1983); and Paula Richman, *Many Ramayanas: The Diversity of a Narrative Tradition in South Asia* (Berkeley and Los Angeles: University of California Press, 1991).

3. Ganesh N. Devy has argued eloquently that Indians need to engage in a comparative literature whose parameters are strictly subcontinental, not global, and certainly not colonial. See "Comparative Literature in India," *New Quest* 63 (May–June 1987): 133–47; 64 (July–August 1987): 211–17. For an example of the use of the *Rāmāyaṇa* that bolstered the Indian self-image under colonial rule, see K. S. Ramaswami Sastrigal, "The Rāmāyaṇa as a Guide to a New World-Order," *Journal of Oriental Research* 4 (1930): 368–83; for an example of the continued priority of Greek-Indian comparison, see Lokesh Chandra, "The Cultural Symphony of India and Greece," *Haryana Sahitya Akademi Journal of Indological Studies* 1, no. 1 (1986): 136–48.

4. Kashinath Trimbak Telang, *Was the Rāmāyaṇa Copied from Homer? A Reply to Professor Weber* (1873; reprint, Delhi: Publishers Parlour, 1976). There were, of course, other motives to be addressed. See Arthur Lillie, *Rama and Homer: An Argument That in the Indian Epics Homer Found the Theme of His Two Great Poems* (London: Kegan, Paul, Trench, Trubner, 1912).

5. Amartya Sen has distinguished generally between investigative, magisterial, and exoticist approaches to India ("India and the West," *The New Republic,* June 7, 1993, 27–34). For a history of the European encounter with India that focuses on philosophy, see Wilhelm Halbfass, *India and Europe: An Essay in Understanding* (Albany: SUNY Press, 1988).

6. The quoted phrases are titles; see Clifford Geertz, *Local Knowledge: Further Essays in Interpretive Anthropology* (New York: Basic Books, 1985). "From the Native's Point of View" recalls an attitude perhaps first voiced in these terms by Bronislaw Malinowski in *Argonauts of the Western Pacific: An Account of Native Enterprise and Adventure in the Archipelagoes of Melanesian New Guinea* (London: G. Routledge, 1922), 25: "The final goal, of which an Ethnographer should never lose sight . . . is, briefly, to grasp the native's point of view, his relation to life, to realise *his* vision of *his* world." Geertz has himself written a classic of cultural comparison, *Islam Observed: Development of Religion in Morocco and Indonesia* (Chicago: University of Chicago Press, 1971).

7. In literary studies, see Harry Levin, *Grounds for Comparison* (Cambridge: Harvard University Press, 1972). Also see Lee H. Yearley, *Mencius and Aquinas: Theories of Virtue and Conceptions of Courage* (Albany: SUNY Press, 1990).

8. Jonathan Z. Smith, *Drudgery Divine: On the Comparison of Early Christianities and the Religions of Late Antiquity* (Chicago: University of Chicago Press, 1991).

9. Ibid., 42.

10. Jonathan Z. Smith, *To Take Place: Toward Theory in Ritual* (Chicago: University of Chicago Press, 1987), 14; quoted in *Drudgery Divine,* 47.

11. Smith, *Drudgery Divine,* 51.

12. Ibid., 53.

13. It goes without saying that one can never question everything simultaneously. The important point is that there is nothing that is beyond questioning.

14. See Marshall Sahlins, *Culture and Practical Reason* (Chicago: University of Chicago Press, 1976).

15. There may be other grounds for questioning the term "influence." Michael Baxandall has suggested that "appropriation" more accurately reflects the processes at work (*Patterns of Intention: On the Historical Explanation of Pictures* [New Haven, Conn.: Yale University Press, 1985],

59–60). But Baxandall's view may require an estimate of the artist as autonomous agent that is too optimistic.

16. Thus, Robert Ackerman writes, albeit in a context that is biographical rather than philosophical or methodological: "On the surface of it, the comparative method seems better adapted to studies of cultural diffusion, where careful collocation of variants may indeed give clues as to the manner in which a folktale or motif spread" (*J. G. Frazer: His Life and Work* [Cambridge: Cambridge University Press, 1987], 272).

17. Smith's agenda seems arbitrarily to dismiss diachronic and temporal considerations altogether; consider the following remark on the significance of visionary maps in the prophet Ezekiel, which improperly limits the theoretical to the taxonomic and the synchronic: "It is a question that the approach we have taken will not allow us to answer on the level of the historical (by appealing to matters of redaction and the like); it is a question that can be answered only at the level of theory" (Smith, *To Take Place,* 65). Perhaps we could say that Smith, like Claude Lévi-Strauss, implies a notion of history whose concept of time is much too simplistic and does not correspond with what historians actually do. On Lévi-Strauss, see Johannes Fabian, *Time and the Other: How Anthropology Makes Its Object* (New York: Columbia University Press, 1983), 52–69.

18. Most attempts to make this case are neither very exciting nor very convincing. Perhaps the most detailed attempt is Gregory Nagy, *Comparative Studies in Greek and Indic Meter* (Cambridge: Harvard University Press, 1974).

19. Bruce Lincoln has finally rejected Dumézil's model because of what he sees as its political implications, rooted in Dumézil's own political praxis; see Lincoln's *Death, War, and Sacrifice: Studies in Ideology and Practice* (Chicago: University of Chicago Press, 1991). Although the allegations that Dumézil participated in fascist activities, if true, are serious causes for concern, even more damaging, to my mind, is the conceptual rather than political criticism directed against Dumézil's theory by Colin Renfrew in *Archaeology and Language: The Puzzle of Indo-European Origins* (New York: Cambridge University Press, 1988). Renfrew develops an alternative model to account for the distribution of Indo-European languages, and in doing so raises serious doubts about the presuppositions on which Dumézil's theories rest.

20. Joseph M. Kitagawa, "Religious Studies and the History of Religions," in *The History of Religions: Understanding Human Experience* (Atlanta, Ga.: Scholars Press, 1987), 152.

21. For a fuller development of the ideas presented in this section, see my article, "Wach, Eliade, and the Critique from Totality," *Numen* 35 (July 1988): 108–38.

22. Joachim Wach, *Religionswissenschaft: Prolegomena zu ihrer wissenschaftstheoretischen Grundlegung* (Leipzig, 1924); trans. under the title *Introduction to the History of Religions,* ed. Joseph M. Kitagawa and Gregory D. Alles (New York: Macmillan, 1987), 117–20, 143–50.

23. Joachim Wach, *Types of Religious Experience: Christian and Non-Christian* (Chicago: University of Chicago Press, 1951), 28–29; italics added.

24. See Joachim Wach, *Sociology of Religion* (Chicago: University of Chicago Press, 1944), 17.

25. For Schleiermacher's appropriation of the Pietist heritage, see especially his famous "speeches," which insist that religion is neither metaphysics nor morals but feelings and emotions: F.D.E. Schleiermacher, *Über die Religion: Reden an die Gebildeten unter ihren Verächtern,* ed. Rudolf Otto, 7th ed. (Göttingen: Vandenhoeck & Ruprecht, 1991); trans. Richard Crouter, under the title *On Religion: Speeches to Its Cultured Despisers* (Cambridge: Cambridge University Press, 1988).

26. See Joachim Wach, *The Comparative Study of Religions* (New York: Columbia University Press, 1958), 32–33.

27. Wach, *Types of Religious Experience,* 33.

28. It is also possible to critique Wach's expressive, as opposed to symbolic, view of meaning. See Clifford Geertz, " 'From the Native's Point of View': On the Nature of Anthropological Understanding," in *Local Knowledge,* 55–70.

29. Mircea Eliade, *The Quest: History and Meaning in Religion* (Chicago: University of Chicago Press, 1969), 8.

30. Ibid., 6.

31. Compare Eliade's "technicians of the sacred" with Wach's emphasis on religious authority, and Eliade's *homo religiosus* with Wach's *homines religiosi;* I have discussed both views of the latter in "Homo religiosus," in *Encyclopedia of Religion,* ed. Mircea Eliade et al. (New York: Macmillan, 1987), 6:442–45.

32. The classic works of these writers are so well known that there is almost no need to mention them: Hans-Georg Gadamer, *Truth and Method* (New York: Seabury Press, 1975); Paul Ricoeur, *Hermeneutics and the Human Sciences,* ed. and trans. John B. Thompson (Cambridge: Cambridge University Press, 1981); and Clifford Geertz, *The Interpretation of Cultures* (New York: Basic Books, 1973), esp. "Religion as a Cultural System," 87–125. The most prominent historian of religions influenced by interpretive anthropology is Jonathan Z. Smith.

33. Baxandall, *Patterns of Intention;* David Freedberg, *The Power of Images: Studies in the History and Theory of Response* (Chicago: University of Chicago Press, 1989). I have tried to adapt both strategies to religious studies. See my "Surface, Space, and Intention: The Parthenon and the Kandariya Mahadeva," *History of Religions* 28 (August 1988): 1–36, which utilizes Baxandall's, and "A Fitting Approach to God: On Entering the Western Temples at Khajurāho," *History of Religions* 33 (November 1993): 161–86, which utilizes Freedberg's.

34. Ronald Grimes, *Ritual Criticism: Case Studies in Its Practice, Essays on Its Theory* (Columbia: University of South Carolina Press, 1990), esp. chap. 7, "Narrative and Ritual Criticism," 158–73; Frits Staal, "The Meaninglessness of Ritual," *Numen* 26 (1979): 2–22; and Renato Rosaldo, *Truth and Culture: The Remaking of Social Analysis* (Boston: Beacon Press, 1989), 15. For a critique of Geertz on a topic directly related to the subject of this book, see Peter van der Veer, " 'God must be liberated!': A Hindu Liberation Movement in Ayodhya," *Modern Asian Studies* 21 (1987): 283–301.

At least two answers to the questions raised in the text are possible, but neither satisfies me. According to the first, religion in its entirety is the communication of humanity as a whole. But humanity as a whole is an abstraction. It is not compatible with the basic unit of communicated meaning, the *sententia* or actual statement. Humanity as a whole cannot communicate in "sentences." The alternative answer is "the sacred." If one has a particular "Sacred" in mind (for example, the Christian God), communication is certainly possible, but the investigation of that communication belongs to the theologies which formulate that particular religious vision. If, on the other hand, "the sacred" is taken as a generic category, one encounters once again an abstraction incapable of *sententiae.*

35. In one European language the connection between category and discipline becomes almost tautological: *Geschichte* is an account of *Geschehen.* Quirks of translation and history yield another tautology—"The history of religions is history"—but this tautology is only apparent. "History of religions" has been adopted by the International Association for the History of Religions as the rough English equivalent of the German *Religionswissenschaft.* Because the scope of "science" is narrower than that of *Wissenschaft,* "the science of religion" is a phrase generally avoided. Thus, the statement, "The history of religions is history," is not a tautology because the first "history" does not refer to history, and also because the second "history"—history as I conceive my enterprise—does not refer to the vision of history that led scholars to use that word as a substitute for *Wissenschaft.* "History of religions" became current in English and the romance languages under the impact of the positivistic critical history of the nineteenth and early twentieth centuries (see A. Eustace Hayden, "From Comparative Religion to the History of Religions," *Journal of Religion* 2 [1922]: 577–87). Some still promote essentially this sort of history as the basic method of *Religionswissenschaft* (see Kurt Rudolph, *Historical Fundamentals and the Study of Religions* [New York: Macmillan, 1985], and in more detail *Geschichte und Probleme der Religionswissenschaft*

[Leiden: E. J. Brill, 1992]), but by "history" I mean something different. I mean that mode of understanding humanity whose central category is the event, whatever actual methods the scholar may employ. I do not conceive my break with tradition as a radical beginning *de novo*. I am merely shifting or permuting the tradition by substituting one category—granted, a very fundamental one (event)—for another (meaning).

With a few notable exceptions, such as Wilfred Cantwell Smith, scholars have generally avoided the phrase "history of religion." The use of the singular has tended to connote, as it does still in Smith, an attempt to find the universal truth in all religions.

36. The topic has resonances that may not at first be apparent. The hermeneutics of *Erlebnis, Ausdruck,* and *Verstehen*—experience, expression, and understanding—that Wach adopted and modified contributed significantly to the decline of rhetoric, the art of persuasive verbal activity, in the nineteenth century. In this view, rhetorical activity stands opposed to the genius's pure expression of experience (compare Gadamer, *Truth and Method,* 64). When scholars abandoned the expressionistic model of meaning for a symbolic one, attention continued to focus on semantics and syntactics to the detriment of verbal action, if you will, of pragmatics. For the decline of rhetoric in the French-speaking world, see Gérard Genette, "Rhetoric Restrained," in *Figures of Literary Discourse* (New York: Columbia University Press, 1982), 103–26.

37. In *Myth and Reality,* trans. Willard R. Trask (New York: Harper & Row, 1963), Mircea Eliade speaks of Homer as "neither a theologian nor a mythographer" but a literary genius who used the gods and myths of Greece for his own purposes (see 147–50, esp. 149). But the agency can work both ways. In *Cosmos and History: The Myth of the Eternal Return,* trans. Willard R. Trask (New York: Harper & Row, 1959), 42, Eliade presumes that the subjects of Homeric poetry were originally historical personages who achieved epic stature when they became " 'formed after the image' of the heroes of ancient myth." For Goldman's judgment on the *Rāmāyaṇa,* see his introduction to *The Rāmāyaṇa of Vālmīki,* vol. 1, *Bālakāṇḍa* (Princeton, N.J.: Princeton University Press, 1984), esp. 41–48.

38. An example is his masterful analysis of the intentional variations in the printed versions of some of Blake's poems. See Jerome J. McGann, *Social Values and Poetic Arts* (Cambridge: Harvard University Press, 1988), 152–72. On the general position, compare the following from one of McGann's earlier essays: "When [Roland] Barthes says that literature 'exists only as discourse,' we must forcefully remind ourselves that discourse always takes place in specific and concrete forms, and that those forms are by no means comprehended by the limits of language" (Jerome J. McGann, *The Beauty of Inflections: Literary Investigations in Historical Method and Theory* [Oxford: Clarendon Press, 1985], 95).

39. McGann, *Social Values and Poetic Acts,* 72.

40. McGann, *The Beauty of Inflections,* 157–58; see also 190 and 201, and McGann's *Romantic Ideology: A Critical Investigation* (Chicago: University of Chicago Press, 1983).

41. Leonard Swidler, introduction to *Death or Dialogue? From the Age of Monologue to the Age of Dialogue,* by Leonard Swidler et al. (London: SCM Press, 1990), vii–viii. On the practice of dialogue, see Swidler's "classic" essay, "The Dialogue Decalogue," *Journal of Ecumenical Studies* 20 (Winter 1983): 1–4.

42. Swidler, *Death or Dialogue?* 9. Despite this initial impression, Cobb does not advocate an old-fashioned quest for converts. "The transformation of the other traditions [through dialogue and encounter] ranks higher as a goal than their supersession" (10). Transformation may be more comfortable as a goal than conversion (just how comfortable is it?); still, Cobb's preference looks terribly arbitrary. That is, it looks arbitrary until we remember that Cobb, writing in a tradition of process theology hearkening back to thinkers like Charles Hartshorne and Henry Nelson Weiman, conceives of Christ as nothing more nor less than creative transformation itself. As a result, Cobb can write, "I see myself in this work [the transformation of Buddhism through dialogue] as a servant of Christ" (118).

The second and third interlocutors, Paul Knitter and Monika Hellwig, at times echo Cobb's concerns. In a sense, Knitter even goes a step further by using the bold word "conversion" (23) and asserting programmatically that dialogue should seek not just mutual transformation but "world-transformation" in a liberationist mode (30). But Knitter does not place much weight on persuasion. In fact, he cannot, because he insists that action precede talking: liberate first, enter into dialogue as a second step. Talk of persuasion and confrontation only loosens the audience up, so to speak, for the agenda of liberationist praxis (19–44).

43. Ibid., 109–10. Before making these statements, however, Swidler affirms what he believes his partners meant when they talked of persuasion: all participants in a genuine dialogue bring their own firmly held convictions to the table (109). Swidler does allow one exception to the dialogic attitude, when human rights are being violated. In other words, only issues of moral practice can be subjects of persuasion.

44. Ibid., 148.

45. René Girard, *Things Hidden Since the Foundation of the World* (Stanford, Calif.: Stanford University Press, 1987).

46. René Girard, *Violence and the Sacred,* trans. Patrick Gregory (Baltimore: Johns Hopkins University Press, 1977).

47. Ibid., 15, 53. On sacrificial crisis, see ibid., chap. 2.

48. Ibid., 4, 300, 8, and 271; see also 13, 79. On Girard's notion of the sacred, consider the following: "The sacred consists of all those forces whose dominance over man increases or seems to increase in proportion to man's effort to master them. Tempests, forest fires, and plagues, among other phenomena, may be classified as sacred. Far outranking these, however, though in a far less obvious manner, stands human violence—violence seen as something exterior to man and henceforth as a part of all the other outside forces that threaten mankind. Violence is the heart and secret soul of the sacred" (31).

49. Ibid., 315.

50. Ibid., 306, 310; see also 317: "The modern mind still cannot bring itself to acknowledge the basic principle behind that mechanism which, in a single decisive movement, curtails reciprocal violence and imposes structure on the community. Because of this willful blindness, modern thinkers continue to see religion as an isolated, wholly fictitious phenomenon cherished only by a few backward peoples or milieus."

51. Ibid., 318.

52. Michel Foucault, *The Order of Things: An Archaeology of the Human Sciences* (New York: Vintage Books, 1973).

53. From within the history of religions, see Bruce Lincoln, *Discourse and the Construction of Society: Comparative Studies of Myth, Ritual, and Classification* (New York: Oxford University Press, 1989).

54. The most prominent advocate for the historicity of the world portrayed in Homeric epic has been M. I. Finley; see *The World of Odysseus,* 2d rev. ed. (Harmondsworth, U.K.: Penguin Books, 1979). For a convincing critique, see A. M. Snodgrass, "An Historical Homeric Society?" *Journal of Hellenic Studies* 94 (1974): 114–25.

55. My use of the word "experience" may be open to misunderstanding because there is, of course, a sense in which literary worlds are "experienced." As I use it here, "experience" is equivalent to sense-experience or perception. I am quite deliberate when I call both imagined and experienced worlds real. They are, however, real at different levels, a concept developed fully by Śaṅkarācārya. See the exposition in P. T. Raju, *Structural Depths of Indian Thought* (Albany: SUNY Press, 1985), 389–90.

56. Girard, *Violence and the Sacred,* 35.

57. Carlo Ginzburg, quoted in Perry Anderson, *A Zone of Engagement* (London: Verso, 1992), 228–29.

Chapter 1: When Persuasion Fails

1. Camille Bulcke, "The Genesis of the Vālmīki Rāmāyaṇa Recensions," *Journal of the Oriental Institute, Baroda* 5 (1955–56): 66–94. So far as I can see, the best record available of what constitutes the *Rāmāyaṇa*'s defining narrative is, in fact, the Baroda critical edition.

2. Scholars of an analytical bent have often made their livings and reputations by identifying, through more or less intricate arguments, the books, chapters, and even the very verses that "Homer" and "Vālmīki" originally sang. I refrain from playing this game for two reasons. First, the defining narrative is a set of ideas, themes, and incidents, not a specific set of words. Everything we know about bards such as Homer and Vālmīki—or the groups of bards for whom these names are collective representations—suggests that they would have composed more or less extemporaneously from the sort of general outline that appears at the beginning of the *Rāmāyaṇa.* Second, without exception analytical efforts have failed disastrously. Because no two scholars can agree on the criteria to be used in identifying original material, their results are hopelessly contradictory. Compare, for example, the inconsistent determinations of J. L. Brockington, *Righteous Rama: The Evolution of an Epic* (Delhi: Oxford University Press, 1984), and M. R. Yardi, "A Statistical Study of *Rāmāyaṇa Sundarakāṇḍa, Yuddhakāṇḍa,* and *Uttarakāṇḍa,*" *Annals, Bhandarkar Oriental Research Institute* 70 (1989): 17–32.

Sheldon Pollock gives a good example of how the defining narrative might consist of ideas rather than words. Passage 833*, found in all northern manuscripts of the *Rāmāyaṇa,* and 835*, found in all the southern manuscripts, differ in wording, but express the same idea. Pollock's comment is apposite: "Not only does the census of manuscripts here show that the narrative element is contained in every manuscript used by the critical edition, but this is precisely the type of variation most indicative of the oral stratum of the text, which may claim the greatest antiquity in the history of the transmission of the poem" ("Ātmānaṃ Mānuṣaṃ Manye: Dharmākūtam on the Divinity of Rāma," *Journal of the Oriental Institute, Baroda* 33 [1983/84]: 239). I presume that the *Rāmāyaṇa,* besides being an oral poem, is formulaic in the sense Milman Parry and Albert Lord have applied to the *Iliad;* see Nabaneeta Sen, "Comparative Studies in Oral Epic Poetry and *The Vālmīki Rāmāyaṇa:* A Report on the *Bālākaṇṇa,*" *Journal of the American Oriental Society* 86 (1966): 397–409, and "The *Valmiki-Ramayana* and the *Raghuvamsam:* Stylistic Structure of Oral Poetry as Contrasted to Classical Poetry," *Jadavpur Journal of Comparative Literature* 8 (1968): 85–95. But as in the case of the *Iliad,* the *Rāmāyaṇa*'s formulas are not unambiguous; see J. L. Brockington, "A Note on Mrs. Sen's Article about the Rāmāyaṇa," *Journal of the American Oriental Society* 89 (1969): 412–14.

3. Compare James M. Redfield, *Nature and Culture in the Iliad: The Tragedy of Hektor* (Chicago: University of Chicago Press, 1975), and Jasper Griffin, *Homer on Life and Death* (Oxford: Oxford University Press, 1980). On the first option (although not exactly on Redfield's "tragedy of Hektor"), C. J. Emlyn-Jones expresses my own views precisely: "There is a tendency, prevalent among some modern scholars, to turn Achilles' experience into a tragedy, involving some kind of intellectual or spiritual regeneration, nothing of which has any support in the text" (*The Ionians and Hellenism: A Study of the Cultural Achievement of the Early Greek Inhabitants of Asia Minor* [London: Routledge & Kegan Paul, 1980], 78). He adds in a note: "At no time does Achilles resemble the later tragic hero in his consciousness of what he has done or basic regret for it" (196 n. 76). The best introduction to most issues pertaining to the *Iliad* for the general reader is Mark W. Edwards, *Homer: Poet of the Iliad* (Baltimore: Johns Hopkins University Press, 1987).

4. For detailed discussion of the issues, see James M. Redfield, "The Proem of the *Iliad:* Homer's Art," *Classical Philology* 74 (1979): 95–110.

5. *Il.* 9.517, 19.35, 19.75.

6. Another notorious example of Homer's apparent inability to sing the poem he announces is the *Dios boulē* (the plan of Zeus) of *Il.* 1.5, for Zeus seems to change his mind about halfway through. See Redfield, "The Proem of the *Iliad,*" 105–8.

7. Gregory Nagy, *The Best of the Achaeans: Concepts of the Hero in Archaic Greek Poetry* (Baltimore: Johns Hopkins University Press, 1979), 80.

8. Compare Jeffrey M. Hurwit, *The Art and Culture of Early Greece, 1100–400 B.C.* (Ithaca, N.Y.: Cornell University Press, 1985), 71–73. For more general comments on the interrelations of grief and anger, see Rosaldo, *Culture and Truth,* 1–21.

9. Also marked similarities. Especially striking is the similar pattern of attempted persuasion in each tale. There are three unsuccessful attempts to persuade Meleagros: by representatives of the leading men, who offer gifts (9.574–80), by his father (581–85), and by his comrades in arms (585–87). Only the subsequent entreaties of Cleopatra succeed (590–95). The three unsuccessful speeches in *Iliad* 9 replicate the pattern of the unsuccessful speeches addressed to Meleagros: first Odysseus offers gifts, then Phoinix speaks as a substitute father, then Ajax presses the claims of comradeship. After a lengthy interval, Patroklos, Achilles' *hetairos,* delivers an ambiguously persuasive speech.

10. Oswyn Murray points out the distinctive lack of kinship terminology in Homeric social organization in emphasizing the symposium as an instrument of social control ("The Symposium as Social Organization," in *The Greek Renaissance of the Eighth Century B.C.: Tradition and Innovation,* ed. Robin Hägg, Acta Instituti Atheniensis Regni Sueciae, ser. 4, no. 30 [Stockholm, 1983], 195–99). See the comments by Marinatos in the discussion that follows, for a needed reminder of the continued religious and social role of the family throughout Greek history.

11. For example, *Il.* 1.269, 9.315, 345, 386; 18.126.

12. Those who wish to be free from the shackles of Indian tradition generally read the *Rāmāyaṇa* in ways that cater to modern Northern (if you prefer, Western) tastes: as folklore, as psychological projection, as a political tool. To them, the *Rāmāyaṇa*'s traditional interpretations, in fact, its traditional versions, often appear overburdened with later brahminical encrustations that diligent scraping must remove. But no one has offered a reliable method for identifying any stage of the poem's prehistory. Furthermore, no one has yet offered a compelling reason why the poet or poets who composed the *Rāmāyaṇa*'s defining narrative could not have done so as self-conscious brahmins. Indeed, the contrast with the *Daśaratha-jātaka* (developed in the next section) supports the view that the ancient *Rāmāyaṇa* was distinguished from other Rāma stories precisely by its brahminical moral content.

13. Indeed, given the ancient traditions of Paraśurāma and Balarāma, one might say that Rāma was a heroic figure whom ancient Indians realized under two different valorizations. One set of traditions, prominent in the northeast, emphasized Rāma's virtue; another set, prominent in the northwest and west, emphasized his physical prowess.

14. See the translation in E. B. Cowell, ed., *The Jātaka or Stories of the Buddha's Former Births* (London: Pali Text Society, 1957), *Jātaka* 461, 4:78–82.

The *jātakas* resemble the *Rāmāyaṇa* in several ways. Like it, they record tales that are set in Northeast India (where and when they were composed is disputed) and tell of one of India's two major mythological dynasties, the Sūryavaṃśa or "sun-dynasty," more particularly, the descendants of the legendary king Ikṣvāku. Although the *jātakas* are mostly Prakrit prose and the *Rāmāyaṇa* is entirely Sanskrit verse, the two works, like the two languages, are close. They share many narrative themes and typical scenes, such as typical descriptions and speeches. They even share some actual verses, allowing of course for the inevitable minor variations between Prakrit and Sanskrit.

Previous comparisons of the *Daśaratha-jātaka* and the *Rāmāyaṇa* have usually been plagued by the concern, informed by sectarian loyalties, to establish the genealogical priority of one or the other. See, for example, D. C. Sircar, "The Rāmāyaṇa and the Daśaratha Jātaka," *Journal of the Oriental Institute, Baroda* 26 (1976–77): 50–55.

15. At the beginning of the defining narrative, Rāma's righteousness pointedly precludes anger and antagonism, even in circumstances in which most of us would consider righteous anger an

appropriate response. Contrast Daśaratha's reaction in the *jātaka* that bears his name, quoted in section 9 of this chapter.

16. The correlation of truth, nature, and *dharma* and of appearance, sensation, and *adharma* hints at a central opposition in the *smṛti*s, the traditional Indian treatises on *dharma*. Subtle and hidden, *dharma* is a manifestation of one's true inner being; *adharma,* manifest and enticing, constitutes the commonsense approach to the world. See Robert Lingat, *The Classical Law of India,* trans. J. Duncan M. Derrett (Berkeley and Los Angeles: University of California Press, 1973), 156–57 (*kāma* and *artha* are *dṛṣṭārtha, dharma adṛṣṭārtha*).

17. By detailing the encounter between Kaikeyī and Mantharā, Vālmīki is able from the very beginning to dramatize the conflict between these two options. Initially, Kaikeyī represents disinterested behavior in accord with *dharma,* Mantharā behavior in the interests of *artha.*

18. Contrast the account of the *Daśaratha-jātaka,* which has no such obsessions (discussed in section 9 of this chapter).

19. That the *Rāmāyaṇa* develops in two stages was noted early on by Hermann Jacobi. He, however, distinguished the first stage as natural in its mode of presentation, the second as fantastic. See *The Ramayana,* trans. S. N. Ghosal (Baroda, India: Oriental Institute, 1960).

20. Vālmīki tries to establish an intimate connection between the two threats. On the one hand, he treats the beneficent effects of Rāma's banishment as the result of an unexpressed purpose. When the forest-dwelling sages beseech Rāma for help against the *rākṣasa*s, Rāma scolds them for thinking they had to ask. He has come to the forest, he says, of his own free will in order to benefit the sages: to kill their enemies, the *rākṣasa*s, in battle (*Rām.* 3.5.19–20). Similarly, when Bharata complains about his mother Kaikeyī's perversity to Bharadvāja, the sage mollifies him: "Rāma's forest-dwelling will result in happiness [*sukha*]" (*Rām.* 2.86.28). On the other hand, the abduction of Sītā is counted as part and parcel of what Kaikeyī intended. As soon as Rāma, Sītā, and Lakṣmaṇa enter Daṇḍaka forest, a demon (*rākṣasa*) named Virādha seizes Sītā. Rāma exclaims: "Today Kaikeyī's desires have been fulfilled. That someone else should touch Sītā is my greatest misfortune, every bit the equal of my father's death and the loss of the kingdom" (*Rām.* 3.2.18–19). The incident clearly foreshadows the encounter with Rāvaṇa. Similarly, when Sītā has been abducted by Rāvaṇa, Rāma laments: "If I die because of Sītā, and you, Lakṣmaṇa, are gone, won't Kaikeyī rejoice, her wish fulfilled?" (*Rām.* 3.56.7). And when right before the battles Rāvaṇa shows Sītā a conjured-up image of Rāma's severed head, Sītā's first words berate Kaikeyī: "Now you've got what you wanted, Kaikeyī! The delight of the family is dead!" (*Rām.* 6.23.4). Bharata echoes a similar sentiment when he calls his mother a *rākṣasī* (*Rām.* 2.68.9).

21. In Sanskrit, *uvāca, pratyuvāca, papraccha,* and *ninideṣa.*

22. For a general, wide-ranging discussion, see Harvey P. Alper, ed., *Mantra* (Albany: SUNY Press, 1989).

23. This is not quite the same as, although it is similar to, problems of evil, for which see especially Max Weber, *The Sociology of Religion* (Boston: Beacon Press, 1964), 138–50; Geertz, "Religion as a Cultural System," in *The Interpretation of Cultures;* Paul Ricoeur, *The Symbolism of Evil* (New York: Harper & Row, 1967); and Wendy Doniger O'Flaherty, *The Origins of Evil in Hindu Mythology* (Berkeley and Los Angeles: University of California Press, 1976).

24. Adkins's classic statement is *Merit and Responsibility* (Oxford: Oxford University Press, 1960). Further elaboration in " 'Friendship' and 'Self-Sufficiency' in Homer and Aristotle," *Classical Quarterly,* n.s., 13 (1963): 30–45; "*Euchomai, euchōlē,* and *euchos* in Homer," *Classical Quarterly,* n.s., 19 (1969): 20–33; "Threatening, Abusing, and Feeling Angry in the Homeric Poems," *Journal of Hellenic Studies* 89 (1969): 7–21; "Homeric Values and Homeric Society," *Journal of Hellenic Studies* 91 (1971): 1–14; "Truth, *kosmos,* and *aretē* in the Homeric Poems," *Classical Quarterly,* n.s., 22 (1972): 5–18; "Homeric Gods and the Values of Homeric Society," *Journal of Hellenic*

Studies 92 (1972): 1–19; and "Art, Beliefs, and Values in the Later Books of the *Iliad*," *Classical Philology* 70 (1975): 239–54.

25. Cowell, ed., *The Jātaka,* 4:79.

Chapter 2: Poetic Works and Their Worlds

1. See Finley, *The World of Odysseus,* and S. N. Vyas, *India in the Rāmāyaṇa Age: A Study of the Social and Cultural Conditions in Ancient India as Described in Vālmīki's Rāmāyaṇa* (Delhi: Atma Ram, 1967).

2. Recall, for example, the old judgment of Richard Bentley (1662–1742), disputing the claim that Homer "designed his poems for eternity to please and instruct mankind": "Take my word for it, poor Homer never had such aspiring thoughts. He wrote a sequel of songs and rhapsodies, to be sung by himself for small earnings and good cheer, at festivals and other days of merriment. The Iliad he made for the men and the Odyssey for the other sex" (quoted in Rudolf Pfeiffer, *History of Classical Scholarship from 1300 to 1850* [Oxford: Clarendon Press, 1976], 158).

3. For poems that arise in an oral context, as the *Iliad* and the *Rāmāyaṇa* both seem to have done, one can postulate a fairly direct relationship between the length of the composition and the delight of the audience. On the one hand, a positive reaction from the audience will induce a poet to elaborate her or his efforts. On the other, a poem that does not please will lose its audience and thus not be perpetuated.

4. Eric Havelock, *Preface to Plato* (Cambridge: Harvard University Press, 1963); see his more recent book, *The Muse Learns to Write: Reflections on Orality & Literacy from Antiquity to the Present* (New Haven, Conn.: Yale University Press, 1986). The *locus classicus* for "Homer the educator" is, of course, Plato, who disapproved of Homer's lessons.

5. See Jasper Griffin, "The Epic Cycle and the Uniqueness of Homer," *Journal of Hellenic Studies* 97 (1977): 39–53. Similarly, the narrative of the *Rāmāyaṇa,* traditionally classed as *kāvya* (high letters), is much more unified (in a loose, Aristotelian sense of poetic unity) than the *Mahābhārata* and other works of *itihāsa-purāṇa* (the mythological collections known as *Purāṇas*).

6. The *Daśaratha-jātaka,* as an occasion and demonstration story, seems (like all *jātakas*) to have a clearly didactic, moral purpose. One difficulty with including the *Rāmāyaṇa* in this class is, why then would Vālmīki have framed his narrative as problem and resolution, rather than as occasion and demonstration? Compare, too, the stories from the *Pañcatantra* and, in a Greek context, Aesop. The relatively brief compass of all these stories and the *jātakas* also tends to indicate that simple, moral didacticism is not a sufficient reason to generate a monumental poem: the same lesson can be taught more quickly and more directly in a poem of shorter compass. In fairness one should note that at least other ages would have vehemently disagreed with this assertion. Howard Clarke summarizes the views of Philip Sidney, John Dryden, and above all Torquato Tasso: "Tragic heroes teach us what vices we must avoid, epic heroes teach us what virtues we must imitate" (Howard Clarke, *Homer's Readers: A Historical Introduction to the Iliad and the Odyssey* [Newark: University of Delaware Press, 1981], 113).

7. Compare Ian Morris, "The Use and Abuse of Homer," *Classical Antiquity* 5 (1968): 128: "The Homeric poems are an example of ideology by analogy, . . . using the analogy of the Heroic Age to legitimize an eighth-century dominance structure." Yet Morris is absolutely correct when he insists that we can read the *Iliad* as only analogous to the situation of the poet and his contemporaries. Unfortunately for the historian (but fortunately for the history of literature), the analogy between the poem and its audience can work with any number of specific forms of sociopolitical organization.

8. Ian Morris, *Burial and Ancient Society: The Rise of the Greek City-State* (Cambridge: Cambridge University Press, 1987).

9. On funerals, see J. N. Coldstream, *Geometric Greece* (New York: St. Martin's Press, 1977), 349–52, and "Hero-Cults in the Age of Homer," *Journal of Hellenic Studies* 96 (1976): 8–17; but see also the sources cited at note 45. On names, see G. L. Huxley, *The Early Ionians* (New York: Humanities Press, 1966), 43; and compare Stefan Hiller, "Possible Historical Reasons for the Rediscovery of the Mycenaean Past in the Age of Homer," in Hägg, ed., *The Greek Renaissance,* 9–15, esp. 11–12, on the Aeneids and Glaucids. On narrative heroic art, see Coldstream, *Geometric Greece,* 352–56, and Anthony M. Snodgrass, "Poet and Painter in Eighth Century Greece," *Proceedings of the Cambridge Philological Society* 205 (1979): 118–30. On Mycenaean cults as familial, see Anthony M. Snodgrass, *Archaeology and the Rise of the Greek State: An Inaugural Lecture* (Cambridge: Cambridge University Press, 1977), 30–31; but compare Coldstream, *Geometric Greece,* 346–48, and "Hero-Cults," and Theodora Hadzisteliou Price, "Hero-Cult and Homer," *Historia* 22 (1973): 129–44.

10. Morris, "The Use and Abuse of Homer," 127–28.

11. Anthony M. Snodgrass, "Towards the Interpretation of the Geometric Figure-Scenes," *Mitteilungen des deutschen archäologischen Instituts, Athenische Abteilung* 95 (1980): 51–58, esp. 53. For more detail, see Snodgrass, "Poet and Painter," which discusses inscriptions, sanctuaries, and other evidence to suggest pointedly that "non-Homeric epic [was] a focus of public interest [in the eighth century], and . . . that influences could also have existed outside the sphere of poetry altogether" (125). For a briefer discussion, see "Central Greece and Thessaly," in *The Cambridge Ancient History,* 2d ed., ed. John Boardman, I.E.S. Edwards, N.G.L. Hammond, and E. Sollberger (Cambridge: Cambridge University Press, 1982), vol. 3, part 1, pp. 657–95, esp. 686.

12. Hans Robert Jauss, "Interaction Patterns of Identification with the Hero," in *Aesthetic Experience and Literary Hermeneutics,* trans. Michael Shaw (Minneapolis: University of Minnesota Press, 1982), 152–88.

13. Ibid., 159, 167–72.

14. D. C. Sircar, in V. Raghavan, ed., *The Rāmāyaṇa Tradition in Asia,* 325–26.

15. On the elections, see *India Today* (International Edition), May 31, 1991, 77 and 79; August 15, 1991, 70–72. Much recent literature alludes to these events, but it is still too early to see where the saga will end. For recent information, see almost any edition of the news magazine, *India Today,* or Indian newspapers such as *The Times of India, Indian Express,* or *The Hindu.* For accounts of events leading up to the demolition of the Babri Masjid on December 6, 1992, see Sarvepalli Gopal, ed., *Anatomy of a Confrontation: The Babri Masjid-Ramjanmabhumi Issue* (New Delhi: Viking Penguin, 1991), and, in a broader context, Ainslee T. Embree, *Utopias in Conflict: Religion and Nationalism in Modern India* (Berkeley and Los Angeles: University of California Press, 1990), Daniel Gold, "Organized Hinduisms: From Vedic Truth to Hindu Nation," in *Fundamentalisms Observed,* ed. Martin E. Marty and R. Scott Appleby (Chicago: University of Chicago Press, 1991), 531–83, Barbara Stoler Miller, "Presidential Address: Contending Narratives—The Political Life of the Indian Epics," *Journal of Asian Studies* 50 (November 1991): 783–92, and Peter van der Veer, *Religious Nationalism* (California, 1994).

16. Romila Thapar, *Exile and the Kingdom: Some Thoughts on the Ramayana* (Bangalore: The Mythic Society, 1978); see also her "Origin Myths and the Early Indian Historical Tradition," in *History and Society: Essays in Honour of Professor Niharranjan Ray,* ed. Debiprasad Chattopadhyaya (Calcutta: K. P. Bagchi, 1978), 271–94.

17. Consider the notion that the *Rāmāyaṇa* was composed to legitimate a dynasty in southern Kośala, perhaps the most crucial assumption of all. If legitimation of a southern kingdom were the narrative's purpose, we would expect the establishment of that kingdom to be a major, well-developed component of the story. But in our *Rāmāyaṇa,* Vibhīṣaṇa's inauguration is only incidental. It occupies only eleven lines in the critical edition (*Rām.* 6.100.8–18), and of these eleven, only

half (9–14) are really concerned with the inauguration itself. The incident is easily overlooked in favor of other, more important events. Of course, Thapar postulates a prior version of the poem, but this version is both hypothetical and unnecessary. We can imagine the *Rāmāyaṇa* being produced without recourse to an origin myth for southern Kośala, and there is not a shred of evidence that Vibhīṣaṇa's coronation ever occupied a more prominent position in the poem.

18. I am not averse on principle to finding legitimatory efforts in a poet's work or even in Vālmīki's work. For example, the scenario I have sketched in the text begins to resemble some of the Viśvāmitra episodes of the *Bāla-kāṇḍa*. Later in this chapter, I suggest that when Guha, the local prince (*rāja*) of Śṛṅgaverapura, lays all he has at Rāma's feet (*Rām* 2.44, esp. *śloka*s 12, 14–15), his behavior speaks in favor of close economic relations on the part of Śṛṅgaverapura, a site of strategic economic importance in ancient India, with Ayodhyā as opposed to, say, Kauśāmbī, which was perhaps Ayodhyā's closest competitor for the city's loyalties. But these instances are isolated; they hardly motivate the composition of the *Rāmāyaṇa*'s narrative.

19. Compare *Rām.* 2.23.11, in which Vālmīki hints that the events which bring about Rāma's exile silence the efforts of praise poets.

20. It is possible, I suppose, to posit a hypothetical, prior stage in the poem's genesis and attribute a legitimatory function to that stage. But it strikes me as senseless to discuss a hypothetical stage for which there is neither evidence nor any demonstrable need.

21. Huxley, *The Early Ionians,* 42. On the Homeridae, see Thomas W. Allen, *Homer: The Origins and the Transmission* (Oxford: Clarendon Press, 1924), chap. 2.

22. J. M. Cook, "Greek Settlement in the Eastern Aegean and Asia Minor," in *The Cambridge Ancient History,* ed. I.E.S. Edwards et al. (Cambridge: Cambridge University Press, 1975), vol. 2, part 2, pp. 773–804, esp. 776.

23. Snodgrass, "Towards the Interpretation of the Geometric Figure-Scenes," 57.

24. See in general J. M. Cook, *The Greeks in Ionia and the East* (New York: Praeger, 1963); idem, "East Greece," in *The Cambridge Ancient History,* 2d ed., vol. 3, part 1, pp. 745–53; idem, "Greek Settlement," and idem, "The Eastern Greeks," in *The Cambridge Ancient History,* 2d ed., vol. 3, part 3, pp. 196–221; Emlyn-Jones, *The Ionians and Hellenism;* and Huxley, *The Early Ionians.* See also the major archaeological report by John Boardman, *Excavations in Chios, 1952–1955: Greek Emporio,* British School of Archaeology at Athens, suppl. vol. 6 (Oxford, 1967).

On oriental influences generally, see Coldstream, *Geometric Greece,* 358–65; Oswyn Murray, *Early Greece* (Sussex: Harvester Press, 1980), 80–99; *Oxford History of the Classical World,* 26–27; and Walter Burkert, *The Orientalizing Revolution: Near Eastern Influence on Greek Culture in the Early Archaic Age,* trans. Margaret E. Pinder and Walter Burkert (Cambridge: Harvard University Press, 1992), and more specifically, "Oriental Myth and Literature in the *Iliad,*" in Hägg, ed., *The Greek Renaissance,* 51–56.

25. Huxley, *The Early Ionians,* 33.

26. Emlyn-Jones, *The Ionians and Hellenism,* 69.

27. M. R. Popham and L. H. Sackett, *Excavations at Lefkandi, Euboea, 1964–66* (British School of Archaeology at Athens, 1968); Popham, Sackett, and P. G. Themelis, *Lefkandi, The Iron Age* (London: Thames & Hudson, 1979); and Popham, Sackett, and E. Touloupa, "Further Excavations of the Toumba Cemetery at Lefkandi, 1981," *Bulletin of the British School of Archaeology at Athens* 77 (1982): 213–48, and "The Hero of Lefkandi," *Antiquity* 56 (1982): 169–74. For a general, preliminary discussion of the site's possible significance, see *Oxford History of the Classical World,* 20.

28. Boardman, *Excavations in Chios;* compare *Il.* 11.807–08. On urbanization in Ionia, see Snodgrass, *Archaic Greece,* 32, as well as Cook, *The Greeks in Ionia and the East,* "Greek Settlement," "East Greece," and "The Eastern Greeks." David Rupp observes that elaborately constructed altars do not appear in Greece until the second half of the seventh century; he sees the eighth century's concern with temples and votive offerings as "a tangible means of showing for all to

see the cohesion, wealth, and importance of the growing political body" ("Reflections on the Development of Altars in the Eighth Century B.C." in Hägg, ed., *The Greek Renaissance,* 101–7, esp. 107).

29. Coldstream, *Geometric Greece,* 303–4.

30. Cook, *The Greeks in Ionia,* 34–35; for a revision of the date, see Cook, "East Greece," 749–50.

31. For example, McGann, *Beauty of Inflections,* chap. 1, in which elements of Keats's "To Autumn" are linked to specific events in England in 1819.

32. Emlyn-Jones, *The Ionians and Hellenism,* 14 and passim.

33. The *oikos* as the fundamental unit of society was first emphasized by M. I. Finley in *The World of Odysseus.* For a recent survey, see Chester G. Starr, *Individual and Community: The Rise of the Polis 800–500 B.C.* (New York: Oxford University Press, 1986), 27–33. Bjørn Qviller has analyzed the shift from *oikos* to *polis* in economic terms borrowed from social anthropology; see his "Dynamics of the Homeric Society," *Symbolae Osloenses* 56 (1981): 109–55.

34. For a discussion of this move in the context of modern experimental psychology, see Stanley Milgram, *Obedience to Authority: An Experimental View* (New York: Harper & Row, 1974), esp. 47–49, and 135–64.

35. See the last paragraph of section 3 in this chapter. One might also speak of a "community of persuasion," because the communities are structured in such a way that joint activity must be accomplished through the persuasion of relative equals.

Walter Donlan has provided a more finely tuned analysis of authority in the *Iliad* from a sociological point of view that is consistent with what I mean here by a "community of consensus." See his "Structure of Authority in the *Iliad,*" *Arethusa* 12 (1979): 51–70. According to Donlan, the structure of authority in the *Iliad* is tripartite; its constituent elements are "established social position," "standing based on ability," and "collective authority" or "collegial cooperation." Inherent in this model is tension between the competing claims of position and standing, which must be mediated by "collegial cooperation." For Donlan, the argument between Achilles and Agamemnon is a paradigm of this conflict.

Donlan admits that his analysis is structural, not literary. But from the literary structure of the *Iliad,* it would seem that Donlan's structural analysis does not give us the entire picture. He makes sense of Achilles' conflict with Agamemnon and the restoration of collegial cooperation in the funeral games of *Iliad* 23, but he can do very little with what to me is the more striking part of the poem: the conflict between Achilles and Hektor and the restoration of harmony in *Iliad* 24.

36. See, for example, Hägg, ed., *The Greek Renaissance.* The word "renaissance" was initially proposed because it was presumed that the appeal to Mycenaean antiquity inspired the cultural revival.

37. Anthony M. Snodgrass, *Archaic Greece: The Age of Experiment* (Berkeley and Los Angeles: University of California Press, 1980), 20–24, 35–37; Morris, *Burial and Ancient Society.* For a critique of Snodgrass's methods and views, see Chester G. Starr, *The Economic and Social History of Early Greece, 800–500 B.C.* (New York: Oxford University Press, 1977), 43–46; and Coldstream, *Geometric Greece,* 313–14. Snodgrass replies briefly in "Two Demographic Notes," in Hägg, ed., *The Greek Renaissance,* 167–71. See also Starr, *Individual and Community,* 38–40.

38. For these developments in general, see Murray, *Early Greece,* 69–79 and 100–119, and *The Oxford History of the Classical World.* Among specific studies, see esp. John Boardman, *The Greeks Overseas* (Baltimore, Md.: Penguin, 1964).

39. For a brief, general account of this development, see the *Oxford History of the Classical World,* 19–26.

40. These three are conveniently discussed together in Snodgrass, *Archaeology and the Rise of the Greek State,* 24–33.

41. Because the relation between the world of the *Iliad* and that of Homer's audience is at most that of analogy, the precise sociological forms cannot be determined from the *Iliad* but only from historical studies. For an alternative to traditional views of developments during this period, see Morris, *Burial and Ancient Society.* Starr discusses various anthropological models applied to the period in *Individual and Community,* 42–46.

42. Snodgrass, *Archaic Greece,* 61, and *Archaeology and the Rise of the Greek State,* 9. Compare Murray, *Early Greece,* 36–68.

43. Murray, *Early Greece,* 60. See my "Verbal Craft and Religious Act in the *Iliad,*" *Religion* 18 (1988): 293–309, for an analysis of *Il.* 11.807–8.

44. On allegory, see Robert Lamberton, *Homer the Theologian: Neoplatonist Allegorical Reading and the Growth of the Epic Tradition* (Berkeley and Los Angeles: University of California Press, 1986).

45. The best example of the former is Robert P. Goldman's introduction to his translation *The Rāmāyaṇa of Vālmīki,* vol. 1, *Bālakāṇḍa,* 14–23. The latter date was advocated by the premier Indian archaeologist, H. D. Sankalia, in *Ramayana: Myth or Reality?* (New Delhi: People's Publishing House, 1973); but see his reassessment in *The Ramayana in Historical Perspective* (Delhi: Macmillan India, 1982).

46. Gregory D. Alles, "Reflections on Dating 'Vālmīki,' " *Journal of the Oriental Institute, Baroda* 38 (March–June 1989): 217–44.

47. Ibid., 227.

48. Arthur Berriedale Keith, "The Date of the Ramayana," *Journal of the Royal Asiatic Society* 47 (1915): 318–28; Camille Bulcke, "About Vālmīki," *Journal of the Oriental Institute, Baroda* 8 (1958–59): 121–31, and "More About Vālmīki," ibid., 346–48.

49. The first Maurya, Candragupta, was also the first grand unifier in Indian history. As a result, he can be made into a kind of the grand ancestor of the modern Indian state. See K. A. Nilakanta Sastri, ed., *A Comprehensive History of India,* vol. 2, *The Mauryas and Satavahanas, 325 B.C.–A.D. 300* (Bombay: Orient Longmans, 1957); R. C. Majumdar, ed., *The Age of Imperial Unity,* vol. 2 of *The History and Culture of the Indian People* (Bombay: Bharatiya Vidya Bhavan, 1968); and Jawaharlal Nehru, *Discovery of India* (New York: John Day, 1946), 123–26 (note esp. the quotation from H. G. Wells on 126). On Aśoka, see the classic study by Romila Thapar, *Aśoka and the Decline of the Mauryas* (Oxford: Oxford University Press, 1961), which also translates the edicts. For a general collection of the edicts, see G. Srinivasa Murti and A. N. Krishna Aiyangar, *Edicts of Aśoka (Priyadarśin),* intro. K. V. Rangaswami Aiyangar (Madras: Adyar Library, 1950).

50. Niharranjan Ray, *Maurya and Post-Maurya Art: A Study in Social and Formal Contrasts* (New Delhi: Indian Council of Historical Research, 1975); D. C. Sircar, *Inscriptions of Aśoka,* 3d rev. ed. (New Delhi: Government of India, 1975), and *Asokan Studies* (Calcutta: Indian Museum, 1979).

51. Minor Rock Edict 1.7–8 (Sircar, *Aśokan Studies,* 11).

52. Consider Aśoka's program carefully. He banned killing, which precluded brahminical sacrifices (Rock Edict 1.2). Rāma kills demons who prevent the sages in the forest from sacrificing. Aśoka banned religious assemblies (*samājās*) except for those that propagate his *dhamma* (Rock Edict 1.3–5; Rock Edict 9.7–9), and he looked down on religious festivals and women's rites (Rock Edict 9.2–6). Vālmīki says that festivals and assemblies (*utsavāśca samājāśca*) thrive in a state with a king (2.61.13). Aśoka propagated his *dhamma,* at times personally, through images of celestial cars, elephants, and hell-fire and through abstract moral discourses, just the opposite of Vālmīki's approach (Rock Edict 4.3). The minor edict at Bhabra recommended didactic rather than narrative discourse: in addition to *dhamma,* sermons on "the Excellence of the Discipline, the Lineage of the Noble One, the Future Fears, the Verses of the Sage, the *Sūtra* of Silence, the Questions of Upatissa, and the Admonition spoken by the Lord Buddha to Rāhula on the subject of false speech" (Thapar, *Aśoka,* 261). And of course Aśoka appointed *Dharma-mahāmātras* active in all religious

groups (he singles out brahmins for special mention) to insure his *dhamma* is propagated and obeyed (Rock Edict 5.9–15, esp. 10–11 and 14).

53. S. P. Gupta, *The Roots of Indian Art* (Delhi: B. R. Publishing, 1980).

54. For the Śuṅga period generally, with copious citations of the documentary evidence, see Bindeshwari Prasad Sinha, *The Comprehensive History of Bihar* (Patna: Kashi Prasad Jayaswal Research Institute, 1974), vol. 1, part 1; Binod Chandra Sinha, *History of the Śuṅga Dynasty* (Varanasi: Bharatiya Publishing House, 1977); and Nilakanta Sastri, ed., *A Comprehensive History of India,* vol. 2, *The Mauryas and Satavahanas.*

55. B. B. Lal and K. N. Dikshit, "Sringaverpura: A Key-Site for the Protohistory and Early History of the Central Ganga Valley," *Puruttatva* 10 (1978–79): 1–8; also see the successive progress reports in *Indian Archaeology—A Review,* for the years 1977–78, 1982–83, 1983–84, and 1984–85.

56. Lal confirmed the identity of these coins in a personal conversation, May 1989, Purana Qila, Delhi.

57. G. R. Sharma, *The Excavations at Kauśāmbī (1957–1959): The Defences and the Śyenaciti of the Puruṣamedha* (Allahabad: University of Allahabad, 1960).

58. Especially detailed is Himanshu Ray, *Monastery and Guild: Commerce under the Sātavāhanas* (Delhi: Oxford University Press, 1986). The inscriptions at Bharhūt and Sāñcī would indicate that significant wealth was in the hands of monastics, too. Compare Heinrich Lüders, ed., *Bharhut Inscriptions,* Corpus inscriptionum indicarum, vol. 2, part 2, rev. E. Waldschmidt and M. A. Mehendale (Ootacamund: Archaeological Survey of India, 1963); and Debalal Mitra, *Sanchi,* 2d ed. (New Delhi: Archaeological Survey of India, 1965).

59. See Ray, *Maurya and Post-Maurya Art,* and Gupta, *Roots of Indian Art.*

60. According to the *Aśokavadāna,* Aśoka became extremely generous in his old age and as a result was removed from office; see Thapar, *Aśoka and the Decline of the Mauryas,* 192.

61. For such speculations, see the general histories cited in note 54. H. D. Sankalia has even suggested that the dissolution extended far beyond the royal court. He noted a marked increase in the evidence of drinking and the import of Roman wine into India during the first century B.C.E. See Sankalia, *The Ramayana in Historical Perspective,* 47–48, 94. Unfortunately, Sankalia did not detail the statistical calculations necessary to support his conclusion. It is important to note, however, that they are not invalidated by an occasional Roman wine-jug that happened to find its way to India prior to the first century.

62. See, for example, Aśoka's First Minor Rock Edict.

63. Ayodhyā stone inscription of Dhana[deva], in D. C. Sircar, *Select Inscriptions Bearing on Indian History and Civilization,* vol. 1, *From the Sixth Century B.C. to the Sixth Century A.D.,* 2d ed. (Calcutta: University of Calcutta Press, 1965), 95.

64. Madhav M. Deshpande, *Sociolinguistic Attitudes in India: A Historical Reconstruction* (Ann Arbor, Mich.: Karoma Publishers, 1979), 7, ascribes a similar attitude to Kātyāyana, according to whom *dharma* can be acquired only through using Sanskrit.

65. I doubt very much whether the *śramaṇas,* the wandering mendicants who followed heterodox traditions like Buddhism, would have criticized brahminical *dharma* much. For all their differences, they at least had one thing in common with the advocates of a brahminical *dharma:* the ideal of *dharma* itself, action not motivated by a desire for results.

True, Buddhists may have had better days to look back on. True, too, their later mythographers were harsh on Puṣyamitra. But relations between Buddhists and brahmins cannot have been quite so strained as later generations remembered. All along the trade routes patrons of Buddhism, together with Buddhist clerics, built great monuments that still astound people today, such as Bharhūt and Sāñcī. We also know that advocates of heterodox and brahminical traditions could and did live side by side in peace, sometimes under the same royal roof.

On *śramaṇa*s in general, G. C. Pande, *Śramaṇa Tradition: Its History and Contribution to Indian Culture* (Ahmedabad: L. D. Institute of Indology, 1978), is tightly packed with insights.

66. See Walter Ruben, "The Minister Jābāli in Vālmīki's Rāmāyaṇa: The Portrait of One of the Indian Materialists," in *Studies in Ancient Indian Thought* (Calcutta: Indian Studies, Past and Present, 1966), 1–24. Long ago K. T. Telang noted that "some of the stanzas in the speech of Jâbâli bear a striking resemblance to some of the stanzas quoted in the *Sarvadarśanasangraha* as belonging to Brihaspati, the ringleader of the Chârvâka movement" (*Was the Rāmāyaṇa Copied from Homer?* 40).

67. Himanshu Ray (*Monastery and Guild*) contains good discussions of the archaeological and literary evidence.

68. On ritual activity out of desire for fruits, see G. U. Thite, *Sacrifice in the Brahmana-texts* (Pune: University of Poona, 1975), esp. 230: "One may have as many desires as one can. It is never too much in desires (*na vai kāmānām atiriktam asti*) (Ś[atapatha-]B[rāhmaṇa] 8.7.2.19; 9.4.2.28, 3.15, 5.1.40)." Compare page 226: "In the Brāhmaṇa-texts, there are so many results [of successful sacrifices] told that it is almost futile to attempt their classification." For Kṛṣṇa's contrary advice, see *Bhagavad-gītā* 2.47. Deshpande points out that the mythology of Paraśurāma would have provided an ideal justification for overthrowing Bṛhadratha (*Sociolinguistic Attitudes in India,* 7, see also 6). Puṣyamitra seems to have come from the regions south and west of the Ganges, but if he was a Śuṅga, as at least one later relative was, he belonged to the lineage of Bharadvāja, not Bhṛgu. For an as yet tentative identification of an anti-Bhārgava faction in the *Mahābhārata,* and one whose concerns are reminiscent not only of the *Rāmāyaṇa* but also of Aśoka's edicts (a similar phrase appears in the edicts), see Norvin Hein, "Epic *Sarvabhūtahite Ratah*: A Byword of Non-Bhārgava Editors," *Annals, Bhandarkar Oriental Research Institute* 67 (1986): 17–34.

69. For actual evidence of this wealth, see H. Lüders, ed., *Bharhut Inscriptions.* Gregory Schopen has pointed out how these inscriptions leave no doubt some Buddhist clerics were wealthy, although that would violate the precepts given by the texts; see "Archaeology and Protestant Presuppositions in the Study of Indian Buddhism," *History of Religions* 31 (August 1991): 1–23.

70. Readers without Sanskrit may consult the translation by Edwin Gerow in the wonderful *Theater of Memory: The Plays of Kālidāsa,* ed. Barbara Stoler Miller (New York: Columbia University Press, 1984), 253–312.

71. Quoted from Romila Thapar, *Aśoka and the Decline of the Mauryas,* 266.

72. Romila Thapar, *From Lineage to State: Social Formations in the Mid-First Millennium* B.C. *in the Ganga Valley* (Bombay: Oxford University Press, 1984).

73. Vālmīki's efforts adopted a literary and artistic form that achieved new popularity in the Śuṅga period, the monumental narrative. But within the parameters of that form he managed to invoke the self-evidence of age-old tradition. He mystified the conflict implicit in a brahminical conception of *dharma* by employing distinctly recognizable and venerable brahminical themes. To be sure, a gulf separates Vālmīki's citified brahminism from the older brahminical ritualism, associated with a village-based lineage-society. Vālmīki has virtually no use for the Vedic gods. He is more well disposed to sacrifice, but his attitudes are ambiguous. Rāma may protect brahminical sacrificers; but demons, too, sacrifice successfully (cf. Indrajita), and results everyone longs for—the results of Rāma's rule—are obtained only when Rāma's ritual installation is interrupted. Nevertheless, as Madhusudan Madhavlal Pathak notes in his *Similes in the Ramayana* (Vadodara, India: Maharaja Sayajirao University of Baroda, 1968), Vālmīki's metaphors show him to be a brahminical loyalist. Of greater significance here, the architecture of the *Rāmāyaṇa*'s defining narrative quotes five important brahminical motifs.

First, Vālmīki's world, like that of the Vedic sacrificers, was at its very core bipartite. It consisted of the inhabited world, where a person enjoyed the fruits of action (in the Vedas the village, for Vālmīki the city), and the uninhabited world where one acted by way of renouncing enjoyment (the sacrificial ground, the jungle).

Second, in contrast to the heterodox *śramaṇas*, who rejected violence, Vālmīki, like the ancient Vedic seers (*ṛṣis*), discerned in violence the source of human good (e.g., the famous *puruṣa-sūkta, Ṛg-veda* 10.90). In Vedic tradition, violence and division created the world; in the *Rāmāyaṇa*—and in the Vedas, too—violence and division recreated the world.

Third, in both Vedic practice and Vālmīki's virtue one acquires the fruits of action in the same, paradoxical manner: *tyāga,* renunciation. As a result, Rāma's actions are strikingly reminiscent of the sacrifices he takes pains to protect: he renounces, and through renunciation he receives even more.

Fourth, Vālmīki adopts the Vedic mythology of evil. He envisions evil as incarnate in the demonic nightstalkers (the *rakṣās* or *rākṣasās*), who defile sacrifices, devour flesh, and, in Rāvaṇa's case, desecrate *dharma.* Unlike Buddhist storytellers, neither the Vedas nor Vālmīki hold out much hope for persuading these demons. They must be killed.

Fifth, the effects of observing *dharma* are similar to those of Vedic practice: both eliminate faults (*doṣas*). But whereas the purity gained from Vedic practice accrues primarily to the sponsor of the rites, the purity of observing *dharma* is available to all. Later Indians would tell how Rāma's victory eliminated evil and initiated a wonderful new age.

In the *Rāmāyaṇa,* Vālmīki objectified and enacted the threat that brahminical *dharma* would, if taken seriously, lead to society's dissolution. Then he used the resources of ancient brahminical tradition to construct a narrative that transmuted the problems into opportunities. In the forests of renunciation Rāma faced and defeated the demons of personal desire. In this way, Vālmīki provided ancient Indians with a convincing social fiction.

On the Vedic tradition generally, see esp. J. C. Heesterman, *The Inner Conflict of Tradition: Essays in Indian Ritual, Kingship, and Society* (Chicago: University of Chicago Press, 1985); Brian K. Smith, *Reflections on Resemblance, Ritual, and Religion* (New York: Oxford University Press, 1989); Frits Staal, *Agni: The Ritual of the Fire Altar* (Berkeley, Calif.: Asian Humanities Press, 1983); and more prosaically, Thite, *Sacrifice in the Brahmana-texts.*

74. See D. C. Sircar, "The Decline of Buddhism in Bengal," in *Studies in the Religious Life of Ancient and Medieval India* (Delhi: Motilal Banarsidass, 1971), 183–205.

75. See Walter Ruben, *Die homerischen und die altindischen Epen,* Sitzungsberichte der Akademie der Wissenschaften der DDR, Jahrgang 1973, no. 24 (Berlin: Akademie-Verlag, 1975); see also *Die gesellschaftliche Entwicklung im alten Indien,* 6 vols. (Berlin: Akademie-Verlag, 1967–74).

Chapter 3: Hiding One's Limitations

1. I have developed the analysis in this and the next section in greater detail in "Epic Persuasion: Religion and Rhetoric in the *Iliad* and Vālmīki's *Rāmāyaṇa*" (Ph.D. diss., University of Chicago, 1986); for a similarly concise summary, with a somewhat different application, see my "Verbal Craft and Religious Act in the *Iliad.*" On Homer's treatment of speeches, see further Dieter Lohmann, *Die Komposition der Reden in der Ilias* (Berlin: Walter de Gruyter, 1970). The literature on rhetoric in ancient Greece more generally is immense; see esp. George A. Kennedy, *The Art of Persuasion in Greece* (Princeton, N.J.: Princeton University Press, 1963), and with greater specificity, "The Ancient Dispute over Rhetoric in Homer," *American Journal of Philology* 78 (1957): 23–35; other helpful, general works include Charles S. Baldwin, *Ancient Rhetoric and Poetic* (New York: Macmillan, 1924); Harry Caplan, *Of Eloquence: Studies in Ancient and Medieval Rhetoric,* ed. Anne King and Helen North (Ithaca, N.Y.: Cornell University Press, 1970): Marcel Delaunois, "Comment parlent les héros d'Homère: La Question de l'enchaînement des idées dans l'éloquence grecque," *Les Études Classiques* 20 (1952): 80–92; Eric A. Havelock and Jackson P. Hershbell, eds., *Communication Arts in the Ancient World* (New York: Hastings House, 1978); and

Marsh McCall, *Ancient Rhetorical Theories of Simile and Comparison* (Cambridge: Harvard University Press, 1969).

2. The effect centers on the identical metrical placement of the nearly homonymous antonyms, *achos* (grief, affliction), and *akos* (remedy). Phonetic similarity is confined to the neighborhood of the virtual homonyms: both are preceded by a syllable containing a short, front vowel followed by a sibilant and a dental, aspirated where the following guttural is aspirated, nonaspirated where the following guttural is not aspirated. In both lines, elision bridges the penthemimeral caesura, the lost vowels completing an e-i pair with the vowel in the preceding syllable. Both near homonyms are followed by a verb that begins with epsilon (one in a diphthong), but now aspiration is reversed. *Ch* is followed by a smooth breathing, *k* by a rough breathing. Colometrically, the lines are identical: trithemimeral and penthemimeral caesurae and bucolic diaereseis. Both phrases after the diaereseis are enjambed quite necessarily, and both begin new clauses. The only metrical difference is in the fourth foot: the verb in the first line is dactylic, in the second, spondaic.

3. Trivial exceptions are those where repetition is given in the structure of the language itself and so cannot be attributed to rhetorical effort, for example, the repeated enclitic *te* meaning "and."

4. Note, too, that one figure is noticeably absent. Homer's renowned simile is almost never found in speeches that attempt to persuade. In seeking to persuade, Homer's characters make comparisons only with items that fall within the same general systems of relations as those whom they are trying to persuade; that is, they make comparisons only with (exemplary) human beings and with the gods.

5. For an analysis of speaking in the *Rāmāyaṇa* that relies on the Southern Recension rather than the critical edition, see Renate Söhnen, *Untersuchungen zur Komposition von Reden und Gesprächen im Ramayana,* 2 vols., Studien zur Indologie und Iranistik, 6 (Reinbek: Verlag für orientalistische Fachpublikationen, 1979). Studies of rhetoric in South Asia are much more limited than are those in ancient Greece, largely because formal rhetoric was a Greek invention. For the broader context, see Robert T. Oliver, *Communication and Culture in Ancient India and China,* (Syracuse, N.Y.: Syracuse University Press, 1971), and the rather unsatisfactory (because unanalytical) volume by S. C. De, *Public Speeches in Ancient and Medieval India (Based on Sanskrit and Prakrit Literature),* rev. ed. (Delhi: Ajanta Publications, 1976).

6. As Sheldon Pollock also notes in his translation of the *Ayodhyā-kāṇḍa,* 368, note pertaining to 20.32.

7. Because the Sanskrit word for fate (*daiva*) derives from the word for god (*deva*), this verse essentially articulates a variety of humanism. The proper end of man (*puruṣa*) is determined by manliness (*pauruṣam*), not fate (*daiva*).

8. The four parts of the verse are also thematically distinct. The first quarter-verse describes Lakṣmaṇa (literally, "today . . . of me, possessor of powerful weapons"); the third describes Daśaratha ("to make the king powerless"); the fourth describes Rāma ("and you powerful, oh powerful one"). The second quarter-verse states the act of manifestation that brings these three together ("the power will appear"). The initial word, *adya,* "today," also begins the next verse, each of whose four parts is a phrase in apposition to the words that refer to Lakṣmaṇa in the first quarter-verse above.

9. Other speeches in the *Rāmāyaṇa* are even more eloquent and polished than this one, and they show these traits to an even higher degree. See, for example, the speech in which Sītā beseeches Rāvaṇa, if that is the right verb, in Janasthana, *Rām.* 3.45.29–43. Perhaps Vālmīki wanted us to see in Lakṣmaṇa's lack of supreme eloquence a sign of the tense situation, or better yet, of the agitated manner in which Lakṣmaṇa responds to it.

10. There is a simple illustration of the difference. A standard topic in Homeric metrics is the extent to which Homer's lines are enjambed: that is, the extent to which Homer comes to a full stop at the end of the line. See, for example, Albert B. Lord, "Homer and Huso III: Enjambement in Greek and Southslavic Song," *Transactions and Proceedings of the American Philo-*

logical Association 79 (1948): 113–24, which started many discussions. The question would never arise in Vālmīki, for he invariably comes to what Homer scholars would consider a full stop at the end of each verse, even in those relatively rare occasions when the next verse continues the thought.

11. I use the cumbersome adjective "individuated" rather than "individual," because I do not wish to invoke any connotations of European "individualism." By "individuated" I mean that power comes in distinct, isolated units. The appropriate noun to associate with the adjective is not "the individual" but the neuter, characterless "individuum."

12. The central human repository of power provides a concise study in the contrast with the *Iliad.* In Homer, the king is *anax andrōn,* literally, "sovereign of men" (that is, "of males"); in the *Rāmāyaṇa,* he is, to be sure, *nṛpa,* "protector of human beings," but he is also *mahīpati,* "lord of the earth," and *bandhur lokasya,* "relative of the world."

13. In implying that *dharma* is individuated I mean to point to two characteristics: (1) each person must follow his or her own *dharma,* specified by a number of defining characteristics (as Kṛṣṇa teaches in the *Mahābhārata,* no one else's *dharma* will do); (2) in determining *dharma* the kinds of social concerns that Homer's heroes raise routinely are not allowed.

14. It was not, of course, impossible for Homer and Vālmīki to have composed speeches that violate established patterns of persuasion. Many poets have used words, arguments, and images that violate the way speech is normally configured, among other reasons, because audiences find such violations significant or disturbing or both. An obvious example is the way later Greeks used verbal repetition and nonempirical, nonsocial verbal effects to image the foreign both outside their societies (barbaric speech) and within them (the so-called Asiatic modes of discourse and, in more extravagant form, the mutterings of witches). The Greek word *barbaros* (from which English "barbaric" derives) was constructed simply by putting an adjective ending on repetitious babble: *bar + bar + os.*

15. In English, the Sanskrit compound *dharmabandhaḥ* (literally, "*dharma*-bind") is best translated as a phrase, "the bind of *dharma.*" It is possible to construe the genitive in this phrase ("of *dharma*") in one of two ways. The more obvious rendering, in terms of classical European grammar, is as a subjective genitive (as in the phrase, "the government's interdiction"). In this case, "bind of *dharma*" refers to the constraint with which *dharma* (subject) binds Daśaratha. But one may also construe the phrase as an objective genitive (as in the phrase, "the interdiction of murder") and produce a more subtle reading. In that case "bind of *dharma*" refers to the constraint that binds *dharma* (object) itself. Naturally, Sanskrit grammar has its own terms for analyzing compounds. In these terms, the first rendering of *dharmabandhaḥ* is a *karmadhāraya,* a compound that postulates a relationship of identity between the first and second elements ("the bind is *dharma*"). The second rendering is a *tatpuruṣa,* a compound that postulates an oblique relationship—some relationship other than identity—between the final element and the element that precedes it ("the constraint of or on *dharma*").

16. Many Indians are profoundly disturbed by this scene, so much so that many scholars have tried to argue that the incident is a perverse, later addition. See, for example, Camille Bulcke, "The Repudiation of Sītā," *Journal of the Oriental Institute, Baroda* 1 (1951–52): 48–50; Nilmadhav Sen, "The Fire-Ordeal of Sītā—A Later Interpolation in the Rāmāyaṇa?" *Journal of the Oriental Institute, Baroda* 1 (1951–52): 201–6; and G. H. Bhatt, "The Fire-Ordeal of Sītā: An Interpolation in the Vālmīki-Rāmāyaṇa," *Journal of the Oriental Institute, Baroda* 5 (1955–56): 292. During the televised "Ramayan," the portrayal of Sītā's fire ordeal sparked civil unrest. I am somewhat embarrassed to confess that I find the incident rather to my tastes, not because I do not find the treatment of Sītā repulsive, but precisely because I do. Through most of the epic, I find Rāma to be a rather flat and uninteresting character. His refusal to accept Sītā provides some of the ambiguity, complexity, indeed, genuine humanity in which I take aesthetic delight. At the same time, I hardly think Vālmīki wrote this section to indulge my tastes.

17. Eliade's views on cosmogony, like most of his views, are repeated in a variety of books. Perhaps the most important are *Cosmos and History; Myth and Reality;* and *The Sacred and the Profane: The Nature of Religion,* trans. Willard R. Trask (New York: Harcourt, Brace, & World, 1959). For Charles Long's views, see his earlier book, *Alpha: The Myths of Creation* (New York: George Braziller, 1963), and his later article, "Cosmogony," in *The Encyclopedia of Religion,* ed. Mircea Eliade (New York: Macmillan, 1987), 4:94–99.

18. For a brief but excellent summary, see William LaFleur, "Biography," in *The Encyclopedia of Religion,* ed. Mircea Eliade (New York: Macmillan, 1987), 2:220–24. See further Frank E. Reynolds and Donald Capps, eds., *The Biographical Process: Studies in the History and Psychology of Religion* (The Hague: Mouton, 1976). On Muhammad, see especially Annemarie Schimmel, *And Mohammed Is His Messenger: The Veneration of the Prophet in Islamic Piety* (Chapel Hill: University of North Carolina Press, 1985), and William A. Graham, *Divine Word and Prophetic Word in Early Islam: A Reconsideration of the Sources, with Special Reference to the Divine Saying or Hadith Qudsi* (The Hague: Mouton, 1977).

19. See note 37 to the introduction. Eliade's views are anticipated by the Cambridge Ritualists, who found Homer's Olympian religion to be devoid of genuine religious content. See Gilbert Murray, *The Rise of the Greek Epic,* 3d ed., rev. and enl. (Oxford: Clarendon Press, 1924), most pointedly 265, "The Homeric religion . . . was not really religion at all," and *Five Stages of Greek Religion* (Boston: Beacon Press, 1951), esp. chap. 2.

Actually, Jacobi's view, like Eliade's, is somewhat more complicated. Because Sītā appears as a figure in later Vedic mythology, Jacobi postulated a relationship between Rāma and the Vedic god Indra that was later lost. But unlike the notion of a later Vaiṣṇava redaction, this view has few takers today. For further elaboration, see J. L. Brockington, "Religious Attitudes in Vālmīki's *Rāmāyaṇa,*" *Journal of the Royal Asiatic Society* (1976): 108–29, and "Rāmo dharmabhṛtāṃ varaḥ," *Indologica Taurinensia* 5 (1977): 55–68. It is possible, of course, to question the specifics of these views. For example, Sheldon Pollock has argued—convincingly, I think—that the issue of Rāma's divinity is rather more complex than Jacobi and Goldman wish to think. See Sheldon Pollock, "Atmānaṃ Mānuṣaṃ Manye," and "The Divine King in the Indian Epic," *Journal of the American Oriental Society* 104 (1984): 505–28.

20. I am quite deliberate when I speak of different levels of reality instead of truth and falsity. It might be worth recalling an argument John Hick made many years ago when logical positivists were pronouncing Christian teachings meaningless because they violated the criterion of verifiability. Teachings of an afterlife are indeed verifiable, Hick wrote; but they are only verifiable after death. (Of course, these teachings may not be falsifiable.) See John Hick, "Theology and Verification" reprinted in Hick, ed., *The Existence of God* (New York: Macmillan, 1964), 252–74, and the broader discussion in *Philosophy of Religion,* 2d ed. (Englewood Cliffs, N.J.: Prentice-Hall, 1973), 84–96, esp. 90–95.

21. See introduction, n. 53. The most recent major philosophical source for talk about language, or better, about literature constructing worlds is Martin Heidegger, who picks up on phrases of a poet like Friedrich Hölderlin (1770–1843): *dichterisch wohnet der Mensch* ("poetically man dwells") and *seit ein Gespräch wir sind* ("since we are a conversation"). Among other works, see the collected essays in *Poetry, Language, Thought,* trans. Albert Hofstadter (New York: Harper & Row, 1971), for example, "The Origin of the Work of Art," 15–87. There Heidegger baldly asserts: "The work [of art] opens up a *world* and keeps it abidingly in force. To be a work means to set up a world" (44); "The temple-work, in setting up a world, does not cause the material to disappear, but rather causes it to come forth for the very first time and to come into the Open of the work's world. The rock comes to be and rest and so first becomes rock" (46); and further, "Truth happens in the temple's standing where it is. This does not mean that something is correctly represented and rendered here, but that what is as a whole is brought into unconcealedness and held therein" (56). Although the example that Heidegger discusses throughout much of this essay is the Greek

temple, he eventually grants priority to poetry: "The linguistic work, the poem in the narrower sense, has a privileged position in the domain of the arts. . . . Language alone brings what is, as something that is, into the Open for the first time" (73).

This perspective contrasts, as Heidegger intimates, with an aesthetic that conceives of poetry as an imitation, or better, representation of reality. This latter trend derives paradigmatically from Plato and especially Aristotle. In *Poetics* 2 and 5.7–11 (trans. W. Hamilton Fyfe [Loeb Classical Library, 1953]), Aristotle distinguishes epic as a variety of representation (*mimēsis*). A classic modern work on the subject, Erich Auerbach's *Mimesis: The Representation of Reality in Western Literature,* trans. Willard R. Trask (Princeton: Princeton University Press, 1953), begins by contrasting Homer with the Hebrew Bible as one typical manner of representing reality in European literature.

Chapter 4: Texts, Meanings, and Social Acts

1. We do not know the titles of all of Sophocles' plays. Of those we do know, over a third pertain to the Trojan cycle.

2. Clarke, *Homer's Readers,* 133.

3. As mentioned in Chapter 2 (at note 11), the same pattern typifies the use of materials from the Trojan cycle by vase painters in the eighth century. According to Anthony Snodgrass's account, only about 10 percent of the illustrations represent scenes from the *Iliad* and the *Odyssey.*

4. The Achilles saga is recounted in ample detail in Wilhelm Roscher's *Ausführliches Lexikon der griechischen und römischen Mythologie* (Leipzig: B. G. Teubner, 1884–1937), s.v. "Achilleus."

5. For an account of the *Odyssey*'s literary descendants, see W. B. Stanford, *The Ulysses Theme: A Study in the Adaptability of a Traditional Hero* (Oxford: Basil Blackwell, 1954); see also Elisabeth Frenzel, *Stoffe der Weltliteratur: Ein Lexikon dichtungsgeschichtlicher Längsschnitte,* 4th ed. (Stuttgart: Kröner, 1976).

6. In English the most important of these talents have probably been Thomas Hobbes, Alexander Pope, and William Cowper. John Dryden and William Congreve translated parts of the poem. And no one should overlook the widely influential Elizabethan translator George Chapman.

7. Quoted in Alexander Pope, *The Iliad of Homer: Books I–IX,* ed. Maynard Mack et al., Twickenham Edition of the Poems of Alexander Pope (London: Methuen, 1967), 7:xlii. Samuel Johnson called Pope's effort "the noblest version of poetry which the world has ever seen" (ibid.). Perhaps more to the point is the comment of Pope's modern editor: "Whatever Bentley may have meant (or said), Pope's Homer was indeed the Homer of Bentley's day" (lxxvii).

8. Quoted in Matthew Arnold, *Essays Literary and Critical* (London: J. M. Dent, 1906), 224.

9. In ibid., 210–75. Compare in the same volume Francis W. Newman, "Homeric Translation in Theory and Practice: A Reply to Matthew Arnold," 276–336, and Arnold's "Last Words on Translating Homer: A Reply to Francis W. Newman," 337–80.

10. Arnold, *Essays Literary and Critical,* 250.

11. The distinction may be somewhat arbitrary. The dual service of Hellenistic literati as both poets and scholars is emphasized in Rudolf Pfeiffer, *A History of Classical Scholarship from the Beginnings to the End of the Hellenistic Age* (Oxford: Clarendon Press, 1986). Pfeiffer sees Callimachus as the preeminent example, a poet who needed original, "pure" sources if his work were to be authentic. In the earliest days, when Homeric poetry was the preserve of the rhapsodes, it does not make much sense to distinguish textual artists from textual scholars.

12. Pfeiffer cites Plato (?) *Hipparchos* 228B, and Diogenes Laertius 1.57 (ibid., 8).

13. See ibid., part 2, chaps. 2, 3, 5, and 6. For the pre-Alexandrian efforts of Antimachos of Colophon (fl. 464–410), and the division between city-texts (*hai kata tas poleis* [*ekdoseis*]) and texts

associated with a specific editor (*hai kat' andra*), see ibid., 94; but compare J. E. Sandys, *A History of Classical Scholarship,* 3 vols. (reprint, New York: Hafner, 1967), 1:34. According to Sandys, Zenodotos's work with Homer was the first attempt to restore the original of any text (1:121).

14. P. C. Divanji, "Influence of the Rāmāyaṇa on the Gujarati Literature," *Journal of the Oriental Institute, Baroda* 4 (1954–55): 46–57. See also the works cited in note 2 to the introduction.

15. The number of pages occupied in Growse's translation provides a rough gauge of each book's importance. Book 1 occupies 224 pages; book 2, 194 pages; book 3, only 44 pages; book 4 even fewer, 26 pages; book 5, a mere 42 pages; book 6, 92 pages; and book 7, 96 pages. See *The Rāmāyaṇa of Tulasīdāsa,* trans. F. S. Growse, rev. R. C. Prasad, 2d rev. ed. (Delhi: Motilal Banarsidass, 1987). For an exemplary account of the ways Tulsi's *Ramcaritmanas* is realized, see Philip Lutgendorf, *The Life of a Text: Performing the Ramcaritmanas of Tulsidas* (Berkeley and Los Angeles: University of California Press, 1991).

16. Exact figures for each *kāṇḍa* are given by U. P. Shah in his introduction to the seventh volume of the Baroda critical edition (Baroda: Oriental Institute, 1975), 51. According to Shah, the vulgate of the Southern Recension (the Bombay edition) contains 24,049 *grantha*s (primarily *śloka*s), the critical edition 18,766.

17. The additions actually represent eleven lines, 503*, 504*, and 507* in the critical edition. I have computed the percentage as eleven lines added to an original sixty-two (taking verse 35 as two lines).

18. This section, 503*, is from Goldman et al., 366 n. 8, and was translated by Sheldon Pollock.

19. If we compare Vālmīki's *Rāmāyaṇa* with a summary such as the *Rāmopākhyāna* in the *Mahābhārata,* we can see that one of the fundamental principles guiding the composition of Vālmīki's poem is full statement, complete manifestation, or total articulation. Every detail, each sequence, was (like Rāma himself) to be fully realized.

20. As one might expect, the contrast has good Vedic precedent. Mīmāmsā philosophers propound a conventionalist view of all language *except* the Vedic texts, particularly the Vedic injunctions, whose words, they say, are eternal and necessary. See P. T. Raju, 47.

21. Perhaps a personal incident will illustrate this concern. Standing in line in Pune for a ticket on the Deccan Queen to Bombay, I entered into conversation about the *Rāmāyaṇa* with the man behind me. The broadcast of Ramanand Sagar's serial *Ramayan* on Indian television had, he said, confused his mother. For all her life she had heard certain incidents told one way, but Sagar portrayed them differently. What, he asked me, really happened? I doubt that he was satisfied when I replied Sagar was doing nothing that other poets had not done with the story throughout history. Reports in the Indian news media reveal that this woman was not the only one confused.

22. Certain regional prejudices also motivate the critique. The critical edition of the *Mahābhārata* was made in Maharashtra (at Pune); the critical edition of the *Rāmāyaṇa* was made in Gujarat (at Baroda).

23. For a careful and generally convincing explication of these hints, see Pollock, "Ātmānaṃ Mānuṣaṃ Manye" and "The Divine King."

24. "Rāmam viddhi paraṃ brahma sac-cid-ānandam advayam / sarvopādhi-vinirmuktaṃ sattā-mātram agocaram" (*Adhyātma Rāmāyaṇa: The Spiritual Version of the Rama Saga,* ed. Swami Tapasyananda [Madras: Sri Ramakrishna Math, 1985], 1.1.32).

25. The most important differences are listed in ibid., 369–76.

26. Hans Bakker, *Ayodhyā* (Groningen: Egbert Forsten, 1986).

27. A. N. Jani translated a summary recently printed in Gujarati for me during a conversation at his home in Baroda, January 1989.

28. See Walter Burkert, *Greek Religion,* trans. John Raffan (Cambridge: Harvard University Press, 1985), 204.

29. So Hildebrecht Hommel, who argues that the cult of Achilles in the Black Sea represents worship of a lord of the dead who was originally entirely independent of Achilles' biography. See *Der*

Gott Achilleus (Heidelberg: Carl Winter, 1980). If he is correct, that could account for the appearance of an untamable Achilles in the *Iliad*'s defining narrative. But other explanations are possible. Walter Burkert suggests that Achilles' divinity derived from his Nereid mother (*Greek Religion,* 205). Older critics, most notably L. R. Farnell, emphasized the role of the epics; see Farnell's *Greek Hero Cults and Ideas of Immortality* (1921; reprint, Oxford: Clarendon Press, 1970).

30. Burkert, *Greek Religion,* 204.

31. On the tomb (*taphos*) of Achilles at Elis, see Pausanias 6.24.1; there are, in fact, sub-Mycenaean tombs at Elis, and perhaps one was attributed to Achilles. Other sites of the Achilles cult in mainland Greece include a sanctuary (*hieron*) on the Sparta-Arcadia road (3.20.8), a sanctuary at Brasiae in Laconia where an Achilles festival took place every year (3.24.5), and a cenotaph in Elis where, at the instructions of the oracle, women would mourn Achilles at sundown on a specified day (6.23.2). Pausanias also knows the temple of Achilles at Ister on the Black Sea (3.19.11–13).

32. For the minimalist position, see Pfeiffer, *History of Classical Scholarship from the Beginnings to the End of the Hellenistic Age,* esp. 35. According to J. E. Sandys, moral allegory is ascribed to Anaxagoras of Clazomenae, but it was probably practiced only by Anaxagoras's pupils such as, for example, Metrodorus (*History of Classical Scholarship,* 1:30). For more generous but more speculative assessments, see N. J. Richardson, "Homeric Professors in the Age of the Sophists," *Proceedings, Cambridge Philological Society* 201 (1975): 65–81, and Lamberton, *Homer the Theologian.*

33. Many treatments of classical scholarship ignore allegorical readings as "unscholarly." I have relied heavily on Clarke, *Homer's Readers.*

34. Don Cameron Allen, *Mysteriously Meant: The Rediscovery of Pagan Symbolism and Allegorical Interpretation in the Renaissance* (Baltimore, Md.: Johns Hopkins University Press, 1970), 80. See also Clarke, *Homer's Readers;* Allen, *Mysteriously Meant,* 90 and 96; and Lamberton, *Homer the Theologian,* 224.

35. J. Tate tries to make an even larger case, that allegory was never popular among the Greeks. See "On the History of Allegorism," *Classical Quarterly* 28 (1934): 105–15, esp. 110, and 110 n. 4. But Tate's contention is too sweeping.

36. On Homer's paganism, we should keep in mind that his description of the activities of the gods contrasted sharply with the lack of religious interest displayed in Dares's and Dictys's Latin accounts of the Trojan war, the accounts that were responsible for knowledge of the Homeric epic during the Western European middle ages. See Clarke, *Homer's Readers,* chap. 1.

Renaissance humanists used allegory to demonstrate that Homer contained veiled references to Christian truth and even to important figures in the Jewish and Christian traditions. See Allen, *Mysteriously Meant,* 100–105.

37. An example is Anne Dacier (1654–1720), translator of Homer and coeditor of the Delphin edition of Latin texts. In the so-called battle of the ancients and moderns (a literary dispute over the respective merits of ancient and innovative styles, satirized by Jonathan Swift in *The Battle of the Books*), Dacier was an ardent defender of the ancients. Among her keenest weapons was allegory, which she used to protect Homer's gods. These efforts were widely attacked. See Clarke, *Homer's Readers,* 73–77, 123–31.

38. Clarke, *Homer's Readers,* 106–7.

39. Horace *Ars poetica,* lines 359–60.

40. Alexander Pope, *Essay on Criticism,* 1.179–80 (Alexander Pope, *Pastoral Poetry and an Essay on Criticism,* ed. Emile Audra and Aubrey Williams [London: Methuen, 1961]). On this passage Pope's editors cite similar sentiments from John Dryden's work *The Author's Apology for Heroic Poetry:* "Ought they not rather, in modesty, to doubt of their own judgments, when they think this or that expression in Homer, Virgil, Tasso, or Milton's *Paradise,* to be too far strained, than positively to conclude that 'tis all fustion, and mere nonsense?" (p. 261, note on 1.180).

41. There had been hints of the coming cold. For example, in a book published posthumously, *Conjectures Académiques ou Dissertation sur l'Iliade* (1715), François Hédelin, the abbé d'Aubignac (1604–76), voluminously catalogues the *Iliad*'s defects and inconsistencies. He does so to argue that the poet Homer was only a product of later imagination and that the Homeric epics were nothing more than shorter poems clumsily stitched together. See the extensive summary and discussion in Clarke, *Homer's Readers,* 150–55.

42. For the standard works, see Adam Parry, ed., *The Making of Homeric Verse: The Collected Papers of Milman Parry* (Oxford: Clarendon Press, 1971), and Albert B. Lord, *The Singer of Tales* (Cambridge: Harvard University Press, 1960).

43. Snodgrass, "An Historical Homeric Society?"

44. Xenophon *Symposium* 3.4–6, 4.6–8; see also Lamberton, 40, who also cites Plato *Republic* 598d (n. 142). Later in the *Republic,* Plato calls Homer the "educator of Greece" (*tēn Hellada pepaideuken*), but as is widely known, Plato was not exactly kind to Homer. On the sophists and Homer, see Sandys, *A History of Classical Scholarship,* 1:27–29.

45. Isocrates *Panegyricus,* trans. George Norlin in vol. 1 of the Loeb Classical Library edition of Isocrates (1928). Plutarch *Alexander* 8.2, 15.4–5; see 26 for the alleged role of a vision of Homer in the founding of Pharos. (I have used the text in vol. 7 of *Plutarch's Lives,* ed. Bernadotte Perrin, Loeb Classical Library, 1949.) J. R. Hamilton, *Plutarch, Alexander: A Commentary* (Oxford: Clarendon Press, 1969), 38, note to 15.7.

46. Ulrich Wilcken, *Alexander the Great,* trans. G. C. Richards, with introduction by Eugene N. Borza (New York: W. W. Norton, 1967), 57.

47. Pfeiffer, *A History of Classical Scholarship from the Beginnings to the End of the Hellenistic Age,* 133.

48. For the political uses of the Trojan tale in the Middle Ages, see Jean Seznec, *The Survival of the Pagan Gods: The Mythological Tradition and Its Place in Renaissance Humanism and Art,* trans. Barbara F. Sessions (New York: Pantheon Books, 1953), 24ff.

49. See, for example, J. C. Scaliger's *Poetices libri septem,* discussed in Clarke, *Homer's Readers,* 117–18.

50. Kirsi Simonsuuri, *Homer's Original Genius: Eighteenth Century Notions of the Early Greek Epic (1688–1798)* (Cambridge: Cambridge University Press, 1979).

51. A classical education had never been egalitarian. Elitism was built into the term "classical" itself. In late antiquity Aulus Gellius had distinguished a *scriptor classicus,* a "classical writer," from a *scriptor proletarius,* a "proletarian" one. In the early sixteenth century, classics on the humanistic model were designed to provide aristocrats with invaluable social skills: the language they needed to communicate and the ability to perform well with it in public.

52. Arnold, *Essays Literary and Critical,* 220. On the prominence of the British aristocracy of the eighteenth century, and of how they differed from other European aristocrats in their openness to mercantilism, see Marilyn Butler, *Romantics, Rebels, and Reactionaries: English Literature and Its Background, 1750–1830* (New York: Oxford University Press, 1982).

53. Arnold, *Essays Literary and Critical,* 220.

54. John Cowper Powys, *Homer and the Aether* (London: Macdonald, 1959), 16.

55. James E. Russell, *German Higher Schools,* new ed. (London: Longmans, Green, 1910), 70–75.

56. See Ganesh N. Devy, *After Amnesia: Tradition and Change in Indian Literary Criticism* (New Delhi: Orient Longmans, 1991), for a remarkable initial attempt.

57. Tulsi's *Ramcaritmanas* teaches a similar lesson: "The virtues of Raghunāyak are the source of every blessing. Those who listen to them reverently cross the ocean of existence. They do not need a boat" (*Ramcaritmanas* 5, Dohā 60 [Growse translation]).

58. Compare, for example, the rather rote productions: K. S. Ramaswami Sastri, *Studies in Ramayana,* Kirti Mandir Lecture Series, 9 (Baroda: Baroda State, Department of Education,

[1948?]), and K. Viswanathan, "The Influence of the 'Ramayana' and the 'Mahabharata' on Indian Life and Literature," *Aryan Path* 37 (1966): 276–80.

59. Notice in North American edition of *Hinduism Today,* May 1993, 27.

60. Compare *Adhyātma-rāmāyaṇa* 2.6.64–92.

61. Conversation in A. N. Jani's home, Baroda, January 1989.

62. Rosaldo, *Culture and Truth,* 39–40.

63. The major exception has been, of course, the Baroda critical edition.

Chapter 5: Beyond Dialogue, Violence, and Meaning

1. McGann, *The Beauty of Inflections,* 157–58; compare 190 and 201. See also McGann's *Romantic Ideology.*

2. Swidler et al., *Death or Dialogue?* 104; compare Paul Knitter's comments: "We are on the same team, sharing the same vision, working at the same task" (*Death or Dialogue?* 85).

3. Hans Küng et al., *Christianity and the World Religions: Paths of Dialogue with Islam, Hinduism, and Buddhism,* trans. Peter Heinegg (Garden City, N.Y.: Doubleday, 1986), 443.

4. Anderson is criticizing Berlin's appeal to the human ability to communicate in an attempt to stop liberal pluralism from falling into complete, nihilistic relativism. See Anderson, *A Zone of Engagement,* 245.

5. Ibid., 335.

6. Georges Bataille, *Theory of Religion,* trans. Robert Hurley (New York: Zone Books, 1989), 110.

7. Ibid., 57.

8. Ibid., 100.

9. Girard, *Violence and the Sacred,* 316.

10. Ibid., 19.

11. Ibid., 15.

12. Ibid. But spirals of violence are not entirely unknown in European and European-American theaters (such as theaters of war). When such violence threatens, Girard conveniently forgets the distinction between primitive and civilized. Consider, for example, the end of the book, where Girard asserts that religious violence applies universally (316–17), that "a violent projection of violence . . . truly pertains to all societies including our own" (317), that the thriving of ethnology today "is evidence of a new sacrificial crisis" (318), and that now "the essential violence returns to us in a spectacular manner—not only in the form of a violent history but also in the form of subversive knowledge" (318).

13. Ibid., 46.

14. Murray, *Early Greece,* 60. For a more ethnographic account of vengeance, see Rosaldo, "Grief and a Headhunter's Rage," in *Truth and Culture,* 1–21.

15. There may be other reasons, too, why Girard is not entirely convincing. See, for example, Ivan Strenski, *Religion in Relation: Method, Application, & Moral Location,* Studies in Comparative Religion (Columbia: University of South Carolina Press, 1992).

16. Prominent exponents of this current have included members of the so-called Chicago school, Joachim Wach, Mircea Eliade, and Joseph Kitagawa.

17. Mircea Eliade, *Patterns in Comparative Religion,* trans. Rosemary Sheed (New York: New American Library, 1963).

18. See, for example, Smith's devastating criticism in chapter 1 of *To Take Place.*

19. In, for example, Kurt Rudolph, "Eliade und die 'Religionsgeschichte,' " in *Geschichte und Probleme der Religionswissenschaft,* 381–411.

20. Eliade, *Patterns in Comparative Religion,* 5–6.

21. Mircea Eliade, "The History of Religions in Retrospect: 1912 and After," in *The Quest,* 21. This article was originally published in *The Journal of Bible and Religion* 31 (1963): 98–107.

22. Charles H. Long, *Significations: Signs, Symbols, and Images in the Interpretation of Religion* (Philadelphia: Fortress Press, 1986). For a balanced, recent assessment of Eliade's possible fascism, see David Cave, *Mircea Eliade's Vision for a New Humanism* (New York: Oxford University Press, 1993), 5–11 and 13 n. 5, and at much greater length Mac Linscott Ricketts, *Mircea Eliade: The Romanian Roots, 1907–1945,* 2 vols. (Boulder, Colo.: East European Monographs, 1988).

23. Long, *Significations,* 196 and 79–91. As one might expect, Long invokes Hegel's celebrated master-slave dialectic: " 'The master is trapped by his own power, which he can only seek to maintain. . . . Only the slave, therefore, has the potentiality for escaping an unbalanced reciprocity and for becoming truly free' " (168–69). In Long's eyes, the Enlightenment ancestry of the history of religions is ambiguous. On the one hand, there was a universalizing impetus to find religion and religious truth everywhere; on the other, it participated in the dynamics of conquest and signification that I mention in the text. This ambiguity is mirrored in Long's own relationship to the discipline. As he notes in the introduction, as a graduate student in the 1950s he "was attracted to this scholarly orientation, for it was the only discipline that responded to the religious experience and expressions of my origins in the black community of this country" (8). Perhaps for this reason, Long can write, immediately after the sentence quoted in the text, "Opaque theologies in their deconstructive tasks will be able to make common cause with folklorists, novelists, poets, and many other nontheological types who are involved in the discernment of these meanings" (196). Indeed, Long's use of Rudolf Otto's thought is strong and striking. When Long writes that communities of color "have had to face the ultimacy of reality as a daily experience in the modern world" (197), there is an unmistakable echo of his discussion of the "radical contingency" that W.E.B. DuBois faced and the *mysterium tremendum* evident in the religions of oppressed peoples more generally (165, 162–63).

In *Death or Dialogue?* 38, Knitter also talks about a "hermeneutical privilege of the poor," but with much less nuance and sense for life's ambiguities than Long is able to muster.

24. In English, see Kurt Rudolph, *Historical Fundamentals and the Study of Religions;* at greater length, see his *Geschichte und Probleme der Religionswissenschaft.*

25. Lucretius *De rerum natura* 1.101 (*Selections from Lucretius,* ed. G. E. Benfield and R. C. Reeves [London: Oxford University Press, 1967]).

26. Jonathan Z. Smith, "The Bare Facts of Ritual," in *Imagining Religion: From Babylon to Jonestown* (Chicago: University of Chicago Press, 1982), 53–65, esp. 63.

27. Joachim Wach, "Religionswissenschaft," in *Die Religion in Geschichte und Gegenwart,* 2d ed., ed. Hermann Gunkel and Leopold Zscharnack (Tübingen: J.C.B. Mohr, 1930), vol. 4, cols. 1954–59; trans. Gregory D. Alles, under the title "The History of Religions (Religionswissenschaft)," in *Introduction to the History of Religions,* ed. Joseph M. Kitagawa and Gregory D. Alles (New York: Macmillan, 1987), 159–67.

28. "Sie gilt es zu erforschen, zu verstehen, und darzustellen" (Wach, "Religionswissenschaft," col. 1955; "History of Religions," 162).

29. Joachim Wach, *Das Verstehen: Grundzüge einer Geschichte der hermeneutischen Theorie im 19. Jahrhundert,* 3 vols. (Tübingen: J.C.B. Mohr [Paul Siebeck], 1926–33).

30. David Hume, *The Natural History of Religion,* ed. H. E. Root (Stanford, Calif.: Stanford University Press, 1957), 21.

31. David Hume, *Dialogues Concerning Natural Religion* (Harmondsworth, U.K.: Penguin Books, 1990), 103.

32. Compare, for example, the Second Presidential Address of William Jones, who exhorts members of the Asiatic Society to pursue "truth unadorned by rhetorick" (quoted in Garland

Cannon, *The Life and Mind of Oriental Jones: Sir William Jones, the Father of Modern Linguistics* [Cambridge: Cambridge University Press, 1990], 224).

33. Hume, *Dialogues Concerning Natural Religion,* 115.

34. Schleiermacher—not Schleiermacher himself, but his reception among historians of religions—is another good, early example of the exclusion of persuasion about religious truth from academic discourse. Historians of religions have tended to neglect the full range of Schleiermacher's career: the educational reformer, the scholar of Plato, the lecturer on hermeneutics, the Christian theologian. Instead, they have focused attention on the youthful Schleiermacher, who wrote in *On Religion* five speeches to religion's "cultured despisers." Their use of these speeches is curious. Schleiermacher himself aims for rhetorical irresistibility. He wants to convince educated people who despise religion that they despise it for the wrong reasons, that they are themselves capable and worthy of religious practice. When historians of religions write about these speeches, they write as if Schleiermacher's aim had been to give a disinterested account of the role of internal experience in religious life. In other words, although for Schleiermacher the content was a tool for his rhetoric, historians of religions attempt to distill the content from the rhetoric. In the early twentieth century it became fashionable to justify this and similar attitudes by loosely appealing to the phenomenological slogan of "bracketing."

35. For example, Rudolf Otto, *The Philosophy of Religion Based on Kant and Fries,* trans. E. B. Dicker, foreword by W. Tudor Jones (London: Williams & Norgate, 1931), and, better known, *The Idea of the Holy,* trans. John W. Harvey (Oxford: Oxford University Press, 1923).

36. As a form of discourse, the history of religions is subject to the varieties of rhetorical criticisms applied to the humane study of cultures since the late seventies. Prominent examples include Hayden V. White, *Metahistory: The Historical Imagination in Nineteenth-Century Europe* (Baltimore, Md.: Johns Hopkins University Press, 1973); James Clifford and George Marcus, eds., *Writing Culture: The Poetics and Politics of Ethnography* (Berkeley and Los Angeles: University of California Press, 1986); and Clifford Geertz, *Works and Lives: The Anthropologist as Author* (Stanford, Calif.: Stanford University Press, 1989).

37. Wilfred Cantwell Smith, "A Universal Theology of Religion," in *Toward a Universal Theology of Religion,* ed. Leonard Swidler (Maryknoll, N.Y.: Orbis Books, 1987), 51–72, esp. 67. Two other quotations from the same article succinctly elaborate the point: "The Church does indeed sorely need, and an understanding of the world-wide history of religion can indeed provide, an intellectually strong, rationally coherent, empirically based, inductively argued, logically persuasive, transcendentally adequate, integrative theory to do justice to our faith and to our work" (56); "Any other starting-point for the journey of one's mind towards a true theology inevitably omits something. Most starting-points omit much. The history of religion omits nothing" (57).

38. Frank E. Reynolds and David Tracy, eds., *Myth and Philosophy* (Albany: SUNY Press, 1990).

39. Smith, *Imagining Religion,* xi.

Selected Bibliography

Ackerman, Robert. *J. G. Frazer: His Life and Work.* Cambridge: Cambridge University Press, 1987.

Adhyātma Rāmāyaṇa: The Spiritual Version of the Rama Saga. Ed. Swami Tapasyananda. Madras: Sri Ramakrishna Math, 1985.

Adkins, Arthur W. H. "Art, Beliefs and Values in the Later Books of the *Iliad.*" *Classical Philology* 70 (1975): 239–54.

———. "*Euchomai, euchōlē,* and *euchos* in Homer." *Classical Quarterly,* n.s., 19 (1969): 20–33.

———. " 'Friendship' and 'Self-Sufficiency' in Homer and Aristotle." *Classical Quarterly,* n.s., 13 (1963): 30–45.

———. *From the Many to the One.* Ithaca, N.Y.: Cornell University Press, 1970.

———. "Homeric Gods and the Values of Homeric Society." *Journal of Hellenic Studies* 92 (1972): 1–19.

———. "Homeric Values and Homeric Society." *Journal of Hellenic Studies* 91 (1971): 1–14.

———. *Merit and Responsibility.* Oxford: Oxford University Press, 1960.

———. *Moral Values and Political Behavior in Ancient Greece: From Homer to the End of the Fifth Century.* New York: W. W. Norton, 1972.

———. "Threatening, Abusing, and Feeling Angry in the Homeric Poems." *Journal of Hellenic Studies* 89 (1969): 7–21.

———. "Truth, *kosmos,* and *aretē* in the Homeric Poems." *Classical Quarterly,* n.s., 22 (1972): 5–18.

Allen, Don Cameron. *Mysteriously Meant: The Rediscovery of Pagan Symbolism and Allegorical Interpretation in the Renaissance.* Baltimore: Johns Hopkins University Press, 1970.
Allen, Thomas W. *Homer: The Origins and the Transmission.* Oxford: Clarendon Press, 1924.
Alles, Gregory D. "Epic Persuasion: Religion and Rhetoric in the *Iliad* and Vālmīki's *Rāmāyaṇa.*" Ph.D. diss., University of Chicago, 1986.
______. "A Fitting Approach to God: On Entering the Western Temples at Khajurāho." *History of Religions* 33 (November 1993): 161–86.
______. "Reflections on Dating 'Vālmīki.' " *Journal of the Oriental Institute, Baroda* 38 (March–June 1989): 217–44.
______. "Surface, Space, and Intention: The Parthenon and the Kandariya Mahadeva." *History of Religions* 28 (August 1988): 1–36.
______. "Verbal Craft and Religious Act in the *Iliad.*" *Religion* 18 (1988): 293–309.
______. "Wach, Eliade, and the Critique from Totality." *Numen* 35 (July 1988): 108–38.
Alper, Harvey, P., ed. *Mantra.* Albany: SUNY Press, 1989.
Anderson, Perry. *A Zone of Engagement.* London: Verso, 1992.
Aristotle. *Poetics.* Greek text with English translation. Ed. W. Hamilton Fyfe. With "Longinus" *On the Sublime* and Demetrius *On Style.* Loeb Classical Library, 1953.
Arnold, Matthew. *Essays Literary and Critical.* London: J. M. Dent, 1906.
Auerbach, Erich. *Mimesis: The Representation of Reality in Western Literature.* Trans. Willard R. Trask. Princeton: Princeton University Press, 1953.
Bakker, Hans. *Ayodhyā.* Groningen: Egbert Forsten, 1986.
Baldwin, Charles S. *Ancient Rhetoric and Poetic.* New York: Macmillan, 1924.
Bataille, Georges. *Theory of Religion.* Trans. Robert Hurley. New York: Zone Books, 1989.
Baxandall, Michael. *Patterns of Intention: On the Historical Explanation of Pictures.* New Haven: Yale University Press, 1985.
Bhatt, G. H. "The Fire-Ordeal of Sītā: An Interpolation in the Vālmīki-Rāmāyaṇa." *Journal of the Oriental Institute, Baroda* 5 (1955–56): 292.
Boardman, John. *Excavations in Chios, 1952–1955: Greek Emporio.* British School of Archaeology at Athens, Supplementary volume 6. Oxford, 1967.
______. *The Greeks Overseas.* Baltimore: Penguin Books, 1964.
Brockington, J. L. "A Note on Mrs. Sen's Article about the Rāmāyaṇa." *Journal of the American Oriental Society* 89 (1969): 412–14.
______. "Rāmo dharmabhṛtāṃ varaḥ." *Indologica Taurinensia* 5 (1977): 55–68.
______. "Religious Attitudes in Vālmīki's *Rāmāyaṇa.*" *Journal of the Royal Asiatic Society* (1976): 108–29.
______. *Righteous Rama: The Evolution of an Epic.* Delhi: Oxford University Press, 1984.
Bulcke, Camille. "About Vālmīki." *Journal of the Oriental Institute, Baroda* 8 (1958–59): 121–31.
______. "The Genesis of the Vālmīki Rāmāyaṇa Recensions." *Journal of the Oriental Institute, Baroda* 5 (1955–56): 66–94.
______. "More About Vālmīki." *Journal of the Oriental Institute, Baroda* 8 (1958–59): 346–48.
______. "The Repudiation of Sītā." *Journal of the Oriental Institute, Baroda* 1 (1951–52): 48–50.
Burkert, Walter. *Greek Religion.* Trans. John Raffan. Cambridge: Harvard University Press, 1985.

———. *The Orientalizing Revolution: Near Eastern Influence on Greek Culture in the Early Archaic Age.* Trans. Margaret E. Pinder and Walter Burkert. Cambridge: Harvard University Press, 1992.

Butler, Marilyn. *Romantics, Rebels, and Reactionaries: English Literature and Its Background, 1750–1830.* New York: Oxford University Press, 1982.

Cambridge Ancient History. Vol. 1, parts 1 & 2, and vol. 2, parts 1 & 2. 3d ed. Ed. I.E.S. Edwards et al. Cambridge: Cambridge University Press, 1972–75. Vol. 3, parts 1 & 3. 2d ed. Ed. John Boardman et al. Cambridge: Cambridge University Press, 1982.

Cannon, Garland. *The Life and Mind of Oriental Jones: Sir William Jones, the Father of Modern Linguistics.* Cambridge: Cambridge University Press, 1990.

Caplan, Harry. *Of Eloquence: Studies in Ancient and Medieval Rhetoric.* Ed. Anne King and Helen North. Ithaca, N.Y.: Cornell University Press, 1970.

Cave, David. *Mircea Eliade's Vision for a New Humanism.* New York: Oxford University Press, 1993.

Chandra, Lokesh. "The Cultural Symphony of India and Greece." *Haryana Sahitya Akademi Journal of Indological Studies* 1, no. 1 (1986): 136–48.

Clarke, Howard. *Homer's Readers: A Historical Introduction to the Iliad and the Odyssey.* Newark: University of Delaware Press, 1981.

Clifford, James, and George Marcus, eds. *Writing Culture: The Poetics and Politics of Ethnography.* Berkeley and Los Angeles: University of California Press, 1986.

Coldstream, J. N. *Geometric Greece.* New York: St. Martin's Press, 1977.

———. "Hero-Cults in the Age of Homer." *Journal of Hellenic Studies* 96 (1976): 8–17.

Cook, J. M. *The Greeks in Ionia and the East.* New York: Praeger, 1963.

Cowell, E. G., ed. *The Jātaka or Stories of the Buddha's Former Births.* London: Pali Text Society, 1957.

De, S. C. *Public Speeches in Ancient and Medieval India (Based on Sanskrit and Prakrit Literature).* Rev. ed. Delhi: Ajanta Publications, 1976.

Delaunois, Marcel. "Comment parlent les héros d'Homère: La Question de l'enchaînement des idées dans l'éloquence grecque." *Les Études Classiques* 20 (1952): 80–92.

Deshpande, Madhav M. *Sociolinguistic Attitudes in India: A Historical Reconstruction.* Ann Arbor, Mich.: Karoma Publishers, 1979.

Devy, Ganesh N. *After Amnesia: Tradition and Change in Indian Literary Criticism.* New Delhi: Orient Longmans, 1991.

———. "Comparative Literature in India." *New Quest* 63 (May–June 1987): 133–47; 64 (July–August 1987): 211–17.

Divanji, P. C. "Influence of the Rāmāyaṇa on the Gujarati Literature." *Journal of the Oriental Institute, Baroda* 4 (1954–55): 46–57.

Donlan, Walter. "The Structure of Authority in the *Iliad.*" *Arethusa* 12 (1979): 51–70.

Edwards, Mark W. *Homer: Poet of the Iliad.* Baltimore: Johns Hopkins University Press, 1987.

Eliade, Mircea. *Cosmos and History: The Myth of the Eternal Return.* Trans. Willard R. Trask. New York: Harper & Row, 1959.

———. *Myth and Reality.* Trans. Willard R. Trask. New York: Harper & Row, 1963.

———. *Patterns in Comparative Religion.* Trans. Rosemary Sheed. New York: New American Library, 1963.

———. *The Quest: History and Meaning in Religion.* Chicago: University of Chicago Press, 1969.

———. *The Sacred and the Profane: The Nature of Religion.* Trans. Willard R. Trask. New York: Harcourt, Brace, & World, 1959.

Embree, Ainslee T. *Utopias in Conflict: Religion and Nationalism in Modern India.* Berkeley and Los Angeles: University of California Press, 1990.

Emlyn-Jones, C. J. *The Ionians and Hellenism: A Study of the Cultural Achievement of the Early Greek Inhabitants of Asia Minor.* London: Routledge & Kegan Paul, 1980.

Fabian, Johannes. *Time and the Other: How Anthropology Makes Its Object.* New York: Columbia University Press, 1983.

Farnell, L. R. *Greek Hero Cults and Ideas of Immortality.* 1921. Reprint, Oxford: Clarendon Press, 1970.

Finley, M. I. *The World of Odysseus.* 2d rev. ed. Harmondsworth, U.K.: Penguin Books, 1979.

Foucault, Michel. *The Order of Things: An Archaeology of the Human Sciences.* New York: Vintage Books, 1973.

Freedberg, David. *The Power of Images: Studies in the History and Theory of Response.* Chicago: University of Chicago Press, 1989.

Frenzel, Elisabeth. *Stoffe der Weltliteratur: Ein Lexikon dichtungsgeschichtlicher Längsschnitte.* 4th ed. Stuttgart: Kröner, 1976.

Gadamer, Hans-Georg. *Truth and Method.* Ed. and trans. Garrett Barden and John Cumming. New York: Seabury Press, 1975.

Geertz, Clifford. *The Interpretation of Cultures.* New York: Basic Books, 1973.

———. *Islam Observed: Development of Religion in Morocco and Indonesia.* Chicago: University of Chicago Press, 1971.

———. *Local Knowledge: Further Essays in Interpretive Anthropology.* New York: Basic Books, 1985.

———. *Works and Lives: The Anthropologist as Author.* Stanford, Calif.: Stanford University Press, 1989.

Genette, Gérard. *Figures of Literary Discourse.* New York: Columbia University Press, 1982.

Girard, René. *Things Hidden Since the Foundation of the World.* Stanford, Calif.: Stanford University Press, 1987.

———. *Violence and the Sacred.* Trans. Patrick Gregory. Baltimore: Johns Hopkins University Press, 1977.

Gold, Daniel. "Organized Hinduisms: From Vedic Truth to Hindu Nation." In *Fundamentalisms Observed,* ed. Martin E. Marty and R. Scott Appleby, 531–83. Chicago: University of Chicago Press, 1991.

Goldman, Robert P. "Introduction" to *The Rāmāyaṇa of Vālmīki,* vol. 1, *Bālakāṇḍa.* Princeton: Princeton University Press, 1984.

Gopal, Sarvepalli, ed. *Anatomy of a Confrontation: The Babri Masjid-Ramjanmabhumi Issue.* New Delhi: Viking Penguin, 1991.

Graham, William A. *Divine Word and Prophetic Word in Early Islam: A Reconsideration of the Sources, with Special Reference to the Divine Saying or Hadith Qudsi.* The Hague: Mouton, 1977.

Griffin, Jasper. "The Epic Cycle and the Uniqueness of Homer." *Journal of Hellenic Studies* 97 (1977): 39–53.

———. *Homer on Life and Death.* Oxford: Oxford University Press, 1980.

Grimes, Ronald. *Ritual Criticism: Case Studies in Its Practice, Essays on Its Theory.* Columbia: University of South Carolina Press, 1990.

Gupta, S. P. *The Roots of Indian Art.* Delhi: B. R. Publishing, 1980.

Hägg, Robin, ed. *The Greek Renaissance of the Eighth Century* B.C.*: Tradition and Innovation.* Acta Instituti Atheniensis Regni Sueciae, ser. 4, no. 30. Stockholm, 1983.

Halbfass, Wilhelm. *India and Europe: An Essay in Understanding.* Albany: SUNY Press, 1988.

Hamilton, J. R. *Plutarch, Alexander: A Commentary.* Oxford: Clarendon Press, 1969.

Havelock, Eric. *The Muse Learns to Write: Reflections on Orality & Literacy from Antiquity to the Present.* New Haven: Yale University Press, 1986.

———. *Preface to Plato.* Cambridge: Harvard University Press, 1963.

Havelock, Eric, and Jackson P. Hershbell, eds. *Communication Arts in the Ancient World.* New York: Hastings House, 1978.

Hayden, A. Eustace. "From Comparative Religion to the History of Religions." *Journal of Religion* 2 (1922): 577–87.

Heesterman, J. C. *The Inner Conflict of Tradition: Essays in Indian Ritual, Kingship, and Society.* Chicago: University of Chicago Press, 1985.

Heidegger, Martin. *Poetry, Language, Thought.* Trans. Albert Hofstadter. New York: Harper & Row, 1971.

Hein, Norvin. "Epic *Sarvabhūtahite Rataḥ:* A Byword of Non-Bhārgava Editors." *Annals, Bhandarkar Oriental Research Institute* 67 (1986): 17–34.

Hick, John. *Philosophy of Religion.* 2d ed. Englewood Cliffs, N.J.: Prentice-Hall, 1973.

———, ed. *The Existence of God.* New York: Macmillan, 1964.

Homer. *Iliad.* In *Homeri Opera,* vols. 1 and 2, ed. David B. Monro and Thomas W. Allen, 3d ed. Oxford Classical Text Series. 1920. Reprint, Oxford: Clarendon Press, 1969, 1971. Trans. Richmond Lattimore, under the title *The Iliad of Homer.* Chicago: University of Chicago Press, 1951.

Hommel, Hildebrecht. *Der Gott Achilleus.* Heidelberg: Carl Winter, 1980.

Horatius Flaccus, Quintus. *Satires, Epistles, and Ars Poetica.* Latin text with English translation. Rev. ed. Ed. H. Rushton Fairclough. Loeb Classical Library, 1936.

Hume, David. *Dialogues Concerning Natural Religion.* Harmondsworth, U.K.: Penguin Books, 1990.

———. *The Natural History of Religion.* Ed. H. E. Root. Stanford, Calif.: Stanford University Press, 1957.

Hurwit, Jeffrey M. *The Art and Culture of Early Greece, 1100–400 B.C.* Ithaca, N.Y.: Cornell University Press, 1985.

Huxley, G. L. *The Early Ionians.* New York: Humanities Press, 1966.

Isocrates. Greek text with English translation. Ed. George Norlin. 3 vols. Loeb Classical Library, 1928.

Jacobi, Hermann. *The Ramayana.* Trans. S. N. Ghosal. Baroda, India: Oriental Institute, 1960.

Jauss, Hans Robert. *Aesthetic Experience and Literary Hermeneutics.* Trans. Michael Shaw. Minneapolis: University of Minnesota Press, 1982.

Keith, Arthur Berriedale. "The Date of the Ramayana." *Journal of the Royal Asiatic Society* 47 (1915): 318–28.

Kennedy, George A. "The Ancient Dispute over Rhetoric in Homer." *American Journal of Philology* 78 (1957): 23–35.

———. *The Art of Persuasion in Greece.* Princeton: Princeton University Press, 1963.

Kitagawa, Joseph M. *The History of Religions: Understanding Human Experience.* Atlanta: Scholars Press, 1987.

Küng, Hans, et al. *Christianity and the World Religions: Paths of Dialogue with Islam, Hinduism, and Buddhism.* Trans. Peter Heinegg. Garden City, N.Y.: Doubleday, 1986.

LaFleur, William. "Biography." In *The Encyclopedia of Religion,* ed. Mircea Eliade, 2:220–24. New York: Macmillan, 1987.

Lal, B. B. and K. N. Dikshit. "Sringaverpura: A Key-Site for the Protohistory and Early History of the Central Ganga Valley." *Puruttatva* 10 (1978–79): 1–8.

Lamberton, Robert. *Homer the Theologian: Neoplatonist Allegorical Reading and the Growth of the Epic Tradition.* Berkeley and Los Angeles: University of California Press, 1986.

Levin, Harry. *Grounds for Comparison.* Cambridge: Harvard University Press, 1972.

Lillie, Arthur. *Rama and Homer: An Argument That in the Indian Epics Homer Found the Theme of His Two Great Poems.* London: Kegan, Paul, Trench, Trubner, 1912.

Lincoln, Bruce. *Death, War, and Sacrifice: Studies in Ideology and Practice.* Chicago: University of Chicago Press, 1991.

______. *Discourse and the Construction of Society: Comparative Studies of Myth, Ritual, and Classification.* New York: Oxford University Press, 1989.

Lingat, Robert. *The Classical Law of India.* Trans. J. Duncan M. Derrett. Berkeley and Los Angeles: University of California Press, 1973.

Lohmann, Dieter. *Die Komposition der Reden in der Ilias.* Berlin: Walter de Gruyter, 1970.

Long, Charles H. *Alpha: The Myths of Creation.* New York: George Braziller, 1963.

______. "Cosmogony." In *The Encyclopedia of Religion,* ed. Mircea Eliade, 4:94–99. New York: Macmillan, 1987.

______. *Significations: Signs, Symbols, and Images in the Interpretation of Religion.* Philadelphia: Fortress Press, 1986.

Lord, Albert B. "Homer and Huso III: Enjambement in Greek and Southslavic Song." *Transactions and Proceedings of the American Philological Association* 79 (1948): 113–24.

______. *The Singer of Tales.* Cambridge: Harvard University Press, 1960.

Lucretius Carus, Titus. *Selections from Lucretius.* Ed. G. E. Benfield and R. C. Reeves. London: Oxford University Press, 1967.

Lüders, Heinrich, ed. *Bharhut Inscriptions.* Corpus inscriptionum indicarum, vol. 2, part 2. Rev. E. Waldschmidt and M. A. Mehendale. Ootacamund: Archaeological Survey of India, 1963.

Lutgendorf, Philip. *The Life of a Text: Performing the Ramcaritmanas of Tulsidas.* Berkeley and Los Angeles: University of California Press, 1991.

McCall, Marsh. *Ancient Rhetorical Theories of Simile and Comparison.* Cambridge: Harvard University Press, 1969.

McGann, Jerome J. *The Beauty of Inflections: Literary Investigations in Historical Method and Theory.* Oxford: Clarendon Press, 1985.

______. *The Romantic Ideology: A Critical Investigation.* Chicago: University of Chicago Press, 1983.

______. *Social Values and Poetic Arts.* Cambridge: Harvard University Press, 1988.

Majumdar, R. C., ed. *The Age of Imperial Unity.* Vol. 2 of *The History and Culture of the Indian People.* Bombay: Bharatiya Vidya Bhavan, 1968.

Malinowski, Bronislaw. *Argonauts of the Western Pacific: An Account of Native Enterprise and Adventure in the Archipelagoes of Melanesian New Guinea.* Preface by Sir James George Frazer. London: G. Routledge & Sons, 1922.

Milgram, Stanley. *Obedience to Authority: An Experimental View.* New York: Harper & Row, 1974.

Miller, Barbara Stoler. "Presidential Address: Contending Narratives—The Political Life of the Indian Epics." *Journal of Asian Studies* 50 (November 1991): 783–92.

______, ed. *The Theater of Memory: The Plays of Kālidāsa.* New York: Columbia University Press, 1984.

Mitra, Debalal. *Sanchi.* 2d ed. New Delhi: Archaeological Survey of India, 1965.
Morris, Ian. *Burial and Ancient Society: The Rise of the Greek City-State.* Cambridge: Cambridge University Press, 1987.
———. "The Use and Abuse of Homer." *Classical Antiquity* 5 (1986): 80–138.
Murray, Gilbert. *Five Stages of Greek Religion.* Boston: Beacon Press, 1951.
———. *The Rise of the Greek Epic.* 3d ed., rev. and enl. Oxford: Clarendon Press, 1924.
Murray, Oswyn. *Early Greece.* Sussex: Harvester Press, 1980.
Nagy, Gregory. *The Best of the Achaeans: Concepts of the Hero in Archaic Greek Poetry.* Baltimore: Johns Hopkins University Press, 1979.
———. *Comparative Studies in Greek and Indic Meter.* Cambridge: Harvard University Press, 1974.
Nehru, Jawaharlal. *Discovery of India.* New York: John Day, 1946.
Nilakanta Sastri, K. A., ed. *A Comprehensive History of India.* Vol. 2, *The Mauryas and Satavahanas, 325 B.C.–A.D. 300.* Bombay: Orient Longmans, 1957.
O'Flaherty, Wendy Doniger. *The Origins of Evil in Hindu Mythology.* Berkeley and Los Angeles: University of California Press, 1976.
Oliver, Robert T. *Communication and Culture in Ancient India and China.* Syracuse, N.Y.: Syracuse University Press, 1971.
Otto, Rudolf. *The Idea of the Holy.* Trans. John W. Harvey. Oxford: Oxford University Press, 1923.
———. *The Philosophy of Religion Based on Kant and Fries.* Trans. E. B. Dicker. Foreword by W. Tudor Jones. London: Williams & Norgate, 1931.
The Oxford History of the Classical World. Ed. John Boardman, Jasper Griffin, and Oswyn Murray. Oxford: Oxford University Press, 1986.
Pande, G. C. *Śramaṇa Tradition: Its History and Contribution to Indian Culture.* Ahmedabad: L. D. Institute of Indology, 1978.
Parry, Adam, ed. *The Making of Homeric Verse: The Collected Papers of Milman Parry.* Oxford: Clarendon Press, 1971.
Pathak, Madhusudan Madhavlal. *Similes in the Ramayana.* Vadodara, India: Maharaja Sayajirao University of Baroda, 1968.
Pausanias. *Description of Greece.* Greek text with English translation. Ed. W.H.S. Jones. 5 vols. Loeb Classical Library, 1926–38.
Pfeiffer, Rudolf. *A History of Classical Scholarship from the Beginnings to the End of the Hellenistic Age.* Oxford: Clarendon Press, 1986.
———. *History of Classical Scholarship from 1300 to 1850.* Oxford: Clarendon Press, 1976.
Plutarch. *Plutarch's Lives.* Vol. 7, *Demosthenes and Cicero, Alexander and Caesar.* Greek text with English translation. Ed. Bernadotte Perrin. Loeb Classical Library, 1949.
Pollock, Sheldon. "Ātmānaṃ Mānuṣaṃ Manye: Dharmākūtam on the Divinity of Rāma." *Journal of the Oriental Institute, Baroda* 33 (1983/84): 231–43.
———. "The Divine King in the Indian Epic." *Journal of the American Oriental Society* 104 (1984): 505–28.
Pope, Alexander. *The Iliad of Homer: Books I–IX.* Ed. Maynard Mack et al. Twickenham Edition of the Poems of Alexander Pope, vol. 7. London: Methuen, 1967.
———. *Pastoral Poetry, and An Essay on Criticism.* Ed. Emile Audra and Aubrey Williams. Twickenham Edition of the Poems of Alexander Pope, vol. 1. London: Methuen, 1961.
Popham, M. R., and L. H. Sackett. *Excavations at Lefkandi, Euboea, 1964–66.* British School of Archaeology at Athens, 1968.

Popham, M. R., L. H. Sackett, and P. G. Themelis. *Lefkandi, The Iron Age.* London: Thames & Hudson, 1979.
Popham, M. R., L. H. Sackett, and E. Touloupa. "Further Excavations of the Toumba Cemetery at Lefkandi, 1981." *Bulletin of the British School of Archaeology at Athens* 77 (1982): 213–48.
———. "The Hero of Lefkandi." *Antiquity* 56 (1982): 169–74.
Powys, John Cowper. *Homer and the Aether.* London: Macdonald, 1959.
Price, Theodora Hadzisteliou. "Hero-Cult and Homer." *Historia* 22 (1973): 129–44.
Qviller, Bjørn. "The Dynamics of the Homeric Society." *Symbolae Osloenses* 56 (1981): 109–55.
Raghavan, V., ed. *Ramayana, Mahabharata, and Bhagavata Writers.* Cultural Leaders of India Series. New Delhi: Government of India, 1978.
———. *The Ramayana Tradition in Asia: Papers Presented at the International Seminar on the Ramayana Tradition in Asia. New Delhi, December, 1975.* New Delhi: Sahitya Akademi, 1975.
Raju, P. T. *Structural Depths of Indian Thought.* Albany: SUNY Press, 1985.
Ramaswami Sastri, K. S. *Studies in Ramayana.* Kirti Mandir Lecture Series, 9. Baroda: Baroda State, Department of Education, [1948?].
Ramaswami Sastrigal, K. S. "The Rāmāyaṇa as a Guide to a New World-Order." *Journal of Oriental Research* 4 (1930): 368–83.
Ray, Himanshu. *Monastery and Guild: Commerce under the Sātavāhanas.* Delhi: Oxford University Press, 1986.
Ray, Niharranjan. *Maurya and Post-Maurya Art: A Study in Social and Formal Contrasts.* New Delhi: Indian Council of Historical Research, 1975.
Redfield, James M. *Nature and Culture in the Iliad: The Tragedy of Hektor.* Chicago: University of Chicago Press, 1975.
———. "The Proem of the *Iliad:* Homer's Art." *Classical Philology* 74 (1979): 95–110.
Renfrew, Colin. *Archaeology and Language: The Puzzle of Indo-European Origins.* New York: Cambridge University Press, 1988.
Reynolds, Frank E., and Donald Capps, eds. *The Biographical Process: Studies in the History and Psychology of Religion.* The Hague: Mouton, 1976.
Reynolds, Frank E., and David Tracy, eds. *Myth and Philosophy.* Albany: SUNY Press, 1990.
Richardson, N. J. "Homeric Professors in the Age of the Sophists." *Proceedings, Cambridge Philological Society* 201 (1975): 65–81.
Richman, Paula, ed. *Many Ramayanas: The Diversity of a Narrative Tradition in South Asia.* Berkeley and Los Angeles: University of California Press, 1991.
Ricketts, Mac Linscott. *Mircea Eliade: The Romanian Roots, 1907–1945.* 2 vols. Boulder, Colo.: East European Monographs, 1988.
Ricoeur, Paul. *Hermeneutics and the Human Sciences.* Ed. and trans. John B. Thompson. Cambridge: Cambridge University Press, 1981.
———. *The Symbolism of Evil.* New York: Harper & Row, 1967.
Rosaldo, Renato. *Truth and Culture: The Remaking of Social Analysis.* Boston: Beacon Press, 1989.
Roscher, Wilhelm. *Ausführliches Lexikon der griechischen und römischen Mythologie.* Leipzig: B. G. Teubner, 1884–1937.
Ruben, Walter. *Die gesellschaftliche Entwicklung im alten Indien.* 6 vols. Berlin: Akademie-Verlag, 1967–74.
———. *Die homerischen und die altindischen Epen.* Sitzungsberichte der Akademie der Wissenschaften der DDR, Jahrgang 1973, no. 24. Berlin: Akademie-Verlag, 1975.

———. "The Minister Jābāli in Vālmīki's Rāmāyaṇa: The Portrait of One of the Indian Materialists." In *Studies in Ancient Indian Thought,* 1–24. Calcutta: Indian Studies, Past and Present, 1966.
Rudolph, Kurt. *Geschichte und Probleme der Religionswissenschaft.* Leiden: E. J. Brill, 1992.
———. *Historical Fundamentals and the Study of Religions.* Haskell Lectures Delivered at the University of Chicago. New York: Macmillan, 1985.
Russell, James E. *German Higher Schools.* New ed. London: Longmans, Green, 1910.
Sahlins, Marshall. *Culture and Practical Reason.* Chicago: University of Chicago Press, 1976.
Sandys, J. E. *A History of Classical Scholarship.* 3 vols. Reprint, New York: Hafner, 1967.
Sankalia, H. D. *The Ramayana in Historical Perspective.* Delhi: Macmillan India, 1982.
———. *Ramayana: Myth or Reality?* New Delhi: People's Publishing House, 1973.
Schimmel, Annemarie. *And Mohammed Is His Messenger: The Veneration of the Prophet in Islamic Piety.* Chapel Hill: University of North Carolina Press, 1985.
Schleiermacher, Friedrich. *On Religion: Speeches to Its Cultured Despisers.* Trans. Richard Crouter. Cambridge: Cambridge University Press, 1988.
Schopen, Gregory. "Archaeology and Protestant Presuppositions in the Study of Indian Buddhism." *History of Religions* 31 (August 1991): 1–23.
Sen, Amartya. "India and the West." *The New Republic,* June 7, 1993, 27–34.
Sen, Nabaneeta. "Comparative Studies in Oral Epic Poetry and *The Vālmīki Rāmāyaṇa:* A Report on the *Bālākaṇḍa.*" *Journal of the American Oriental Society* 86 (1966): 397–409.
———. "The *Valmiki-Ramayana* and the *Raghuvamsam:* Stylistic Structure of Oral Poetry as Contrasted to Classical Poetry." *Jadavpur Journal of Comparative Literature* 8 (1968): 85–95.
Sen, Nilmadhav. "The Fire-Ordeal of Sītā—A Later Interpolation in the Rāmāyaṇa?" *Journal of the Oriental Institute, Baroda* 1 (1951–52): 201–6.
Seznec, Jean. *The Survival of the Pagan Gods: The Mythological Tradition and Its Place in Renaissance Humanism and Art.* Trans. Barbara F. Sessions. New York: Pantheon Books, 1953.
Sharma, G. R. *The Excavations at Kauśāmbī (1957–1959): The Defences and the Śyenaciti of the Puruṣamedha.* Allahabad: University of Allahabad, 1960.
Simonsuuri, Kirsi. *Homer's Original Genius: Eighteenth Century Notions of the Early Greek Epic (1688–1798).* Cambridge: Cambridge University Press, 1979.
Sinha, Bindeshwari Prasad. *The Comprehensive History of Bihar.* Vol. 1, part 1. Patna: Kashi Prasad Jayaswal Research Institute, 1974.
Sinha, Binod Chandra. *History of the Śuṅga Dynasty.* Varanasi: Bharatiya Publishing House, 1977.
Sircar, D. C. *Asokan Studies.* Calcutta: Indian Museum, 1979.
———. "The Decline of Buddhism in Bengal." In *Studies in the Religious Life of Ancient and Medieval India,* 183–205. Delhi: Motilal Banarsidass, 1971.
———. *Inscriptions of Aśoka.* 3d rev. ed. New Delhi: Government of India, 1975.
———. "The Rāmāyaṇa and the Daśaratha Jātaka." *Journal of the Oriental Institute, Baroda* 26 (1976–77): 50–55.
———. *Select Inscriptions Bearing on Indian History and Civilization.* Vol. 1, *From the Sixth Century* B.C. *to the Sixth Century* A.D. 2d ed. Calcutta: University of Calcutta Press, 1965.
Smith, Brian K. *Reflections on Resemblance, Ritual, and Religion.* New York: Oxford University Press, 1989.

Smith, Jonathan Z. *Drudgery Divine: On the Comparison of Early Christianities and the Religions of Late Antiquity.* Chicago: University of Chicago Press, 1991.

———. *Imagining Religion: From Babylon to Jonestown.* Chicago: University of Chicago Press, 1982.

———. *To Take Place: Toward Theory in Ritual.* Chicago: University of Chicago Press, 1987.

Smith, Wilfred Cantwell. "A Universal Theology of Religion." In *Toward a Universal Theology of Religion,* ed. Leonard Swidler, 51–72. Maryknoll, N.Y.: Orbis Books, 1987.

Snodgrass, Anthony M. *Archaeology and the Rise of the Greek State: An Inaugural Lecture.* Cambridge; Cambridge University Press, 1977.

———. *Archaic Greece: The Age of Experiment.* Berkeley and Los Angeles: University of California Press, 1980.

———. "An Historical Homeric Society?" *Journal of Hellenic Studies* 94 (1974): 114–25.

———. "Poet and Painter in Eighth Century Greece." *Proceedings of the Cambridge Philological Society* 205 (1979): 118–30.

———. "Towards the Interpretation of the Geometric Figure-Scenes." *Mitteilungen des deutschen archäologischen Instituts, Athenische Abteilung* 95 (1980): 51–58.

Söhnen, Renate. *Untersuchungen zur Komposition von Reden und Gesprächen im Ramayana.* 2 vols. Studien zur Indologie und Iranistik, 6. Reinbek: Verlag für orientalistische Fachpublikationen, 1979.

Srinivasa Iyengar, K. R., ed. *Asian Variations in Ramayana. Papers Presented at the International Seminar on Variations in Ramayana in Asia: Their Cultural, Social, and Anthropological Significance (New Delhi, January 1981).* New Delhi: Sahitya Akademi, 1983.

Srinivasa Murti, G., and A. N. Krishna Aiyangar. *Edicts of Aśoka (Priyadarśin).* Intro. K. V. Rangaswami Aiyangar. Madras: Adyar Library, 1950.

Staal, Frits. *Agni: The Ritual of the Fire Altar.* Berkeley, Calif.: Asian Humanities Press, 1983.

———. "The Meaninglessness of Ritual." *Numen* 26 (1979): 2–22.

Stanford, W. B. *The Ulysses Theme: A Study in the Adaptability of a Traditional Hero.* Oxford: Basil Blackwell, 1954.

Starr, Chester G. *The Economic and Social History of Early Greece, 800–500 B.C.* New York: Oxford University Press, 1977.

———. *Individual and Community: The Rise of the Polis 800–500 B.C.* New York: Oxford University Press, 1986.

Strenski, Ivan. *Religion in Relation: Method, Application, & Moral Location.* Studies in Comparative Religion. Columbia: University of South Carolina Press, 1992.

Swidler, Leonard. "The Dialogue Decalogue." *Journal of Ecumenical Studies* 20 (Winter 1983): 1–4.

Swidler, Leonard, et al. *Death or Dialogue? From the Age of Monologue to the Age of Dialogue.* London: SCM Press, 1990.

Tate, J. "On the History of Allegorism." *Classical Quarterly* 28 (1934): 105–15.

Telang, Kashinath Trimbak. *Was the Rāmāyaṇa Copied from Homer? A Reply to Professor Weber.* 1873. Reprint, Delhi: Publishers Parlour, 1976.

Thapar, Romila. *Aśoka and the Decline of the Mauryas.* Oxford: Oxford University Press, 1961.

———. *Exile and the Kingdom: Some Thoughts on the Ramayana.* Bangalore: The Mythic Society, 1978.

———. *From Lineage to State: Social Formations in the Mid-First Millennium* B.C. *in the Ganga Valley*. Bombay: Oxford University Press, 1984.

———. "Origin Myths and the Early Indian Historical Tradition." In *History and Society: Essays in Honour of Professor Niharranjan Ray*, ed. Debiprasad Chattopadhyaya, 271–94. Calcutta: K. P. Bagchi, 1978.

Thite, G. U. *Sacrifice in the Brahmana-texts*. Pune, India: University of Poona, 1975.

Tulsi Das. *Ramcaritmanas*. Trans. F. S. Growse, under the title *The Rāmāyaṇa of Tulasīdāsa*. Rev. R. C. Prasad. 2d rev. ed. Delhi: Motilal Banarsidass, 1987.

The Vālmīki-Rāmāyaṇa, Critically Edited for the First Time. Ed. G. H. Bhatt et al. 7 vols. Vadodara, India: The Oriental Institute, M. S. University of Baroda, 1958–75. Translated by Robert P. Goldman et al., under the title *The Rāmāyaṇa of Vālmīki: An Epic of Ancient India*. 4 vols. to date. Princeton, N.J.: Princeton University Press, 1984–.

van der Veer, Peter. *Religious Nationalism*. California, 1994.

———. " 'God must be liberated!': A Hindu Liberation Movement in Ayodhya." *Modern Asian Studies* 21 (1987): 283–301.

Viswanathan, K. "The Influence of the 'Ramayana' and the 'Mahabharata' on Indian Life and Literature." *Aryan Path* 37 (1966): 276–80.

Vyas, S. N. *India in the Rāmāyaṇa Age: A Study of the Social and Cultural Conditions in Ancient India as Described in Vālmīki's Rāmāyaṇa*. Delhi: Atma Ram, 1967.

Wach, Joachim. *The Comparative Study of Religions*. New York: Columbia University Press, 1958.

———. *Introduction to the History of Religions*. Ed. Joseph M. Kitagawa and Gregory D. Alles. New York: Macmillan, 1987.

———. "Religionswissenschaft." In *Die Religion in Geschichte und Gegenwart*, 2d ed., ed. Hermann Gunkel and Leopold Zscharnack, vol. 4, cols. 1954–1959. Tübingen: J.C.B. Mohr, 1930.

———. *Sociology of Religion*. Chicago: University of Chicago Press, 1944.

———. *Types of Religious Experience: Christian and Non-Christian*. Chicago: University of Chicago Press, 1951.

———. *Das Verstehen: Grundzüge einer Geschichte der hermeneutischen Theorie im 19. Jahrhundert*. 3 vols. Tübingen: J.C.B. Mohr (Paul Siebeck), 1926–33.

Weber, Max. *The Sociology of Religion*. Boston: Beacon Press, 1964.

White, Hayden V. *Metahistory: The Historical Imagination in Nineteenth-Century Europe*. Baltimore: Johns Hopkins University Press, 1973.

Wilcken, Ulrich. *Alexander the Great*. Trans. G. C. Richards. Intro. Eugene N. Borza. New York: W. W. Norton, 1967.

Xenophon. *Anabasis IV–VII; Symposium and Apology*. Greek text with English translation. Trans. C. L. Brownson and O. J. Todd. Loeb Classical Library, 1947.

Yardi, M. R. "A Statistical Study of *Rāmāyaṇa Sundarakāṇḍa, Yuddhakāṇḍa,* and *Uttarakāṇḍa*." *Annals, Bhandarkar Oriental Research Institute* 70 (1989): 17–32.

Yearley, Lee H. *Mencius and Aquinas: Theories of Virtue and Conceptions of Courage*. Albany: SUNY Press, 1990.

Index